2nd Fully Revised & Updated Edition

Question Bank in Extension Education

2nd Fully Revised & Updated Edition

Question Bank in Extension Education

Asif Mohammad
Eastern Regional Station of ICAR
National Dairy Research Institute
Kalyani, West Bengal

K. Ponnusamy
Principal Scientist (Agricultural Extension)
ICAR-National Dairy Research Institute
Karnal, Haryana

Rajiv Baliram Kale
Agricultural Extension
ICAR- Directorate of Onion and Garlic Research
Rajgurunagar, Pune, Maharashtra

nipa® books for everyone
PAPERBACKS
New Delhi – 110 034

nipa books for everyone
PAPERBACKS

A Paperback Division of

NEW INDIA PUBLISHING AGENCY

101, Vikas Surya Plaza, CU Block, LSC Market
Pitam Pura, New Delhi 110 034, India
Phone: + 91 (11) 27 34 17 17 Fax: + 91 (11) 27 34 16 16
Email: info@nipabooks.com
Web: www.nipabooks.com

Feedback at feedbacks@nipabooks.com

ISBN: 978-93-89130-48-5

Composed and Designed by NIPA

Preface to the Second Edition

The role and importance of agricultural extension is ever increasing in view of the impending need to increase farm productivity, create an opportunity for income and employment generation and facilitate farmers in the midst of challenges including climate change. As a professional discipline, its contribution is well established across the world addressing poverty, malnutrition and sustainability. With the changing pattern of competitive examination, nature of preparation for success in those examinations has also changed. In the discipline of extension education, many new concepts have emerged in the recent past which should be known/understood for sure success in those examinations.

We feel great pleasure to introduce the thoroughly revised and enlarged edition of the book entitled 'Question Bank in Extension Education'. The first edition found highly beneficial for students aspiring for competitive exams in extension education. The efforts are taken to enhance the quality of the content as per the feedback and suggestion given by the students and scholars. Previous question papers of ICAR- NET, JRF, SRF, ASRB examinations and entrance test of deemed universities have been incorporated for better understanding of trends in the questions commonly asked in the competitive examination. Twelve chapters pertaining to different facets of extension education have been incorporated in the book and attempts have been made to include probable questions for future examinations. Special attention has been made to improve the quality of the questions and minimize errors. We are hopeful that, after going through this book, students can sharpen their analytical skill, enhance their chances of success in the examination and prosper in their future endeavour.

The authors greatly acknowledge all the sources of references from where this book has been compiled.

Asif Mohammad
K. Ponnusamy
Rajiv Baliram Kale

Preface to the First Edition

Agricultural extension as a discipline and profession is progressing in all dimensions. Focus of its attention is always directed at socio-economic transformation of entire farming community. It also motivates various stakeholders who directly or indirectly contribute to the success of farming as well as better livelihood of farm families.

In tune with the advancement of agricultural science, it is equally important to take forward the innovations from research works to the ultimate end-users in order to bring the change in the method of farming and livelihood of farmers. For transferring technologies effectively and efficiently, trained manpower is necessary who can channelize research according to the needs of farmers, industries or all the stakeholders who are likely to use the technology/ innovations. Increasing demand for innovation in agricultural sector would also create opportunities for extension specialists for effective transfer of technologies. Students who are aspiring to become experts in the field of extension science, this book will be quite helpful for them to prepare for all competitive exams including ARS and PG entrance examination.

In this book, ardent care has been taken to incorporate all the relevant topics pertaining to extension science including Concepts and Principles of Extension, Developmental Schemes in India and Abroad, Rural Sociology and Psychology, Research Methodology, Management, Programme Planning and Evaluation, Diffusion of Innovation, Process of Communication, Information and Communication Technology, Training for Development, Farm Journalism and Women empowerment and Gender Mainstreaming. We hope that this book will fulfill the long standing demand of the social science students aspiring for bright future in the field of extension education.

The authors would place on record to acknowledge the various sources of references from where this book is compiled.

Asif Mohammad
K. Ponnusamy
Rajiv Baliram Kale

Contents

1

Concepts and Principles of Extension

1 In which country, the use of the word "extension" started getting importance from an educational development perspective during the second half of the nineteenth century ?

a. England
b. USA
c. India
d. Japan

2 ________ was an influential advocate of formal education for the poor and mass adult education who founded the Society for the Diffusion of Useful Knowledge in 1826.

a. J P Leagans
b. Rogers
c. Auguste Comte
d. Lord Henry Brougham

3 Which crisis led to establishment of the first agricultural extension service in 1845?

a. Heavy drought
b. Outbreak of potato blight
c. Food shortage
d. Farmers suicides

4 Extension education is viewed as the____

a. Participatory process
b. Formal education
c. Distance education process
d. None of the above

5 Which denotes 'expression of the ends towards which our efforts are directed'?

a. Goals
b. Objectives
c. Targets
d. Motives

6 ___is the distance in any given direction one is expected to go during a given period of time.

a. Aim
b. Target
c. Goal
d. Focus

7 According to Kelsey and Hearne, basic philosophy of extension education is to teach peopie is ______

a. How to think
b. What to think
c. Both a and b
d. None of the above

8 The function of extension education is to bring about desirable changes in

a. Knowledge
b. Skill
c. Attitude
d. All the above

9 Extension teaching must result in effective ____________

a. Learning
b. Mentoring
c. Coaching
d. None of the above

10 Extension teaching requires a suitable _______

a. Learning situation
b. Farmers
c. Students
d. Teacher

11 Learning for adults should be __________

a. Problem centered
b. Experience centered
c. Must be meaningful to the learner
d. All the above

12 Learning is an active process on the part of the learners. This statement supports which of the following principles of learning?

a. Principle of association
b. Principle of transfer
c. Principle of self activity
d. Principle of disassociation

13 A favourable attitude accelerates ________

a. Learning
b. Teaching
c. Choice
d. All the above

14 Perfection is seldom achieved without _____

a. Practice
b. Direction
c. Vision
d. Thinking

15 What percentage we tend to remember when we hear and see?

a. 30%
b. 50%
c. 20%
d. 70%

16 _______ is the application of knowledge for practical purposes

a. Technology b. Innovation

c. Invention d. Theory

17 Extension over the imaginary space created by the interconnected telecommunication and computer networks a _______

a. Mobile extension b. Virtual extension

c. Cyber extension d. All the above

18 Need satisfying and goal seeking behavior is referred as_______.

a. Motivation b. Achievement

c. Adoption d. All the above

19 Motivation which generates from within one's own self are known as _______motivation.

a. Extrinsic b. Intrinsic

c. Induced d. Selfish

20 Extension teaching is a planned and deliberate act on the part of the_______.

a. Farmers b. Teacher

c. Audience d. Extension agent

21 Which one of the following denotes the process of consciously choosing courses of action from available alternatives?

a. Decision making b. Adoption

c. Motivation d. Planning

22 To produce lasting change, the extension efforts should produce which type of results?

a. Temporary b. Perfect

c. Satisfying d. Enchanting

23 Which type of evaluation gathers information for development of an extension programme?

a. Formative b. Summative

c. Self-checking d. Do-it-yourself

24 The term 'Extension Education' was first used in 1873 by_______.

a. Cambridge University b. Oxford University

c. Due pond company d. 4-H club

25 The main responsibility of extension service is with the________.

a. State Government b. Central Government

c. State Agricultural Universities d. ICAR

26 ______is the pursuit of wisdom, a body of general principles or laws of a field of knowledge.

a. Behaviour b. Psychology

c. Philosophy d. Culture

27 ______is a professional appointed from outside, by an organisation to work with the rural people.

a. Sarpanch b. President of cooperative society

c. Extension agent d. All the above

28 Which groups have greater motivation towards work, more member satisfaction and greater productivity?

a. Autocratic b. Democratic

c. Laissez- faire d. All the above

29 Who pointed out nine areas of programme emphasis, which indicate the scope of agricultural extension?

a. Kelsey and Hearne b. Lynton and Pareek

c. J P Leagans d. Viswesvaraya

30 Which of the following is a set of assemblage of units interconnected, or interdependent, so as to form a complex unity?

a. Community b. Cluster

c. System d. Society

31 The principal systems in agricultural extension are the client system and the _______.

a. Change agent system b. Farming system

c. Consumer system d. Research system

32 Knowledge is generated through _______.

a. Communication b. Research

c. Diffusion d. Society

33 ________is a lifelong educational process

a. Informal education b. Formal education

c. Adult education d. Extension education

34 Which of the following is true about 'Non formal education'?

a. Organized b. Systematic

c. Educational activity d. All of these

35 Extension education is primarily considered as

a. Formal education b. Informal education

c. Non-formal education d. Adult education

36 Extension teaching can be compared to which of the following?

a. Commercial salesmanship b. Unprofitable venture

c. Both a & b d. None of these

37 Extension means_____

a. Extra tension b. Stretching out

c. Social work d. Expansion

38 Extension word is derived from

a. Ex and tensio b. Extra and tension

c. Extend and sion d. None of these

39 Who among the following said 'The individual is supreme in democracy'?

a. Mildred Horton b. Aristotle

c. Pluto d. Auguste Comte

40 Who among the following said "India lives in its villages"?

a. Jawaharlal Nehru b. Narendra Modi

c. Vinoba Bhave d. Mahatma Gandhi

41 What is the primary aim of all types of cooperative enterprises?

a. To end human exploitation b. To promote co-habitation

c. To earn more profit d. To develop business

42 Whose recommendation leads to launch of Panchayat Raj Institutions in India in 1957?

a. Balwant Rai Mehta Committee b. Asoka Mehta Committee

c. S.K.Dey Committee d. Mohan Singh Mehta Committee

43 How many phases of Panchayati Raj were identified in Asoka Mehta's (1978) report of the Committee of Panchayati Raj Institutions (PRIs)?

a. Two b. Four

c. Three d. Five

44 Which was the core focus in Constitution Seventy-Third Amendment Act 1992?

a. Women empowerment b. Panchayati Raj Institution

c. Self Help Groups d. Child labour

45 In which year the use of the term 'extension' originated in England ?

a. 1883 b. 1865

c. 1886 d. 1866

46 According to Ensminger (1957) extension is________.

a. education b. service

c. transfer of technology d. All the above

47 Who conceptualized extension education as an applied science?

a. Berlo b. K N Singh

c. J.P. Leagans d. Ensminger, D

48 The National Commission on Agriculture (1976) refers to extension as an ________

a. Farmers' field school b. Informal education

c. Formal education d. Out-of-school education

49 Who has written the book- A Guide to Community Development?

a. Dey, S.K b. Ensminger, D

c. Supe, S.V d. D.K. Berlo

50 The book Cooperative Extension Work is written by whom?

a. Kelsey, L.D. and Hearne, C.C. b. Singh, K.N

c. Leagans, J.P d. Ensminger, D

51 Who has written the book Extension Education in Community Development?

a. Schoempeter b. Dey, S.K.

c. Leagans, J.P. d. Ray, G.L.

52 IPM extension approach is based on which of the following?

a. Community Radio b. School on Air

c. Farmer Field Schools (FFS) d. Participatory Rural Appraisal

53 Key Production Area (KPA) development approach is used in which of the following country?
a. Philippines
b. Sri Lanka
c. USA
d. China

54 Which of the following country is noted for its University-based extension?
a. England
b. Philippines
c. United States of America
d. India

55 The extension worker must be a_____.
a. Teacher
b. Friend
c. Farmer
d. Officer

56 In which extension teaching method, separate identity of each person is maintained?
a. Individual method
b. Group method
c. Mass method
d. None of these

57 In *'Farmers' Call'*, who among the following will make the call?
a. Extension agent
b. Subject Matter Specialist
c. Farmer
d. Bankers

58 In which method, farmers are motivated for adoption of a new practice by showing its distinctly superior result?
a. Method demonstration
b. Result demonstration
c. Front line demonstration
d. Component demonstration

59 Which of the following is a relatively short-time demonstration given before a group?
a. Method demonstration
b. Result demonstration
c. Front line demonstration
d. Component demonstration

60 Result demonstrations are carried out in which place?
a. Laboratory
b. Research farm
c. Farm or home of selected individuals
d. Office of line departments

61 Which demonstration is carried out under close supervision of scientist?
a. Method demonstration
b. Result demonstration
c. Frontline demonstration
d. Component demonstration

62 Which one of the following method is the least expensive?

a. Individual contact
b. Group Contact
c. Mass contact
d. Farm and Home visit

63 In case of Vanamahostava (tree planting) which of the following method can be best utilized?

a. Campaign
b. Mass meeting
c. Folder
d. Leaflet

64 For creating general awareness among the people, which of the following contact method is most useful?

a. Individual
b. Group
c. Mass
d. Combination of group and individual

65 Who among the following gave Traditional model of extension?

a. Compton
b. Bergman
c. Leagans
d. Shoemaker

66 Which among the following included the educational element of extension?

a. Informal
b. Non-Formal
c. Both a & b
d. Formal

67 Farming Systems Perspective (FSP) involves seeing things from the ___________

a. Farmers' View-Point
b. Researcher view-point
c. Extension agents' View point
d. Industries' View point

68 Small farmers are normally operate in the farm household with _______________ objectives.

a. Single
b. Dual
c. Multiple
d. Specific

69 In which type of participation major objective is to provide specific services?

a. Consultative
b. Collegial
c. Contractual
d. Both a & b

70 In which type of participation major objective is to get information?

a. Consultative b. Collegial

c. Contractual d. Both a & b

71 In which type of participation major objective is to strengthen farmer research?

a. Consultative b. Collegial

c. Contractual d. Both a & b

72 Which type of research is a research philosophy/approach that specifically focuses on 'learning by doing'?

a. Action b. Modification

c. Ex-post facto d. Historical

73 Which of the following takes place in real-world situations?

a. Contrived b. Action research

c. Laboratory experiment d. None of these

74 NARS concept is which type of concept?

a. Hard System b. Viscous system

c. Soft System d. Desertion system

75 Action research typically involves which component in the methodology?

a. Intervention b. Superficial

c. Interference d. Negligence

76 Who among the following was the first to describe the properties of an Agricultural Knowledge System (AKS) in detail?

a. Rollings b. U. Nagel

c. Biggs d. Cess Leewis

77 The basic premise of which of the following is that research and extension should not be seen as separate institutions?

a. AKIS b. ICT4D

c. MANAGE d. ARIS

78 __________________is a process in which two or more organizations collaborate to achieve shared goals

a. Networking b. Friendship

c. Sharing d. Rivalry

79 Which of the following are some of the most common methodologies to assess the impact of network?

a. SWOT analysis b. Logical Framework Analysis

c. Outcome Mapping d. All of these

80 Poverty generally is regarded as ______________ in nature.

a. Multidimensional b. Uni-dimensional

c. Dimensionless d. None of these

81 The Green Revolution is generally considered to have been a tremendous success in which part of the globe?

a. Latin America b. Asia

c. Both a & b d. Africa

82 Positive Deviance (PD) is a departure from the norm, that results in __________

a. Positive Outcome b. Negative outcome

c. Un predictive outcome d. Conflict

83 The US extension system is structured as which type of system?

a. Mass-media system b. Cooperative System

c. Profitable system d. Voluntary system

84 Experimenting with 'Telecentres' was observed in which of the following countries?

a. Lao People's Democratic Republic

b. Vietnam

c. Mali

d. All of the above

85 Soya-Choupal website floated by whom?

a. ITC b. TATA

c. Reliance d. Wipro

86 In which state, 'Computer on Wheels (COW)' programme was initiated in several districts?

a. Andhra Pradesh b. Madhya Pradesh

c. Maharashtra d. West Bengal

87 Which of the following organisation was the first to introduce extension as a compulsory subject at undergraduate level?

a. BAU b. IARI

c. IVRI d. AAU

88 In which year, Master's programme in Agricultural extension was introduced?

a. 1947-48 b. 1965-66

c. 1955-56 d. 1970-71

89 Indian Journal of Extension Education started publication from which year?

a. 1965 b. 1967

c. 1968 d. 1972

90 The Grow More Food Enquiry committee submitted its report in which year ?

a. 1948 b. 1952

c. 1955 d. 1954

91 Directed contact change is caused by which of the following?

a. Insiders b. Opinion leaders

c. Outsiders d. Sarpanch

92 Which of the following factor is important for rural development?

a. Human b. Socio-cultural

c. Organizational d. All of these

93 Who among the following classified educational objectives?

a. Bloom b. Leagans

c. Rogers d. Wilson and Gallup

94 According to Helsey, 'Ability+ Motivation' results in __________

a. Output b. Perfection

c. Improvement d. Performance

95 According to Knowles, 'Needs or motivating forces + Experience and ability' = ?

a. Behaviour b. Skill

c. Knowledge d. Personality

96 Who among the following reviewed the system of communication flow?

a. Rogers b. Shoemaker

c. Katz d. Aristotle

97 According to Coombs, rural development means________________

a. Rural transformation b. Rural up-liftment

c. Rural reconstruction d. Urbanization

98 In Philippines Rural Reconstruction Movement- the man- power has inspired from whom?

a. Politicians b. Scientists

c. College graduate d. Extension agents

99 Who is considered as the 'Father of Extension' in India?

a. K.N. Singh b. R.N. Singh

c. G.L. Ray d. S.N.Singh

100 Who is the 'Father of University Extension'?

a. Rogers b. James Stewart

c. Shoemaker d. K.N. Singh

101 Who is the 'Father of Demonstration'?

a. J.P.Leagans b. Rolling

c. Seamann A. Knapp d. Hawkins

102 The term 'Extension' having its root in which of the following languages?

a. Greek b. German

c. Roman d. Latin

103 Who used the term 'Extension' first time?

a. J.P. Leagans b. Aristotle

c. Pluto d. Vorhees

104 Who among the following proposed the concept of 'Farmer First'?

a. Kelsey and Hearne b. Robert Chambers

c. Mildred Horton d. Wilson and Gallup

105 Who is considered as the father of 'Group Dynamics'?

a. Emiel Durkhiem b. Cess Leewis

c. Kurt Lewin d. Peter Drucker

106 Which among the following is considered as the basic unit of Extension Work?

a. Family b. Society

c. Individual d. Village

107 Extension is __________

a. One way process b. Two way process

c. Top Down process d. Autocratic process

108 Voorliching means __________

a. Farming b. Lighting the path

c. Study d. Education

109 In French language 'Extension' is referred as __________

a. Voorliching b. Capacitation

c. Vulgurisation d. Beratung

110 In German language 'Beratung' means-

a. Extension b. Training

c. Advisory work d. Teaching

111 In which country 'Give illumination in dark' is referred as 'Penyuluhan'?

a. Malaysia b. Thailand

c. Indonesia d. Bhutan

112 Who among the following is considered as the 'Father of Extension Education'?

a. James Stewart b. J.P. Leagans

c. Auguste Compte d. Ferdinand Tonnies

113 Which committee recommended 'Out of school education' should be given to rural people to stop migration?

a. New York Committee b. London Committee

c. Philadelphia Committee d. Missouri Committee

114 In which of the following country Agro-Ecosystem Analysis was first introduced?

a. Thailand b. Burundi

c. Malaysia d. Uganda

115 Which of the following famine commission recommended the revival of agriculture?

a. Famine Commission 1900 b. Famine Commission 1927

c. Famine Commission 1880 d. Famine Commission 1866

116 Which Govt. of India Act led to agricultural development as a state subject?

a. Govt. of India Act 1990 b. Govt. of India Act 1927

c. Govt. of India Act 1917 d. Govt. of India Act 1919

117 Which one of the following was not the outcome of recommendation of Famine Commission 1901?

a. Establishment of ICAR

b. Establishment of agriculture colleges

c. Indian Agriculture Services

d. Establishment of IVRI

118 Under whose recommendation, recruitment to the Indian Agricultural Service ceased to function?

a. Royal Commission 1924 b. Famine Commission 1901

c. Govt. of India Act 1919 d. Farmers Commission 2003

119 Who wrote the book on 'A theory of human motivation'?

a. A H Maslow b. F L Brayne

c. Fredrick Taylor d. B F Skinner

120 'Extension Teaching Methods' book has been written by which of the following author?

a. D K Berlo b. A S Sandhu

c. Wilson and Gallup d. Walt Disney

121 Which one of the following is not the characteristic of learning?

a. Satisfying b. Purposeful

c. Challenging d. Mysterious

122 The major goal of teaching is ___________

a. Salary b. Motivation

c. Learning d. Social service

123 What is the ultimate purpose of teaching?

a. To inform b. To transform

c. To punish d. To dignify

124 Which one of the following is the aim of extension?

a. Development of individual
b. Development of country
c. Development of world
d. Development of industry

125 The major objective of extension can be categorized in which of the following categories?

a. Material
b. Educational
c. Socio cultural
d. All of these

126 Which of the following is true about extension teaching?

a. Largely Vertical
b. Largely Horizontal
c. Formal
d. Deductive

127 The concept of extension educational process was given by________

a. J P Leagans
b. D K Berlo
c. Kelsey and Hearne
d. Rogers

128 Extension Education is a ________

a. Art
b. Philosophy
c. Semi-social science
d. Physical science

129 Which of the following is the basic concept of extension?

a. Motivation
b. Education
c. Training
d. None of these

130 The concept of 'Cone of Experience' given by Edgar Dale was modified by whom?

a. Sheal
b. D K Berlo
c. Likert
d. Rogers

131 Asia- Pacific Association of Agricultural Research Institution is headquartered at

a. Bangkok
b. New Delhi
c. Beijing
d. Jakarta

132 Extension work is based on the principle of ____________

a. Learning by doing
b. Seeing is believing
c. Both a & b
d. Work for development

133 Who has given the concept of four fundamentals of learning which includes drive, cue, response and reward?

a. J P Leagans
b. Miller and Dollard
c. Likert
d. Aristotle

134 Six steps in teaching learning process was given by ______

a. J P Leagans
b. Miller and Dollard
c. G L Ray
d. Wilson and Gallup

135 Learning is an active process on the part of whom?

a. Learner
b. Teacher
c. Extension worker
d. All of these

136 Who among the following is considered as the 'Father of learning'?

a. Thomson
b. J P Leagans
c. Thorndike
d. Miller

137 The level of objective in extension includes which of the following?

a. Fundamental
b. General
c. Working
d. All of these

138 Which of the following extension approach is followed in India?

a. Description
b. Prescription
c. Advocacy
d. All of these

139 In India the main responsibility of extension service is with whom?

a. State Government
b. Central Government
c. Both a & b
d. ICAR

140 Who among the following is considered as father of PRA?

a. James Stuart
b. J P Leagans
c. Thorndike
d. Robert Chamber

141 What is the full form of ARYA

a. Attracting and Retaining Rural Youth in Agriculture
b. Attracting and Respecting Youth in Agriculture
c. Attracting Rural Youth in Agriculture
d. Attracting and Reorienting Rural Youth in Agriculture

142 Who among the following has given the concept of 'Satellite Model of Extension'?

a. Vikram Sarabhai b. G Perumal

c. M S Swaminathan d. Abdul Kalam

143 'Law of imitation' was given by whom?

a. Newton b. Watson

c. Gabriel Tarde d. Swanson

144 'A guide to community development' was written by whom?

a. Watson b. S V Supe

c. Swanson d. Ensminger

145 Androgogy is related with

a. School learning b. Farm school

c. Adult learning d. Child learning

146 Who has written the book ' Pedagogy of oppressed' ?

a. Paulo Freire b. Robin Sharma

c. O P Dhama d. Ambedkar

147 What are the fundamental objectives of learning?

a. To do b. For doing

c. By doing d. All of these

148 Who among the following has written the book 'Guide on alternative extension approaches'?

a. Axinn b. Smith

c. Johnson d. Leagans

149 Which among the following is not a tool of PRA?

a. Agro ecosystem Analysis b. Trend analysis

c. Venn diagram d. FLD

150 'Method Demonstration' is falling under which category of extension teaching method?

a. Individual b. Group

c. Mass d. Both a & b

151 'Flag method' is coming under which of the following category?

a. Spoken method b. Written method

c. Visual method d. None of these

152 Which of the following method provides first-hand knowledge at farm?

a. Method demonstration b. Campaign

c. Farm and home visit d. Result Demonstration

153 Which of the following depends on the 'Learning by Doing' Principle?

a. Method demonstration b. Result demonstration

c. Campaign d. Circular letter

154 To show the effect of vermi-compost on crops which of the following method is suitable?

a. Method demonstration b. Exhibition

c. Result Demonstration d. Kisan mela

155 To teach famer about the seed treatment before sowing which method is most appropriate?

a. Method Demonstration b. Result demonstration

c. Circular letter d. Campaign

156 To disseminate information about 'Rinder pest' eradication within a short span of time which of the following method can be used?

a. Field day b. Exhibition

c. Mela d. Campaign

157 When there is a shortage of manpower, fund and time which of the following method is most feasible?

a. Individual method b. Group contact method

c. Mass method d. Both a & b

158 'Media forum' is falling under which of the following category?

a. Individual method b. Group method

c. Mass method d. Both a & b

159 Which of the following method is used for confidence building of farmers?

a. Result demonstration b. Farmers' call

c. Exhibition d. Circular letter

160 In which method, there is no consideration of group boundaries?

a. Campaign b. Method demonstration

c. Farm and home visit d. Circular letter

161 In which of the following crop Seaman A Knapp conducted result demonstration?

a. Maize b. Cotton

c. Wheat d. Mango

162 'Seeing is believing' under this principle which of the following method works?

a. Field day b. Method demonstration

c. Result demonstration d. Field visit

163 A systematic display of models, charts, specimens etc. around a theme in a sequential manner is done in which of the following?

a. Campaign b. Method demonstration

c. Exhibition d. Field day

164 Which of the following extension teaching aid involve more than one sensory organ?

a. Radio b. Television

c. Newspaper d. Poster

165 A visual aid is an ______________

a. Instructional Device b. Communicational device

c. Both a & b d. None of these

166 Who among the following has written the book 'Audio visual methods in teaching'?

a. A A Reddy b. Edgar Dale

c. G L Ray d. D.K. Berlo

167 Which of the following is true about audio visual aids?

a. Improving teaching b. Increasing efforts

c. Reducing learning d. Distraction of message

168 Which of the following visual aids comes under the category of non projected aid?

a. Flannel graphs b. Flash cards

c. Posters d. All of these

169 Which of the following visual aids comes under the category of projected aid?

a. Slides b. Film strips

c. OHP d. All of these

170 Which of the following is not a presentation type of audio visual aids?

a. Flash cards b. Pull chart

c. Film strips d. Models

171 A recognizable imitation of original, but not in working condition is known as ____

a. Model b. Mock up

c. Specimen d. Objects

172 A recognizable imitation of original in working condition is known as ____

a. Model b. Mock up

c. Specimen d. Objects

173 In which of the following real objects when taken out from their natural settings?

a. Model b. Mock up

c. Specimen d. Objects

174 For commercial entertainment which type of films are used?

a. 70 mm b. 35 mm

c. Both a & b d. 16 mm

175 For educational movies which type of film is used?

a. 70 mm b. 35 mm

c. 8 mm d. 16 mm

176 What is the appropriate angle for projection on beaded screen?

a. 20^0 b. 30^0

c. 40^0 d. 50^0

177 What is the appropriate angle for projection on matte screen?

a. 20^0 b. 30^0

c. 40^0 d. 50^0

178 According to a proverb one picture is worth of how many words?

a. 100 b. 1000

c. 10000 d. 500

179 Which among the following is true about posters?

a. Visual aid b. Never used alone

c. Urges for immediate action d. All of these

180 ABC of poster refers to____

a. Accurate, Brief, Clear
b. Attractive, Bold, Clear
c. Attractive, Brief, Clear
d. Attractive, Brief, Colorful

181 Which among the following chart is used to compare quantities at different times?

a. Flow chart
b. Time chart
c. Job chart
d. Bar chart

182 For showing trends and relationship which of the following charts can be used?

a. Line chart
b. Time chart
c. Job chart
d. Bar chart

183 Who gave the concept of 'Cone of Experience'?

a. Edger Dale
b. Auguste Comte
c. Emile Durkheim
d. Masslow

184 In which country, 'Radio Phonics' programme is organized?

a. Latin America
b. Brazil
c. Italy
d. Spain

185 'Telescuola' concept is used in which country?

a. Italy
b. Spain
c. England
d. Russia

186 'Cruzada ABC' can be found in which country?

a. Ghana
b. Brazil
c. Italy
d. Spain

187 Media forum originally developed in which country?

a. China
b. Italy
c. Canada
d. Pakistan

188 In India Media Forums are referred as_____

a. Community Radio
b. Charcha Mandal
c. Kisan Sangosthi
d. Charcha Katta

189 Which of the following letter is written and send to many farmers?

a. Circular letter
b. Personal letter
c. Official letter
d. Postal letter

190 Which one of the following is the oldest form of teaching in extension education?

a. Method demonstration
b. Result demonstration
c. Classroom Lecture
d. Black board teaching

191 Who among the following is called as the Father of The Modern Poster?

a. Dominique Lapaire
b. Christopher Bernard
c. Jules Cheret
d. Samuel Negi

192 In which stage poster is more effective method?

a. Knowledge
b. Persuasion
c. Decision
d. Confirmation

193 Who among the following headed the 'National commission on Agriculture (1976)'?

a. Ram Niwas Mirdha
b. M.S. Swaminathan
c. Acharya N.G. Ranga
d. Narasimha Rao

194 Training about handling of milking machine comes under which of the following method?

a. Result demonstration
b. Method demonstration
c. FLD
d. OFT

195 Models are which type of aid?

a. Display
b. Presentation
c. Traditional
d. Projected

196 The term 'Video' was originated from which Latin word?

a. Videre
b. Videgere
c. Videole
d. Videocon

197 'COIK fallacy' is associated with which of the following?

a. Visual Aids
b. Audio Aids
c. Audio- Visual Aids
d. Hearing Aid

198 Which of the following screen is recommended for projection of 3D movies?

a. Aluminum
b. Beaded
c. Lenticular
d. Plastic

199 Epidiascope is also known as ______

a. LCD Projector
b. Over Head Projector
c. LED Projector
d. Opaque Projector

200 Which of the following is indirect type of projector?

a. LCD Projector
b. Over Head Projector
c. Slide Projector
d. Opaque Projector

201 Which of the following is associated with scenic representation of original?

a. Diorama
b. Panorama
c. Cinerama
d. Scenario

202 The Greek word Diorama refers to ______

a. To project through
b. To speak through
c. To know through
d. To see through

203 Which of the following comes under the category of hot media?

a. Radio
b. Photography
c. Film
d. All of these

204 Who among the following classified media into 'hot' and 'cool'?

a. Marshall McLuhan
b. D. McGregor
c. Merton
d. Rogers

205 Which one of the following is coming under cool media?

a. Television
b. Telephone
c. Both a & b
d. Movie

206 Who is the director of 'Young Professionals for Agricultural Development' (YPARD)?

a. Mariana Peters
b. Amelia Ochoa
c. Martina Graf
d. Courtney Paisley

207 Who among the following is the Chairman of the steering Committee of 'Global Forum for Rural Advisory Services' (GFRAS)?

a. Rasheed Sulaiman
b. Sulekha Dev Burman
c. Andy Hall
d. Van den Ban

208 Who among the following is the Chairman and CEO of Global Youth Innovation Network (GYIK)?

a. Pape Samb
b. Hugo Douglas
c. Nia Arnolin
d. None of these

209 Who among the following is the GYIN India Ambassador?

a. Rakhi Bishnoi b. Sadhna Tripathy

c. Poonam Bajpai d. Tarala Sharma

210 While reading a journal our eyes moves in which pattern?

a. C b. L

c. N d. Z

211 White colour represents which of the following mood?

a. Fresh b. Pure

c. Clean d. All of these

212 Yellow colour does not represent which of the following mood?

a. Warm b. light

c. Youthful d. Ripe

213 Flannel Graph is also known as ____________

a. Khaddar graph b. Motion graph

c. Inverted graph d. Steady graph

214 Isotype charts was developed by______

a. Iceberg b. Otto Neurath

c. Wilson d. Rogers

215 What is full form of 'COIK'?

a. Clear Only Information Known b. Clear Off Individual Knowledge

c. Clear Only If Known d. Care Only If Known

216 According to whom 'A chart is a visual symbol'?

a. Walt Disney b. Edgar Dale

c. G L Ray d. Berlo

217 Which of the following aids are called 'Spark Plugs'?

a. Maps b. Charts

c. Graphs d. All of these

218 Which of the following is the most suitable colour for flannel graphs?

a. Dark Green b. Blue

c. Both a & b d. White

219 Which media is mostly used to create awareness?

a. Television
b. Radio
c. Newspaper
d. All of these

220 DD Gyandashan channel started from which date?

a. 26th January 2000
b. 15th August 2004
c. 15th August 2000
d. 26th January 2005

221 How many components constitute effective learning situation?

a. 4
b. 5
c. 6
d. 7

222 Who was the first chairman of 'National Commission on Farmers' which started functioning in February, 2004?

a. M.S. Swaminathan
b. C.N.R. Rao
c. Som Pal
d. S.S. Acharya

223 In which part of Indian Constitution 'Agricultural Extension' was mentioned?

a. Article 243G
b. Article 243F
c. Article 243I
d. Article 243J

224 Under which of the following taxonomy hierarchy of six levels of cognition—knowledge, comprehension, application, analysis, and evaluation, appears?

a. Linnaeus Taxonomy
b. Bloom's Taxonomy
c. Kranz Taxonomy
d. None of these

225 'Persuasive + Participatory' signifies ________ paradigm of Agricultural Extension.

a. Advisory Work
b. Technology transfer
c. Human resource development
d. Facilitation for empowerment

226 'Educational + Paternalistic' signifies ________ paradigm of Agricultural Extension.

a. Advisory Work
b. Technology transfer
c. Human resource development
d. Facilitation for empowerment

227 The largest extension system in the world is found in

a. East Asia
b. West Asia
c. Southern Asia
d. Northern Asia

228 What is the number of extension agents stated by India in between 2009-12?

a. 90000
b. 120000
c. 70000
d. 80000

229 Extension education is essentially a process of -

a. Innovation
b. Adoption
c. Communication
d. None of these

230 Which form of participation symbolizes work as partners?

a. Consultative participation
b. Collaborative participation
c. Contractual participation
d. Passive participation

231 Which form of participation symbolizes strengthening farmer research?

a. Collegial participation
b. Consultative participation
c. Active participation
d. Functional participation

232 National Agricultural Research Systems (NARS) concept is a

a. Soft system concept
b. Hard system concept
c. Rudimentary concept
d. None of these

233 Participatory Assessment and Planning (PAP) is a tool for

a. Community planning
b. Community management
c. Community development
d. All of these

234 The objective of Participatory Assessment and Planning (PAP) is to build the capacity of

a. Researchers
b. Lay inseminators
c. Farmer leaders
d. None of these

235 Why Participatory Social Appraisal (PSA) is used?

a. Social cohesion
b. Maturity of the community
c. Assess social institutions
d. All of these

236 What is/ are the role of Community Envisioning Exercise?

a. Creating awareness
b. Consensus building
c. Decision making
d. All of these

237 Which of the following is considered as the basis of Participatory Learning and Action?

a. Do-it-yourself
b. Self checking
c. Both a & b
d. None of these

238 The method of Rapid Appraisal of Agricultural Knowledge Systems (RAAKS) was pioneered by which of the following University?

a. Wageningen Agricultural University
b. Indian Agricultural Research Institute
c. Oxford University
d. Stanford University

239 Which of the following is considered as the empowering method?

a. Educating
b. Leading
c. Mentoring and supporting
d. All of these

240 Who has written 'Whose reality counts? Putting the first last'?

a. R. Chambers
b. A. Stoner
c. P.B. Shelly
d. None of these

241 Assertion (A): Learning is a lifelong process. Reason (R): Learning to be useful must be linked with life processes. Choose the correct answer from the following code:

a. Both (A) and (R) are true and (R) is the correct explanation of (A).
b. Both (A) and (R) are true but (R) is not the correct explanation of (A).
c. (A) is true, but (R) is false.
d. (A) is false, but (R) is true.

242 Effectiveness of teaching has to be judged in terms of

a. Course coverage
b. Student's interest
c. Learning outcomes of students
d. Use of teaching aids in the classroom

243 Arrange the training of functionaries in adult education in order these are imparted. Use the codes given below:a) Training of volunteersb) Training of resource personc) Training of master trainersd) Training of key resource personscodes:

a. a, b, c, d
b. d, c, b, a
c. c, d, b, a
d. c, a, d, b

244 "Factors" concerning adult learners are important guideposts for development and formulation of a typology of adult learners.a) Socio-cultural b) Socio-economic c) Psycho-social d) Trends of fashion Codes:

a. a, b & c
b. b & c only
c. a, b & d
d. above all

245 Who of the following is considered as father of university extension?

a. Charles Mc Carthy
b. James Stuart
c. Nuding Grieg
d. William Sewell

246 Which of the following is related to adult learning? a) Morale b) Satisfaction c) Drop out from schools d) FeedbackCodes:

a. a, b & c
b. b & c
c. c & d
d. a, b & d

247 Arrange the following in the order (Top to bottom) for organizing adult training by using the codes given below: a. Master trainer b. Key resource person c. Learner d. Resource persone. VolunteerCodes:

a. a, b, d, e, c
b. b, d, a, e, c
c. a, b, d, c, e
d. b, d, a, c, e

248 "Motivating others to goals" is the function of

a. Leading
b. Auditing
c. Staffing
d. Controlling

249 Long lasting results can be seen if extension focuses more on ___________

a. Input supply
b. Output
c. Credit supply
d. None of these

250 Theory of Cognitive Dissonance was given by

a. Richard Lazarus
b. Leon Festinger
c. Jean Piaget's
d None of these

251 In USA, service related to Extension is provided by

a. Land-grant colleges
b. USDA
c. Extension Council
d. All of the above

252 The market- led extension farmers known as

a. Innovation
b. Entrepreneurs
c. High producers
d. Agripreneurs

253 Who among the following has played important role in validation of ITK?

a. Indian Institute of Medical Science

b. UNESCO

c. National Innovation Foundation

d. National Biodiversity Authority

254 Education plus Health leads to

a. Human development b. Social

c. Political d Economical

255 Who is the social entrepreneur?

a. Ratan Tata b. Mohammad Yunus

c. Anil Ambani d All

256 ITK is

a. Holistic b. Qualitative and practical

c. Experience d All of the above

257 Which cannot be learned quickly?

a. New technologies b. Theoretical

c. Conceptual d All of these

258 How to do vaccination_____________?

a. National demonstration b. Result demonstration

c. Methods demonstration d None of these

259 Which organization is responsible for first-line extension

a. ICRISAT b. CGIAR

c. ICAR d. None of these

Answer Key

1. a	2. d	3. b	4. a	5. b	6. c	7. a	8. d	9. a	10. a
11. d	12. c	13. a	14. a	15. b	16. a	17. c	18. a	19. d	20. d
21. a	22. c	23. a	24. a	25. a	26. c	27. c	28. b	29. a	30. c
31. a	32. b	33. a	34. d	35. c	36. a	37. b	38. a	39. a	40. d
41. a	42. a	43. c	44. b	45. d	46. a	47. c	48. d	49. b	50. a
51. c	52. c	53. a	54. c	55. a	56. a	57. c	58. b	59. a	60. c
61. c	62. c	63. a	64. c	65. a	66. c	67. a	68. c	69. c	70. a
71. b	72. a	73. b	74. c	75. a	76. b	77. a	78. a	79. a	80. a
81. c	82. a	83. b	84. d	85. a	86. a	87. a	88. c	89. a	90. b
91. c	92. d	93. a	94. d	95. a	96. c	97. a	98. c	99. a	100. b
101. c	102. d	103. d	104. b	105. c	106. a	107. b	108. b	109. c	110. c
111. c	112. b	113 c	114. a	115. c	116. d	117. d	118. a	119. a	120. c
121. d	122. c	123. b	124. a	125. d	126. b	127. a	128. c	129. b	130. a
131. a	132. c	133. b	134. d	135. a	136. c	137. d	138. b	139. a	140. d
141. a	142. b	143. c	144. d	145. c	146. a	147. d	148. a	149. d	150. b
151. a	152. c	153. a	154. c	155. a	156. d	157. c	158. b	159. a	160. a
161. b	162. c	163. c	164. b	165. c	166. b	167. a	168. d	169. d	170. d
171. a	172. b	173. c	174. c	175. d	176. a	177. b	178. b	179. d	180. c
181. d	182. a	183. a	184. a	185. a	186. b	187. c	188. b	189. a	190. a
191. c	192. a	193. a	194. b	195. a	196. a	197. c	198. a	199. d	200. b
201. a	202. d	203. d	204. a	205. c	206. d	207. a	208. a	209. c	210. d
211. d	212. c	213. a	214. b	215. c	216. b	217. d	218. c	219. d	220. a
221. b	222. c	223. a	224. b	225. a	226. c	227. c	228. a	229. c	230. b
231. a	232. a	233. d	234. c	235. d	236. d	237. a	238. a	239. d	240. a
241. a	242. c	243. c	244. d	245. b	246. d	247. a	248. a	249. b	250. b
251. d	252. d	253. c	254. a	255. b	256. d	257. c	258. c	259. c	

2

Developmental Schemes in India and Abroad

1 In which year National Horticulture Mission was launched as a centrally sponsored scheme?

a. 2005-06 b. 2001-02

c. 1951-52 d. 1955-56

2 In which of the following state National Horticulture Mission (NHM) has not been implemented?

a. North Eastern States b. Jammu & Kashmir

c. Himachal Pradesh d. All of these

3 What are the components of National Food Security Mission?

a. Rice– Wheat– Pulses b. Rice– Wheat– Legumes

c. Rice– Wheat– Milk d. Rice– Wheat– Cereals

4 National Rural Employment Guarantee Act (NREGA) was enacted in____________.

a. September 2006 b. September 2005

c. January 2006 d. January 2005

5 Sampoorna Grameen Rozgar Yojana (SGRY) and National Food for Work Programme (NFFWP) have been merged with which of the following scheme?

a. National Rural Employment Guarantee Act (NREGA)

b. National Food Security Mission

c. Bharat Nirman

d. Rashtriya Krishi Vikas Yojana (RKVY)

6 Macro Management of Agriculture (MMA) Scheme is a ___________

a. Centrally Sponsored Scheme b. State Sponsored Scheme

c. ICAR Sponsored Scheme d. Non Sponsored Scheme

7 Under Micro Irrigation (MI) Scheme what is the percentage of share born by State Government?

a. 40% b. 10%

c. 75% d. 100%

8 Which scheme promoted creation of scientific storage facility for farmers?

a. Gramin Bhandaran Yojana

b. National Pulses Development Project

c. Rashtriya Krishi Vikas Yojana

d. National Agricultural Technology Project

9 Which is of the followings programme is started with the objective to increase the production of pulses in the country?

a. National Pulses Development Project

b. National Agricultural Innovation Project

c. Rashtriya Krishi Vikas Yojana

d. National Agricultural Technology Project

10 National Agriculture Development Programme (NADP) is best known by ______.

a. National Pulses Development Project

b. National Agricultural Innovation Project

c. Rashtriya Krishi Vikas Yojana

d. National Agricultural Technology Project

11 One of the major aims of RKVY is

a. Achieving 4% annual growth in the Agriculture sector

b. Achieving 9% annual growth in the Agriculture sector

c. Increasing the employment in agriculture

d. None of the above

12 Technology assessment and refinement under different agro-eco systems was done through

a. IDDP b. NAIP

c. IVLP d. RKVY

13 In TAR-IVLP which of the following was the unit of operation?

a. Block b. Village

c. District d. State

14 "To build the critical capacity of the ICAR as a catalyzing agent for management of change in the Indian NARS"- was the objective of ______

a. MGNREGA b. NATP

c. NAIP d. RKVY

15 Which among the following is intended to provide all basic needs of the farmers through a single window service?

a. ATIC b. KGK

c. KVK d. SAU

16 Agricultural Technology Information Centre (ATIC) has been conceived and implanted since 1998-99, under which of the following project?

a. NAIS b. NATP

c. NAIP d. RKVY

17 Who among the followings started Gurgaon project in Haryana?

a. F.L. Brayne b. Daniel Hamilton

c. S K Dey d. Albet Mayer

18 Sir Daniel Hamilton's Scheme of Rural Reconstruction started at which place in Bengal?

a. Sundarban b. Kolkata

c. Shatiniketan d. Hawrah

19 Sevagram experiment was started by Mahatma Gandhi at ______

a. Wardha b. Sabarmati

c. Dandi d. Pune

20 In which of the following year, the Community Development Programme was launched?

a. 1957 b. 1958

c. 1952 d. 1951

21 In which year, India was declared as free of rinderpest?

a. 1996 b. 2006

c. 2016 d. 2000

22 Post Graduation Programme in Agricultural Extension Education was started first in which of the following college?

a. Agricultural College, Sabour, Bihar

b. Agricultural College, Pantnagar, Uttarakhand

c. Agricultural College, Pune, Maharashtra

d. Agricultural College, Hisar, Haryana

23 In the year 1960 which of the following programme was started in agricultural sector?

a. Intensive Cattle Development Project

b. Intensive Agricultural District Programme

c. Intensive Agricultural Area Programme

d. T&V Programme

24 Intensive Cattle Development Project was launched in which of the following year?

a. 1964 b. 1974

c. 1954 d. 1953

25 Technology Mission on Oilseeds was launched in which of the following year?

a. 1983 b. 1992

c. 1985 d. 1986

26 Jawahar Rojgar Yojana was launched in which of the following year?

a. 1983 b. 1989

c. 1985 d. 1991

27 IADP was launched in July 1960 in _______ districts of various states in its first phase and later extended to ______ districts more in second phase during 1963-64.

a. 7 & 9 b. 5 & 7

c. 9 &11 d. 7 & 11

28 Intensive Agricultural Area Programme (IAAP) came into operation in how many districts?

a. 110 b. 100

c. 115 d. 114

29 The HYVP was launched in Kharif 1966-67 with a sole objective to increase the total food production by utilizing which of the following?

a. High yielding seeds of selected crops

b. Improved method of cultivation

c. Farmers' training

d. Increasing the area under cultivation

30 What was the basic objective of DPAP?

a. To reduce the severity of the impact of the drought.

b. To reduce the severity of the impact of the flood.

c. To increase the agricultural productivity

d. To increase the employment in agricultural sector

31 Who conceptualized the Training and Visit (T&V) system?

a. Daniel Benor b. M S Swaminathan

c. F L Brayne d. Albert Mayer

32 The basic objective of which of the following programme was to bridge the gap between the research systems with that of extension system?

a. T&V programme b. NAEP

c. TAR-IVLP d. NATP

33 In August 1952, which was the first systematic attempt to improve the quality and productivity of cattle and buffaloes in the country?

a Key Village Scheme

b. National Extension Service

c. Community Development Programme

d. Intensive Cattle Development Project

34 The Centrally sponsored scheme TRYSEM was launched by Government of India under Department of Rural Development on _______.

a. August 15, 1978 b. January 1, 1979

c. August 15, 1979 d. January 1, 1978

35 Development of Women and Children in Rural Areas (DWCRA) was started in the year 1982 as a sub-scheme which of the following project?

a. IRDP b. NAEP

c. DPAP d. NREP

36 National Rural Employment Programme (NREP) and Rural Landless Employment Guarantee Programme (RLEGP) were merged into which of the following programme?

a. MNREGA b. IRDP

c. IAY d. Jawahar Rozgar Yojana

37 Which country implemented the 'Comilla project'?

a. India b. Pakisthan

c. Bangladesh d. USA

38 The Integrated Pest Management (IPM) programme was launched in 1989 in which of the following country?

a. Indonesia b. India

c. UK d. USA

39 'Schools on the air' a pilot project was established in1992 in which of the following country?

a. Indonesia b. India

c. Philippines d. USA

40 Which one of the following was the first national extension programme of China?

a. 4 H club b. LANDCARE

c. Harvest Programme d. T & V programme

41 Famous programme LANDCARE was launched in which of the following country?

a. USA b. Australia

c. Japan d. England

42 GMF enquiry committee report was submitted in which year?

a. 1952 b. 1954

c. 1955 d. 1948

43 Bharat Yuvak Krishak Samaj was established in which year?

a. 1979 b. 1966

c. 1971 d. 1956

44 What was the motto of 4-H clubs?

a. To make the best better

b. To make the better best

c. To make all the best

d. To join the hands for development

45 Who among the following demonstrated the corn growing against the boll weevil?

a. Seaman A. Knapp
b. Sigmund Freud
c. J P Leagans
d. K N Singh

46 In which year Smith-Lever Act was passed?

a. 1904
b. 1912
c. 1914
d. 1924

47 Who was associated with 4-H club?

a. Seaman A. Knapp
b. Danial Banor
c. J P Leagans
d. O.H. Benson

48 SFDA scheme was introduced in how many districts of India?

a. 46
b. 52
c. 50
d. 45

49 MFAL scheme was introduced in how many districts of India?

a. 46
b. 52
c. 40
d. 45

50 Rural Landless Employment Guarantee Scheme was started in which year?

a. 1984
b. 1978
c. 1990
d. 1983

51 Which one of the following is true about IRDP?

a. Child Development Programme
b. Women Empowerment Programme
c. Anti Poverty Programme
d. Adult Education Programme

52 What was the period of stage 2 of Community Development Block?

a. Five years
b. Ten years
c. Seven years
d. Two years

53 In which of the following state has no Panchayati Raj system?

a. Meghalaya
b. Rajasthan
c. West Bengal
d. Maharashtra

54 Who among the following supervised the T & V programme at the zonal level?

a. Secretary of agriculture b. District collector

c. Sarpanch d. Regional director

55 Which one of the following is the period of pre-extension stage of Community Development Block?

a. One year b. Two years

c. Five years d. Three years

56 Under TRYSEM scheme how many rural youths were intended to be trained?

a. Five lakhs b. Two lakhs

c. One lakh d. Ten lakhs

57 The share of centre and state under NREP scheme was________

a. 50:50 b. 60:40

c. 90:10 d. 80:20

58 The first five year plan was launched in which year?

a. 1951-52 b. 1955-56

c. 1947-48 d. 1952-53

59 First KVK was established in which year?

a. 1974 b. 1976

c. 1975 d. 1965

60 IADP was also known as ______

a. Donation programme b. Package programme

c. Distribution programme d. Green progamme

61 Nalagarh committee report was submitted in which year?

a. 1968 b. 1985

c. 1958 d. 1978

62 Ford Foundation team report was submitted in which year?

a. 1957 b. 1950

c. 1959 d. 1968

63 On the recommendation of which report KVK was established in India?

a. Mohan Kanda 1976 b. K.N Singh 1974

c. C.Prasad 1970 d. Mohan Singh Mehta 1973

64 Agricultural Research Service (ARS) was started in which year?

a. 1971 b. 1973

c. 1977 d. 1975

65 In which ATARI zone, highest number of Krishi Vigyan Kendras are functioning?

a. Zone-II b. Zone-V

c. Zone-III d. Zone-VIII

66 Kisan Call Cente (KCC) was initiated in which year?

a. 2000 b. 2004

c. 2001 d. 2005

67 The first post graduation teaching in extension was started in which year?

a. 1955 b. 1961

c. 1948 d. 1965

68 The first PhD programme in extension in IARI was started in which year?

a. 1955 b. 1961

c. 1948 d. 1965

69 The first agriculture university at Pantnagar was started in which year?

a. 1955 b. 1960

c. 1970 d. 1965

70 The first Agriculture society in USA was established in which place?

a. Philadelphia b. New York

c. Boston d. Chicago

71 The first society of agriculture was established in Scotland in which year?

a. 1778 b. 1828

c. 1728 d. 1928

72 Hatch Act was passed in which year?

a. 1887 b. 1927

c. 1827 d. 1886

73 Land Grand College Act is also known as ______

a. Hatch Act b. Model Act

c. 4-H Act d. Morril Act

74 Who was the first scientist vice president of ICAR?

a. B P Pal b. A Ayappan

c. R S Paroda d. Panjab Singh

75 Imperial Council of Agricultural Research was established in year_____

a. 16th July 1901 b. 16th July 1929

c. 16th June 1901 d. 16th July 1919

76 'Community Development in India' book was written by ________

a. B Mukerji b. S V Supe

c. G L Ray d. A A Reddy

77 The fundamental objective of CD project in India was______

a. Destination man b. Destination women

c. Destination child d. Destination country

78 Under the auspices of the YMCA which of the following programme was started?

a. Shriniketan b. Shantiniketan

c. Gurgaon d. Marthandam

79 Who among the following was the leader of Bhudan movement in India?

a. Mahatma Gandhi b. Vinoba Bhave

c. Jawaharlal Nehru d. Sarojini Naidu

80 Etawah pilot project was financed from United States __________ programme.

a. Point 2 programme b. Point 5 programme

c. Point 4 programme d. Point 10 programme

81 Etawah pilot project was stated in how many villages?

a. 64 b. 60

c. 70 d. 75

82 Who was the president of American Ford foundation during 1951?

a. Paul Hoffman b. Abraham Linkon

c. George Bush d. Fredrick Taylor

83 National Extension Service programme was initiated in____

a. 1952 b. 1955

c. 1953 d. 1961

84 Who among the following described the interrelationship between CD and NES programme?

a. B P Pal b. V T Krishnamachari

c. Vinoba Bhave d. S V Supe

85 'Democracy' word was originated from which language?

a. Greek b. Latin

c. Germen d. Sanskit

86 The state of Madras initiated 'Democratic Decentralization' in which year?

a. 1957 b. 1966

c. 1958 d. 1959

87 Which one of the following is not coming under 4-H ?

a. Head b. Heart

c. Hands d. Height

88 Young Farmers' Association in India was established in which year?

a. July 1966 b. April 1956

c. April 1966 d. April 1976

89 Young Farmers' Association was formed under whose guidance?

a. P S Deshmukh b. Panjabrao Deshmukh

c. Jawaharlal Nehru d. M S Swaminathan

90 'Cooperative Extension Service' was created under which Act in USA?

a. Hatch Act b. Model Act

c. Smith Lever Act d. Morril Act

91 Agricultural Extension Service in Japan was started in which year?

a. 1958 b. 1948

c. 1908 d. 1999

92 ATMA is based on which of the following approach?

a. Community approach b. Individual approach

c. Participatory approach d. Autocratic approach

93 'Firka Development Scheme' was launched in which of the following place?

a. Hyderabad b. Lucknow

c. Gurgaon d. Madras

94 'Sarvodaya Scheme' was operated in which of the following place?

a. Delhi b. Madras

c. Karnataka d. Bombay

95 The concept of 'Village Guide' was introduced by whom and in which project?

a. F L Brayne, Gurgaon project

b. Ravindranath Tagore in Sriniketan project

c. Spencer Hatch, Marthandam project

d. Mahatma Gandhi in Sewagram project

96 The Division of Extension in ICAR headquarters was established in which year?

a. 1972 b. 1971

c. 1961 d. 1955

97 When all the first line TOT projects of ICAR were merged in KVK?

a. 1st April 1974 b. 1st April 1982

c. 1st April 1992 d. 1st April 1976

98 Establishment of 'Rural Universities' was recommended by which committee?

a. University Education Commission

b. University Grant Commission

c. Rural Education Commission

d. University Development Commission

99 Who was the chairman of University Education Commission(1949)?

a. S Radhakrishnan b. Jawaharlal Nehru

c. V T Krishnamachari d. C V Raman

100 Where the first Extension Education Institute was established in 1959?

a. Anand b. Nilokheri

c. Hyderabad d. Jorhat

101 According to Gajendra Gadkar committee recommendation which of the following board was introduced?

a. UPSC b. NDDB

c. ASRB d. NFDB

102 ICAR was made autonomous body in which year?

a. 1955 b. 1966

c. 1948 d. 1965

103 Who among the following was associated with Indian Village Service?

a. F L Brayne b. A T Mosher and B N Gupta

c. Ravindranath Tagore d. Mahatma Gandhi

104 'Grow More Food Campaign' was reviewed in the year 1948 by which of the following committee?

a. Gajendra Gadkar committee b. V T Krishnamachari Committee

c. Thakurdass Committee d. None of these

105 The term 'Community Development' was originated from which place?

a. Cambridge b. London

c. Dhaka d. New York

106 Which of the following project was financed by World Bank?

a. T &V project b. NATP

c. NAIP d. All of these

107 V-AID programme was implemented in

a. Pakistan b. South Africa

c. Vietnam d. Cambodia

108 ATMA governing body is headed by whom?

a. Sarpanch b. Project Director

c. District Collector d. Lead Bank Manager

109 ATMA management committee is headed by _____

a. Sarpanch b. Project Director

c. District Collector d. Lead Bank Manager

110 First organization to start research in extension education was

a. IRRI

b. University of Cambrdige

c. Wageningen University

d. American Society of Cooperative Extension Service

111 Forerunner of CDP was

a. Firka development scheme b. Marthandam project

c. India village scheme d. Etawah pilot project

112 Food production targets were first time introduced in

a. HYVP b. IADP

c. IAAP d. GMFC

113 First mass scale rural upliftment programme was

a. Marthandam project b. Shantiniketan

c. Nilokheri experiment d. Gurgaon experiment

114 Government of India launched National Dairy Plan (NDP-I) in ______________

a. March, 2005 b. March, 2000

c. March, 2010 d. March, 2012

115 National Dairy Plan (Phase-I) was launched in how many states?

a. 10 b. 14

c. 16 d. 26

116 In which year Centrally sponsored scheme 'Intensive Dairy Development Programme' which is operational in non-operation flood area, hilly and backward area, was launched?

a. 1990-91 b. 1995-96

c. 1993-94 d. 1998-99

117 Which of the following scheme was launched in October, 2007, on the basis of resolution taken by National Development Council (NDC) in its 53rd meeting?

a. National Food Security Mission b. National Horticulture Mission

c. National Bamboo Mission d. Nation Agriculture Mission

118 During 12th Five year plan which of the following is/ are the components of National Food Security Mission?

a. NFSM- Rice b. NFSM- Commercial Crops

c. NFSM- Coarse Cereals d. All of these

119 Bringing Green Revolution to Eastern India (BGREI), was implemented during 2010-11 under which of the following Scheme?

a. MGNREGA b. Rashtriya Krishi Vikas Yojana

c. National Food Security Mission d. None of these

120 Bringing Green Revolution to Eastern India (BGREI), was initially launched in 2010-11 in how many states?

a. 4 b. 5

c. 7 d. 10

121 Which one of the following is not coming under the eight national mission on climate change?

a. National Desert Mission
b. National Solar Mission
c. National Water Mission
d. National Mission for Green India

122 When National Initiative on Climate Resilient Agriculture (NICRA) ,a network project of the Indian Council of Agricultural Research (ICAR), was launched ?

a. January,2010
b. June, 2005
c. February, 2011
d. October, 2012

123 National Milk Day is celebrated on which day?

a. 25th January
b. 26th November
c. 15th August
d. 23rd December

124 Who is the current chairman of National Dairy Development Board (NDDB), which was established in 1965?

a. Amrita Patil
b. Mangla Rai
c. T Nanda Kumar
d. S. Ayappan

125 Where the Central Sheep Breeding Farm, which is producing acclimatized exotic/ cross bred superior quality rams, is located?

a. Hissar, Haryana
b. New Delhi
c. Bikaner, Rajasthan
d. Junagarh, Gujarat

126 Under which of the following mission 'Pig Development Scheme' was implemented?

a. National Mission for pig
b. National Mission for meat
c. National Mission for Protein Supplements
d. None of these

127 When ISOPAM yojana was launched to Increase Production & Productivity of Dalhan, Tilhan etc?

a. 1st January,2002
b. 1st January,2004
c. 1st January,2006
d. 1st January,2008

128 Which of the following Finance Minister of India relaunched Kisan Vikas Patra saving scheme?

a. Pranab Mukherjee
b. Jaswant Singh
c. Arun Jaitley
d. Jaswant Sinha

129 Who launched the m-Kisan web portal on 16th July,2013?

a. President of India b. Union Agriculture Minister

c. Home Minister d. Prime Minister

130 Hill Area development programme was implemented in which of the following plan period?

a. Fifth five year pan b. Sixth five year plan

c. Seventh five year plan d. Ninth five year plan

131 Tribal Sub-Plan was initiated during which plan period?

a. Second five year plan b. Third five year plan

c. Fourth five year plan d. Fifth Five Year Plan

132 National Fisheries Development Board was set up at Hyderabad, Andhra Pradesh on ___________

a. 5th September,2007 b. 12th January,2009

c. 10th July,2006 d. 7th August,2011

133 Rural improvement clubs for woman functions in

a. Taiwan b. Vietnam

c. Philippines d. Pakistan

134 Farmers Functional Literacy Programme was a

a. A type of adult education

b. Fully centrally sponsored scheme

c. Linked with development programme like HYV

d. All the above

135 When the Soil Health Card was launched in India?

a. January,2017 b. June,2014

c. February, 2015 d. October,2015

136 The frequency of distribution of 'Soil health card' will be in

a. Every year b. Every 2 years

c. Every 3 years d. Every 4 years

137 Which of the following activities are covered under 'Paramparagat Krishi Vikas Yojana'?

a. Mobilization of farmers b. PGS certification

c. Organic farming d. All of these

138 In which year 'Mission Organic Value Chain Development For North Eastern Region' was launched?

a. 2014 b. 2015

c. 2016 d. 2017

139 Under the scheme 'Paramparagat Krishi Vikas Yojana' how much amount of financial assistance is given for each hectare of land?

a. Rs. 25000 b. Rs. 50000

c. Rs. 75000 d. Rs. 100000

140 On which date National Agriculture Market (e-NAM) scheme was approved?

a. 15th August,2014 b. 30th October,2014

c. 1st July,2015 d. 15th August,2015

141 What is the maximum rate of premium under 'Pradhan Mantri Fasal Bima Yojana' during Kharif season?

a. 1% b. 2%

c. 3% d. 4%

142 'Krishi Sinchayee Yojana' can fulfill the mission of

a. Water conservation b. Mitigation of flood disaster

c. Per drop more crop d. None of these

143 With the aim of "Har Medh Par Ped", which of the following scheme was launched?

a. Sub mission on Agro-forestry b. Briksharopan

c. Silvi-pasture development scheme d. None of these

144 Which of the following is/are the programmes of 'Mahalanobis National Crop ForecastCentre'?

a. CHAMAN (Coordinated Horticulture Assessment and Management)

b. FASAL (Forecasting Agricultural output using Space, Agrometeorology & Land based observations)

c. NADAMS (National Agricultural Drought Assessment and Monitoring System)

d. All of these

145 In which year Reclamation of Problematic Soils was introduced as a sub-scheme of RKVY?

a. 2014-15 b. 2015-16

c. 2016-17 d. None of these

146 The total allocation under National Mission on Bovine Productivity is

a. Rs. 825 crores
b. Rs. 925 crores
c. Rs. 1025 crores
d. Rs. 1125 crores

147 Under 'Pradhan Mantri Fasal Bima Yojana' which of the following risk is not covered?

a. Localized Calamities
b. Planting Risk
c. Post-Harvest Losses
d. Marketing losses

148 Which of the following is/ are the objective of Rashtriya Gokul Mission?

a. Development and conservation of indigenous breeds
b. Enhancing milk production and productivity
c. Breed improvement
d. All of these

149 Rashtriya Krishi Vikas Yojana (RKVY) was launched in the year

a. 2007
b. 2008
c. 2009
d. 2009

150 What is the target of 'Skill India' programme which was launched in 15 July 2015?

a. To train 40 crore Indian
b. To train 75 crore Indian
c. To train 100 crore Indian
d. To train 125 crore Indian

151 Swachh Bharat Abhiyan was officially launched on 02.10.2014 at__________

a. Rajghat, New Delhi
b. Sabarmati Ashram, Gujarat
c. Sewagram, Wardha, Maharashtra
d. India Gate, New Delhi

152 Assertion (A): India has experienced a drastic rise in educational level among its population in the past three decades. Reason (R): The differences in educational attainment between males and females have shrunk.Codes:

a. (A) is correct and (R) is wrong
b. (R) is correct and (A) is wrong
c. Both (A) and (R) are correct and (R) is correct explanation of (A)
d. Both (A) and (R) are correct and (R) is not the correct explanation of (A)

153 AC&ABC is getting adequate support from

a. NABARD b. NAARM

c. IARI d. ICAR

154 'Rythu bazaar' is started in which state

a. AP b. MP

c. UP d. KA

155 Rajiv Gandhi Udyami Mitra Yojna (RGUMY) is for promotion of

a. Small and micro enterprises b. Medium enterprises

c. Large enterprises d. All of these

156 What is the percentage of share capital of National Skill Development Corporation (NSDC) is held by the Government of India through Ministry of Skill Development & Entrepreneurship (MSDE)?

a. 51% b. 49%

c. 75% d 25%

157 AESA organized 1st meeting in which country ?

a. Pakistan (2011) b. India (2011)

c. Bangladesh (2014) d Nepal (2014)

158 BRICS word was coined by

a. Jim O'Neill b. Goldman sachs

c. K.V.Kamat d. Shaktikanta Das

159 In which year, IVLP was started under AP Cess Fund Project

a. 2000 b. 1991

c. 1995 d. 2005

160 IVLP started initially with how many units?

a. 24 b. 42

c. 18 d. 56

161 In IRDP, which category of farmers was not included?

a. Big farmers b. Small farmers

c. Below poverty line farmers d. None of these

162 How much AC & ABC ceiling limit for individual project to avail the subsidy?

a. 22 lakh b. 5 lakh

c. 20 lakh d. 30 lakh

163 AC & ABC would provide

a. Paid services | b. Free training
c. Bank loans | d All of above

164 National Agriculture Insurance Scheme (NAIS) was started in______

a. 1999 | b. 1985
c. 2003 | d. 2010

165 *'Rashtriya Mahila Kosh'* was started in

a. 1860 | b. 1995
c. 1993 | d. 2016

166 Objective of *'Rashtriya Mahila Kosh'* is

a. Credit linking and SHGs
b. To secure maximum outputs with minimum efforts and resources
c. Socio-economic empowerment
d. Enable women to achieve economic independence

167 *'Pradhan Mantri Ujjwala Yojana'* was launched on

a. 1 May 2014 | b. 1 May 2015
c. 1 May 2017 | d 1 May 2016

168 *Roshni* project is related to

a. Women | b. Rural youth
c. Tribal | d Old people

169 Which among the following advocate gender empowerment through Self-help groups?

a. SWADHAR | b. Sewa- shakti
c. Samriddhi | d. None of these

170 Tunis Agenda of Information Society was started in

a. 12 Dec,2003 | b. 18th Nov, 2005
c. 21 Dec, 2001 | d. None of these

171 Maintaining ecological balance is an objective of

a. DPAP | b. SFDA
c. MFAL | d. RLEGP

172 Plantix App- multi-lingual plant disease and pest diagnostic app was initiated by

a. Farmers b. University of California

c. ICRISAT d. None of these

173 National Rural Health Mission was started in

a. 2006 b. 2005

c. 2000 d. 1998

174 NUHM was started in

a. 2013 b. 2010

c. 1998 d. 2000

175 *'Mission Shakti'* was started in which state?

a. Odisha b. Maharashtra

c. Uttarakhand d. Chhattisgarh

176 *'Swayam Siddha'* scheme which is a SHG based programme was launched in which year?

a. 2010 b. 2001

c. 1994 d. 1988

177 ATMA is functioning as————————level agency

a. Block b. State

c. District d. Village

178 *'Balika Samridhi Yojna'* was started in the year

a. 1987 b. 1997

c. 2017 d. 1947

179 The percentage of funding support for Pradhan Mantri Kisan Samman Nidhi from Central Government is

a. 100% b. 90%

c. 75% d. None of these

180 The original name of Dairy Entrepreneurship Development Scheme (DEDS) is

a. Venture Capital Scheme for Dairy and Poultry

b. Dairy Employment Generation scheme

c. Dairy Farmers Empowerment

d. None of the above

181 e-NAM related to

a. Rythu Bazar
b. APMC integration
c. Online shopping
d. None of these

182 International Information System for the Agricultural Science and Technology is maintained by

a. FAO
b. ICAR
c. UNIDO
d. IASRI

183 AGRISNET started in

a. India
b. USA
c. Nepal
d. Pakistan

184 Linkage between stakeholders

a. IRDA
b. TRYSEM
c. NREGA
d. IVLP

185 Which five year plan of India emphasized "Poverty and Social Justice"?

a. 10th five year plan
b. 5th Five year plan
c. 8th five year plan
d. 2nd five year plan

186 "Attending self-sufficiency and improving export" was the main focus in which five year plan?

a. 3rd five year plan
b. 5th five year plan
c. 8th five year plan
d. 10th five year plan

187 Doubling Farmers Income (DFI) committee has recommended strategies to target a farm to non-farm ratio of ________ in the next four years (2019-2022)

a. 60:40
b. 70:30
c. 75:25
d. 80:20

188 National Animal Disease Reporting System (NADRS) is

a. A web based information technology system
b. Record and monitor livestock diseases
c. Initiate preventive and curative action in a timely and speedy manner
d. All of the above

189 SEWP (State Extension Work Plan) comes under the purview of

a. NATP
b. ATMA
c. NAIP
d IVLP

190 Which company is owned by DARE, ICAR?

a. Agri innovate Pvt. Ltd b. AGRINDIA

c. Both d. None of these

Answer Key

1. a	2. d	3. a	4. b	5. a	6. a	7. b	8. a	9. a	10. c
11. a	12. c	13. b	14. c	15. a	16. b	17. a	18. a	19. a	20. c
21. b	22. a	23. b	24. a	25. d	26. b	27. a	28. d	29. a	30. a
31. a	32. b	33. a	34. c	35. a	36. d	37. c	38. a	39. c	40. c
41. b	42. a	43. d	44. a	45. a	46. c	47. d	48. a	49. c	50. d
51. c	52. a	53. a	54. d	55. a	56. b	57. a	58. a	59. a	60. b
61. c	62. c	63. d	64. b	65. c	66. b	67. a	68. b	69. b	70. a
71. c	72. a	73. d	74. a	75. b	76. a	77. a	78. d	79. b	80. c
81. a	82. a	83. c	84. b	85. a	86. a	87. d	88. b	89. a	90. c
91. b	92. c	93. d	94. d	95. a	96. b	97. c	98. a	99. a	100. b
101. c	102. d	103. b	104. c	105. a	106. d	107. a	108. c	109. b	110. d
111. d	112. d	113. d	114. d	115. b	116. c	117. a	118. d	119. b	120. c
121. a	122. c	123. b	124. c	125. a	126. c	127. c	128. c	129. a	130. a
131. d	132. c	133. c	134. d	135. c	136. b	137. d	138. c	139. b	140. c
141. b	142. c	143. a	144. d	145. c	146. a	147. d	148. d	149. a	150. a
151. a	152. d	153. a	154. a	155. a	156. b	157. d	158. a	159. c	160. b
161. a	162. c	163. d	164. a	165. c	166. a	167. d	168. b	169. b	170. b
171. a	172. c	173. b	174. a	175. a	176. b	177. c	178. b	179. a	180. a
181. b	182. a	183. a	184. d	185. b	186. a	187. b	188. d	189. b	190. a

3

Rural Sociology and Psychology

1 Which among the following deals with the science of human relationship?

a. Sociology
b. Psychology
c. Human ecology
d. Agricultural extension

2 A group of people who have lived together long enough, sharing common values and general interests, is referred to as ____________

a. Crowd
b. Family
c. Society
d. Organization

3 Which among the following is a group defined by sex relationship?

a. Caste
b. Marriage
c. Community
d. Family

4 What is a unit of two or more people in reciprocal communication and interaction with each other?

a. Group
b. Society
c. Dyad
d. Family

5 Which type of family is one where determination of descent and property inheritance takes place along the male line?

a. Matrilineal
b. Patrilineal
c. Matrilocal
d. Patrilocal

6 Family which one sets after marriage is known as ____________

a. Family of procreation
b. Family of recreation
c. Individual family
d. All the above

7 An aggregate of more than one primary family is called as ____________

a. Polyandrous family
b. Polygynous family
c. Joint family
d. All the above

8 Which of the following are characterized by intimate face-to- face interaction?

a. Secondary groups b. Primary groups
c. Tertiary group d. Society

9 Youth club is an example of which of the following?

a. Voluntary group b. Formal group
c. Involuntary group d. None of these

10 Which of the followings is an example of involuntary group?

a. Youth club b. Cooperative society
c. Neighbourhood d. Fun club

11 ________ is one to which the persons feel they belong and with which they identify themselves strongly.

a. An in-group b. An out-group
c. Intergroup d. Secondary group

12 A society where relationships are based on bargaining and clearly defined written agreement is known as ________________

a. Rural society b. The Gemelshaft
c. The Gesellschaft d. Urban Society

13 Which groups are organized with set rules and regulations?

a. Formal groups b. Informal groups
c. Friends club d. Primary group

14 Which are tightly knit group?

a. Society b. Caste
c. Community d. Cliques

15 Which among the following govern the application of means in the attainment of goals?

a. Norms b. Needs
c. Social role d. Taboos

16 What is the process by which an individual is conducted into one's social and cultural world?

a. Urbanization b. Socialization
c. Sanskritization d. Liberalization

17 _______ is defined as a set of interrelated units that are engaged in joint problem solving to accomplish a common goal.

a. Group b. A social system

c. Caste d. Community

18 _______ is the arrangement of individuals or groups into hierarchically arranged strata in a community.

a. Social stratification b. Social mobilization

c. Group management d. Social solidarity

19 Caste system and class system represent basic forms of which of the following?

a. Social stratification b. Social mobilization

c. Social obligation d. Social Polarization

20 Which among the followings refers to the changes in culture that result from continued contact between two cultures?

a. Reculturation b. Transculturation

c. Acculturation d. Cultural conflict

21 Which among the followings is/ are the aspects of Competition?

a. Negative b. Positive

c. Both a & b d. None of these

22 Which among the following can be considered as the most basic social institution?

a. Caste b. Family

c. Marriage d. Community

23 Which among the followings is belief in supernatural?

a. Caste b. Religion

c. Society d. Birth

24 Which among the followings is a political institution?

a. Government b. University

c. School d. Cooperative society

25 _______ is learned, transmitted from generation to generation, universal, static as well as dynamic.

a. Culture b. Etiquettes

c. Talent d. Social goals

26 What is the foundation of indigenous knowledge and technology systems?

a. Scientific knowledge b. Current knowledge

c. Traditional knowledge d. General knowledge

27 _____occurs when some parts of individual's culture do not change at the same rate as do other parts of the culture.

a. Cultural lag b. Acculturation

c. Cultural drift d. Assimilation

28 Which among the followings are closely related with values?

a. Feelings b. Beliefs

c. Caste d. Clan

29 Which of are the followings tend to be culture specific?

a. Beliefs b. Values

c. Both a & b d. None of these

30 ______is subordination of individual accomplishments and goals to those of the family.

a. Familism b. Individualism

c. Feminism d. Socialism

31 _______ is belief in fate, rather than one's own ability to change things.

a. Naturism b. Feminism

c. Fatalism d. Daydreaming

32 Which roles are assigned by culture and society to an individual?

a. Ascribed roles b. Achieved roles

c. Both a & b d. None of these

33 Which roles are earned or achieved by the people through individual effort and competition?

a. Ascribed roles b. Achieved roles

c. Both a & b d. None of these

34 _____are the informal rules of behaviour based on habit and tradition, mostly found in usage.

a. Folkways b. Norms

c. Etiquettes d. Mores

35 What are socially acceptable ways of behaviour that do involve moral standards?

a. Folkways b. Norms

c. Etiquettes d. Mores

36 What are the established behavior patterns for the members of a social system?

a. Folkways b. Norms

c. Etiquettes d. Mores

37 Which of the following are generally grown out of mores?

a. Folkways b. Norms

c. Etiquettes d. Laws

38 ________ is that form of power which is socially accepted and has been legitimized

a. Law b. Autocracy

c. Bureaucracy d. All the above

39 Which leaders emerge out of tradition and stick to tradition?

a. Opinion leaders b. Political leaders

c. Traditional leaders d. Sarpanch

40 Which of the followings recognized as leaders because of their specialized knowledge and function in the society?

a. Functional leaders b. Opinion leaders

c. Local leaders d. Community leaders

41 Which type of leadership is a negative, pessimistic or discouraging approach?

a. Leader centered b. Follower centered

c. Public centered d. All of these

42 Which is a method for identification of leaders and leadership patterns?

a. Psychometric technique b. Delphi method

c. Sociometric technique d. Performance appraisal

43 What is referred as the process of alteration in the structure and function of society?

a. Social change b. Migration

c. Adulteration d. Diffusion

44 Prejudice and feelings of cultural superiority lead to ___________

a. Egocentrism b. Ethnocentrism

c. Xenocentrism d. Terrorism

45 Which of the following concept was given by E.S. Bogardus?

a. Acculturation b. Ethnocentrism

c. Social Distance d. Social mobility

46 The concept of Sanskritization was given by?

a. M N Srinivas b. Emile Durkheim

c. Iravati Karve d. G.S. Ghuriya

47 The term 'Sanskritization' is closely associated with the concept of________

a. Primary group b. Reference group

c. Secondary group d. Out group

48 The term 'social fact' is related with the work of which of the following sociologist?

a. Emile Durkheim b. Auguste comte

c. Sigmund Freud d. Simon

49 The ordered social relationships that grow out of the values, norms, statuses and role to fulfill society's needs are referred as:

a. Communities b. Institutions

c. Associations d. Interest groups

50 ______have direction, are organized in a system, rooted in motivation, prone to change.

a. Attitude b. Personality

c. Folkways d. Norms

51 Who coined the term 'Sociology'?

a. Emile Durkheim b. Auguste Comte

c. Max Weber d. M N Srinivas

52 Who is referred as the 'Father of Sociology'?

a. Karl Marx b. Auguste Comte

c. Max Weber d. Lenin

53 Social structure is composed of which of the followings?

a. Groups b. Individuals

c. Temple d. Bank

54 What are of the major types or forms of social stratification?

a. Caste system b. Class system

c. Religion d. Both a & b

55 What is a closed class?

a. Caste b. Clan

c. Position d. Labour

56 Which of the following is dynamic and continuously changes?

a. Caste b. Culture

c. Both a & b d. Religion

57 Change in which of the following aspect is usually more readily accounted than change in other aspects of culture?

a. Technology b. Values

c. Norms d. Belief

58 Which of the following refers to the preferential feeling we have for the way we do things in our culture?

a. Egocentrism b. Exocentrism

c. Ethnocentrism d. None of these

59 According to MacIver, among the following, which one is the socially accorded (agreed) or accredited (given)?

a. Customs b. Craze

c. Innovations d. Fad

60 Mores are the plural of Latin word ______.

a. More b. Mure

c. Moore d. Movere

61 If 'Folkways' are transmitted by tradition and followed generation after generation may become ________.

a. Custom b. Taboo

c. Culture d. Etiquettes

62 ______are accepted as appropriate but not insisted upon.

a. More b. Taboo

c. Etiquettes d. Folkways

63 Which term is used for those things that are ought not to be done?

a. More b. Taboo

c. Etiquettes d. Folkways

64 Standing during the playing of National Anthem- is an example of which of the followings?

a. More b. Taboo

c. Etiquettes d. Folkways

65 Which term is used for those things that are ought to be done?

a. More b. Taboo

c. Etiquettes d. Folkways

66 'Being polite to others' –is an example of which of the following?

a. Politics b. Communism

c. Convention d. Capitalism

67 Who is a person who exerts an influence over a number of people?

a. Leader b. Follower

c. Manager d. None of these

68 Professional leaders also known as______.

a. Formal leaders b. Informal leaders

c. Autocratic leaders d. Local leaders

69 Which of the followings is also called as huddle system or Phillips 66 ?

a. Symposium b. Brainstorming

c. Buzz session d. Conference

70 Which of the followings involves short series of lectures in which 3 or 4 speakers explain the different parts of a particular subject?

a. Brainstorming b. Symposium

c. Conference d. Buzz session

71 Who among the following gave the concept of rural-urban continuum on the basis of his study of Mexican peasants of Tepoztlain?

a. Robert Redfield b. Lewis Morgan

c. Henry Maine d. Emile Durkheim

72 The concept 'Sociometry' was given by______

a. Bogardus b. Levi Strauss

c. J.L Moreno d. Merton

73 The concept of 'Sociography' is associated with ______

a. Bogardus b. Levi Strauss

c. J.L Moreno d. F Tonnies

74 The concept of 'Cultural lag' was given by

a. Ogburn
b. Sumner
c. Merton
d. Taylor

75 The concept of 'Ethnocentrism' was given by______

a. C.H.Cooley
b. William F. Ogburn
c. William G. Sumner
d. R. K. Merton

76 Who among the following is considered as the founding father of the modern sociology?

a. Emile Durkheim
b. August Comte
c. Talcott Parsons
d. Robert K Merton

77 __________ is a method whereby different societies or cultures are analyzed objectively without using the values of one culture to judge the worth of another.

a. Cultural Relativism
b. Cultural Lag
c. Acculturation
d. Cultural deprivation

78 According to the theory of cultural lag given by William F. Ogburn which culture is change faster?

a. Material than Non material
b. Non material than material
c. Both with same pace
d. None of these

79 __________is the practice of comparing other cultural practices with those of one's own and automatically finding those other cultural practices to be inferior.

a. Xenocentrism
b. Egocentrism
c. Ethnocentrism
d. Cultural Lag

80 _______measures the degree of closeness or acceptance we feel toward other groups.

a. Social distance
b. Sociometry
c. Social mobility
d. Sociogram

81 _______is the system in which each caste group within a village is expected to give certain standardized services to the families of other castes.

a. Barter system
b. Agrarian system
c. Jajmani system
d. Sanskitization

82 Which of the following is the reason for decay of Jajmani system?

a. The decline of belief in caste system

b. The decline of hereditary occupation

c. Modernization

d. All of these

83 Which of the following is/are main features of Jajmani system?

a. Multidimensional relationship b. Hereditary relationship

c. Barter exchange d. All of these

84 In Jajmani system, the person rendering the services or supplying the goods is known as___

a. Kameen b. Prajan

c. Both a & b d. Jajman

85 In Jajmani system, the person to whom the services are rendered is known as___

a. Kameen b. Prajan

c. Both a & b d. Jajman

86 The traditional Jajmani System is based on exchange of______

a. Land b. Goods and services

c. Money d. Labour

87 What are the major socialization agents that teach the gender roles?

a. Family b. Schools

c. Media d. All of these

88 Which of the following term shows the belief that our own products, styles or ideas are necessarily inferior to those which originate elsewhere?

a. Ethnocentrism b. Xenocentrism

c. Egocentrism d. Exocentrism

89 Who among the following has written the book 'Rural Sociology in India'?

a. M N Srinivas b. A R Desai

c. Radhakamal Mukherjee d. G.S Ghurye

90 Who among the following has given the concept of 'Mind, Self and Society'?

a. G. H Mead b. Margaret Mead

c. Sigmund Freud d. James George Frazer

91 Which is the correct sequence of social evolution according to L.H Morgan?

a. Barbarism –Civilization -Savagery

b. Civilization -Savagery - Barbarism

c. Savagery -Barbarism -Civilization

d. Barbarism- Savagery - Civilization

92 Who among the following characterized caste as a closed status group?

a. M N Srinivas b. August comte

c. A R Desai d. Max Weber

93 Status over which the individual has absolutely no choice is ______

a. Achieved status b. Ascribed status

c. Master status d. Prescribed status

94 Which one is the correct sequence of the given socio-cultural processes?

a. Cultural contact-assimilation-accommodation-conflict

b. Cultural contact-conflict-accommodation- assimilation

c. Accommodation-assimilation-cultural contact-assimilation

d. Accommodation-conflict cultural- contact -assimilation

95 The broad meaning of Sanskritization is:

a. Horizontal mobility b. Structural mobility

c. Parochialisation d. Cultural upward mobility

96 __________ is the process by which elements of culture spread from one society to another.

a. Diffusion b. Communication

c. Transportation d. Acculturation

97 Who among the following has classified groups into "in groups" and "out groups"?

a. C. H. Cooley b. W. G. Sumner

c. F. Tonnies d. M. Ginsberg

98 Working through Ideal role incumbents is suggested in_______

a. Progressive village b. Non-progressive village

c. Both a & b d. None of these

99 Working through 'socio-metric Stars' is suggested in_______

a. Progressive village b. Non-progressive village

c. Both a & b d. None of these

100 Who among the following has given the concept of 'primary group'?

a. R K Merton b. W. G. Sumner
c. C. H. Cooley d. James George Frazer

101 Which among the following is not the characteristic of primary group?

a. Face to face relationship b. Mutual aid
c. Companionship d. Largeness of the size

102 The process by which the new born child learns to satisfy its basic needs, prepares himself for different roles at any stage in society is called as__________

a. Socialization b. Aculturation
c. Accommodation d. Assimilation

103 According to G.H Mead 'self-conscious assumption of another's acts or roles' is called as_______

a. Imitation b. Ego
c. Self d. Me

104 The concept of 'Looking Glass Self' is given by______

a. G H Mead b. C.H Cooley
c. Sigmund Freud d. James George Frazer

105 According to Charles Horton Cooley's theory of socialization, formation of self-images on the basis of what we perceive to be others' views of us is called as

a. Looking-glass self b. Development of Self
c. Self consciousness d. Ego

106 The concept of 'Development of Self' is given by______

a. James George Frazer b. R K Merton
c. G.H. Mead d. Sigmund Freud

107 Bhoodan Movement was started after a violent peasant movement, known as________

a. Telangana movement b. Champaran movement
c. Naxalbari movement d. Santhal tribal movement

108 Who among the following has suggested a three-fold division of the agricultural population into Malik, Kisan and Mazdoor?

a. Yogendra Singh Alagh b. Daniel Thorner
c. Amartya Sen d. D.N. Dhanagre

109 Which of the following is the process of merging one culture with the dominant culture?

a. Adaptation b. Accommodation

c. Assimilation d. Acculturation

110 Which one of the following is not a feature of peasant societies?

a. Agriculture as a way of life b. Use of family members as labourers

c. Family as a unit of production as well as consumption d. Complete isolation

111 What is the science of human behaviour?

a. Sociology b. Philosophy

c. Biology d. Psychology

112 What is the correct term for becoming aware or knowing something?

a. Conation b. Connotation

c. Cognition d. Foresight

113 What is the correct term for- to act in a particular way or direction after the feeling?

a. Conation b. Connotation

c. Cognition d. Foresight

114 What is the unique, integrated and organized system of all behaviour of a person?

a. Attitude b. Personality

c. Leadership d. Living standard

115 What is the kind of people whose interests are turned inward upon themselves?

a. Introvert b. Extrovert

c. Ambivert d. Overt

116 Who are the people neither introvert nor extrovert?

a. Assertive b. Aggressive

c. Ambiverts d. Shy person

117 'Dying wisdom' a book authored by____________

a. Anil Agarwal & Sunita Narain b. Bina Agarwal

c. Irom Sharmila d. Medha Patkar

118 What is the ability of an individual to make profitable use of past experience?

a. Common sense b. Technology

c. Stupidity d. Intelligence

119 Intelligence is the product of which of the followings?

a. Heredity b. Environment

c. Both a & b d. None of the above

120 When will be the intelligence remains constant?

a. When conditions remain constant

b. Different individual in same race

c. Different individual in different place

d. Different individual in same sex

121 Which word is originated from the Latin word *Personare* which used to mean the voice of an actor speaking through a mask?

a. Performance b. Politics

c. Personality d. Perception

122 What is usually described as a response to stimulus?

a. Performance b. Attention

c. Motivation d. Perception

123 What is correct term for interpreting and perceiving the object?

a. Cognition b. Sensation

c. Translation d. Prediction

124 What is called as meaningful awareness of object?

a. Sensation b. Numbness

c. Objectivity d. None of the above

125 Which of the following word is originated from the Latin word 'emovere' in which 'e' means out and *movere* means to move?

a. Motivation b. Movement

c. Emotion d. Mobility

126 General Psychology is coming under the discipline of ________

a. Applied science b. Pure science

c. Arts d. Social science

127 According to ________, educational psychology is 'that branch of Psychology which deals with teaching and learning'

a. Sigmund Freud b. Joe Skinner

c. B.F. Skinner d. Simon Jones

128 Educational psychology is concerned with which of the following?

a. The child b. The learning process

c. The learning situation d. All of these

129 Which of the following is not true about 'Educational Psychology'?

a. Applied branch of fundamental Psychology

b. Combines two fields which are education and psychology

c. Natural science

d. A branch of science related to education

130 Which of the following area/s covered by 'Educational Psychology'?

a. The Teaching Situation b. The Learning Situation

c. The Teacher d. All of these

131 A systematic experimental study in psychology was started in Germany in which year?

a. 1895 b. 1890

c. 1875 d. 1879

132 First laboratory of psychology was established by whom?

a. Adam Smith b. William Ouchi

c. William Wundt d. Stephen Gerard

133 The method of self-observation is also known as-

a. Introspection b. Retrospection

c. Selfie d. Soli-lo-quay

134 The word 'Introspection' is made up which language?

a. German b. Greek

c. Roman d. Latin

135 In simple word 'looking outside oneself' is denoted as-

a. Supervision b. Emancipation

c. Observation d. Systematization

136 William Wundt established the first psychological laboratory at which place of Germany?

a. Frankfort
b. Leipzing
c. Dusseldorf
d. Berlin

137 'Handbook of Developmental Psychology'- was written by which of the following author?

a. Sprinthall, C.
b. Sanden Vander W. James
c. Darrow, C.N.
d. Wolrnan, B.B.

138 According to Yoakum & Simpson which one of the following is the characteristic for learning?

a. Learning is growth
b. Product of the environment
c. Organisation of experience
d. All of these

139 Which type of learning is incidental?

a. Formal learning
b. Non-formal
c. Informal learning
d. None of these

140 Which one of the following is the characteristic of formal learning?

a. Intentional
b. Organized
c. Both a & b
d. Intentional

141 The learning which involves primarily the use of muscles it is known as ____________

a. Motor Learning
b. Discrimination learning
c. Verbal learning
d. Sensory learning

142 The learning which involves primarily the use of words it is known as

a. Motor Learning
b. Discrimination learning
c. Verbal learning
d. Sensory learning

143 Which one of the following is the characteristic of learning curve?

a. Plateaus
b. Gradual levelling at the end
c. Sudden increase
d. All of these

144 The concept of 'Operant Conditioning' was given by whom?

a. E.L Thorndike
b. B.F Skinner
c. Pavlov
d. Darrow

145 The concept of 'Trial and Error theory' was given by whom?

a. E.L Thorndike
b. Sanden Vander W. James
c. Ivan Pavlov
d. Sprinthall, C

146 According to Thorndike 'learning takes place only when the learner is prepared to learn' comes under which theory of learning?

a. Law of Readiness b. Law of Exercise

c. Law of Effect d. Law of practice

147 Which one of the following is considered as the most important law of learning?

a. Law of Readiness b. Law of Exercise

c. Law of Effect d. Law of practice

148 Who pioneered the concept of 'Classical Conditioning'?

a. E.L Thorndike b. Sanden Vander W. James

c. Ivan Pavlov d. Sprinthall, C

149 Who among the following was associated with 'Theory of Mental Faculties'?

a. Pavlov b. Aristotle

c. Thorndike d. Maslow

150 Who among the following proposed 'Theory of Identical Elements'?

a. Pavlov b. Woodworth

c. Thorndike d. Both b & c

151 Which one of the following is true about Perception?

a. Mental Process b. Physical effort

c. Feeling about mind d. Physical sensation

152 Who gave the Psychogenic Needs and Viscerogenic Needs concept ?

a. Henry Murray b. Maslow

c. Both a & b d. Thorndike

153 Who wrote the famous book 'Motivation and Personality'?

a. Henry Murray b. Abraham Maslow

c. Oladele, J. O. d. Thorndike

154 If one's I.Q. is less than 20 then he will be considered as-

a. Moron b. Imbecile

c. Genius d. Idiot

155 If one's I.Q. is ranging 50 – 70 then he will fall in which category?

a. Moron b. Imbecile

c. Genius d. Idiot

156 Psychology was initially studied under which discipline?

a. Philosophy
b. Sociology
c. Medicine
d. Mass communication

157 Which one of the following is considered as the most primitive of all emotional response patterns?

a. Readiness
b. Anger
c. Startle
d. Foolishness

158 Attention divides the perceptual field of an individual in how many regions?

a. 2
b. 3
c. 4
d. 5

159 Who among the following has divided all personalities into introverts and extraverts?

a. A Maslow
b. Carl Jung
c. P. Newcomb
d. J. Berg

160 Who among the following proposed the concept of 'General Intelligence'?

a. Armando Colaso
b. Victor Hugo
c. Charles Spearman
d. Dario Foe

161 'General intelligence' is also known as which factor?

a. A
b. B
c. F
d. G

162 Perception can be explained as the process of which of the following?

a. Recalling of past data
b. Reception of sensory data
c. Interpretation of sensory data
d. Storage of sensory data

163 Prejudice, coming from the word 'Prejudicum', which of the following is the meaning of 'Prejudicum'?

a. Forming an image of the person
b. Not liking the person
c. Pronouncing a judgment without evidence
d. None of the above

164 Who among the following has given the first three principles of learning?

a. Simon
b. George Kimble
c. Sigmund Freud
d. Edward Thorndike

165 The degree of concentration and eagerness to learn, reflects which law of learning?

a. Eagerness
b. Effect
c. Readiness
d. Exercise

166 California Achievement Tests are the example of which type of test?

a. Group tests b. Sample test

c. Singular test d. Mono-morphic test

167 The full form of ESB is ____________

a. Erythrocyte Sedimentation Bar

b. Electrical Stimulation of the Brain

c. Electronic Stimulation of Behaviour

d. Emotional Standard Behaviour

168 What is the full form of SBP?

a. Socio-biological Psychology b. Stimulus Brain Psychology

c. State of the Brain Psychology d. Split Brain Psychology

169 In the field of personality studies, the term 'Endomorph' means

a. A tall, thin person b. A short, thin person

c. A short, plump person d. None of these

170 In which concept psychology is known as study of soul?

a. Scientific concept of Psychology b. Historical concept of Psychology

c. Spiritual concept of Psychology d. Modern concept of psychology

171 Who among the following has proposed the concept of 'Triarchic theory of intelligence'?

a. Ivan Pavlov b. Robert Sternberg

c. Malkom Knowles d. David Rocco

172 Analytical intelligence is associated with which of the following?

a. Problem indemnification abilities b. Problem solving abilities

c. Mathematical abilities d. Reasoning abilities

173 The Attitude of a person has as its foundation in which of the following?

a. Beliefs of the person b. Faith of a person

c. Opinion of the individual d. None of the above

174 Which one of the following is true about Attitude?

a. Hypnothetical construct b. Hyperbolic construct

c. Hypothetical construct d. Hypothecated construct

175 Who among the following demonstrated the concept of psychoanalysis ?

a. Sigmund Freud b. Pavlov

c. Carl Jung d. Robert Sternberg

176 Which approach of psychology uses the method of introspection to identify the basic elements?

a. Structuralism b. Psychodynamic

c. Functionalism d. Cognitive

177 Which approach of psychology answer why animals and humans have developed the particular psychological aspects ?

a. Structuralism b. Psychodynamic

c. Functionalism d. Cognitive

178 Who among the following have developed the concept of 'Just Noticeable Difference' (JND)?

a. Plato b. Denis Bergman

c. Aryabhatta d. Gustav Fechner

179 In the nervous system which of the following receive and transmit information?

a. Synapse b. Neuron

c. Soma d. Axon

180 Neurons transmit information by which way?

a. Electrically b. Chemically

c. Verbally d. Both a & b

181 The human body's chemical messengers are known as_______

a. Messenger b. Dictator

c. Neurotransmitters d. Neurotransporters

182 Which one of the following is considered as the most common neurotransmitter?

a. Glutamate b. Serotonin

c. Dopamine d. Endorphins

183 The frontal lobe of human brain controls which of the following activities?

a. Planning b. Thinking

c. Memory d. All of these

184 Which branch of psychology studies the effects of physical stimuli on sensory perceptions?

a. Chemical psychology b. Psychoreflex

c. Psychodynamics d. Psychophysics

185 According to Sigmund Freud what is the primary function of dreaming?

a. Sensation b. Entertainment

c. Wish fulfillment d. Relaxation

186 Which of the following comes under the psychoactive drugs?

a. Stimulants b. Hallucinogens

c. Depressants d. All of these

187 When experiences that can be consciously remembered, it is considered as which type of memory?

a. Explicit Memory b. Implicit memory

c. Long-term memory d. Retrieval

188 Which type of memory is measured by a recall memory test?

a. Explicit Memory b. Implicit memory

c. Long-term memory d. Retrieval

189 Which of the following is type of implicit memory?

a. Procedural memory b. Priming

c. Classical conditioning effects d. All of these

190 Which of the following is also known as Auditory sensory memory?

a. Summative memory b. Structural memory

c. Echoic Memory d. Responsive memory

191 Who among the following is associated with IQ?

a. Binet and Simon b. Rutherford

c. Shoemaker d. None of these

192 Who among the following developed 'Stanford-Binet Intelligence Test'?

a. Robert Stanford b. Simon Binet

c. Lewis Terman d. Binet and Stanford

193 Which one of the following is not the fundamental emotion category?

a. Anger b. Happiness

c. Surprise d. Thirst

194 Which among the following theories says 'emotions and arousal occur at the same time'?

a. James-Biggs theory b. James-Lange theory

c. Lewis Terman Theory d. Cannon-Bard theory

195 Which theory refers 'emotion is the result of arousal'?

a. James-Biggs theory
b. James-Lange theory
c. Lewis Terman Theory
d. Cannon-Bard theory

196 'Phrenology' is associated with which of the following?

a. Measurement of intelligence
b. Measurement of personality
c. Measurement of emotions
d. Measurement of memory

197 Assessing personality from facial characteristics is known as ________

a. Phrenology
b. Polygamy
c. Physiognomy
d. Physionomy

198 According to whom mind is divided into three components namely id, ego, and superego?

a. Sigmund Freud
b. Vernon Phillander
c. Lewis Terman
d. Pavlov

199 Which among the following is not the feature of social movement?

a. It is an effort by a group
b Bringing or resisting a change in society
c. It may be peaceful or violent
d It is permanent in nature

200 Which of the following is the reaction to frustrating situation?

a. Aggression
b. Fantacy
c. Stereotopy
d. All of these

201 Day Dreaming is a____________

a. Artistic thinking
b. Accurate thinking
c. Approximate thinking
d. Ideal thinking

202 Saxon villages of harmony are_______

a. Cooperative villages
b. Authoritative villages
c. Traditional villages
d. Mixed villages

203 Which of the following is/ are the characteristics of common bond group?

a. Face to face interaction
b. Members are bonded to each other
c. Both a and b
d. Less bonding among group members

204 Hirirng based on group membership is known as

a. Group hiring
b. Favoritism
c. Partiality
d. Tokenism

205 When one individual stands out from the background is known as

a. Schims
b. Salience
c. Schemas
d. Pronounce

206 When individual's motivation and effort reduced while working in group this can be termed as ___________

a. Social Loafing
b. Social loathing
c. Social antipathy
d. Social repugnance

207 Discrimination towards single people is known as___________

a. Dualism
b. Hatred
c. Singlism
d. None of these

208 When stimuli or events increase the availability in memory, it is known as ___________

a. Priming
b. Stimulating
c. Increasing
d. Invigorating

209 Simple rule to take complex decision is described in which of the following?

a. Smartness
b. Intelligence
c. Heuristics
d. None of these

210 Bona fide pipeline technique used to measure which of the following?

a. Implicit racial attitudes
b. Knowledge level
c. Intelligence
d. Memory

211 A collective community in Israel that was traditionally based on agriculture is known as

a. Kolkhoz
b. Malili
c. Kibbutz
d. None of these

212 How many villages are there in India?

a. 638588
b. 723569
c. 52369
d. 201453

213 Behavior patterns that are typical of particular species of animals- is known as

a. Biology
b. Ethology
c. Structuralism
d. None of the above

214 Which of the following is coming under basic odors?

a. Caprylic b. Burnt

c. Fragrant d. All of these

215 Which of the following is not coming under basic tastes?

a. Salty b. Sour

c. Hot d. Sweet

216 Learning that occurs but not evident in behavior until favorable conditions appear. It is called as

a. Insight learning b. Perceptual learning

c. Latent learning d. None of these

217 The tip of tongue is often referred as

a. Short term memory b. Long term memory

c. Medium term memory d. Pinnacle memory

218 Profound memory deficit is referred to as

a. Amnesia b. Partial memory

c. Memory loss d. None of these

219 Emotional or evaluative meaning of a word or concept is known as ___________

a. Denotative meaning b. Connotative meaning

c. Sensational meaning d. Conceptual clarity

220 The process of evaluating or testing one's own reasoning is known as

a. Reflective thinking b. Inductive thinking

c. Both a & b d. None of a & b

221 Which of the following is incorrectly matched?

a. Sanguine- Cheerful b. Melancholic- Depressed

c. Phlegmatic- Unexcitable d. Cholesic- Cool tempered

222 Learning in which the subject learns to choose one stimulus and not another is known as

a. Discrimination Learning b. Selective learning

c. Judgmental learning d. Perceptual learning

223 Which of the following traditional drawings not correctly matched?

a. Kolam- Tamil Nadu b. Alpana- West Bengal

c. Aipan- Bihar d. Chowk- Kerala

224 Which of the following folk song not correctly matched?

a. Powada, Lavani- Maharashtra b. Bhatiali- West Bengal

c. Tape, Bolia- Punjab d. Bidesia- Rajasthan

225 Which of the following folk drama is incorrectly matched?

a. Nautanki- Uttar Pradesh b. Jatra- West Bengal

c. Tamasha- Maharashtra d. Veethinatakam- Gujarat

226 Which one of the following is not coming under the ABC of Behaviour?

a. Antecedent b. Behaviour

c. Consequence d. Affection

227 A report of behaviors that are actually performed by persons in a given role is known as

a. Role descriptions b. Role prescriptions

c. Role expectations d. None of these

228 Habitual behaviours are called short-circuiting. Why?

a. Behaviour change ends suddenly

b. Stimulus does not travel over the entire nervous system

c. Both a & b

d. None of these

229 Unprepared student trying to fill the answer book with irrelevant content to increase the volume is known as

a. Sublimation b. Rationalisation

c. Compensation d. Surrender

230 Mood indicates

a. Usually of long duration rather mild

b. Organic condition of the individual

c. Results of events and experiences

d. All the above

231 Village become urban when

a. 75% of population engaged in industry and service

b. Population is 5000 plus

c. Density is 400/ sq. km.

d. All the above

232 Which of the following term is used to mean the capacity to understand and function well in more than one cultural group?

a. Poly cultural b. Semi cultural

c. Bicultural d. Many cultural

233 Characteristics or behavior which violates important social norms is known as

a. Deviance b. Rule braking

c. Taboo d. Deterrence

234 In which type of marriage husband and wife share equally in decision making pertaining to family matters?

a. Egalitarian marriage b. Free marriage

c. Social marriage d. Democratic marriage

235 In ________________ marriage husband and wife both work and share household tasks?

a. Egalitarian b. Social

c. Parallel d. Spontaneous

236 When individual reject culturally valued means and goals is known as

a. Nepotism b. Retreatism

c. Rejection d. Abandonism

237 The study of biological basis of social behavior is coming under the purview of

a. Group biology b. Psychological biology

c. Social psychology d. Sociobiology

238 ________________ is the understanding of the meaning from actor's point of view.

a. Vorlitchin b. Gestalt

c. Verstehen d. Action point

239 Marriage between members of the same category, class or group is known as

a. Endogamy b. Mesogamy

c. Ectogamy d. Ploygamy

240 In which system of social stratification position in a social system is given according to merit?

a. Meritocracy b. Bureaucracy

c. Class d. Caste

241 Correlation between task performance and optimal level of arousal can be explained by which of the following laws?

a. Yerkes-Dodson law   b. Charles Hopkin's law
c. Sigmund Freud's law   d. Bennet's law

242 Which of the following indicates false perception?

a. Somnambulism   b. Escapism
c. Day dreaming   d. Hallucination

243 In echoic memory which of the following sensory information are stored?

a. Audio   b. Visual
c. Smell   d. Taste

244 In iconic memory which type of sensory information are stored?

a. Visual   b. Audio
c. Taste   d. Smell

245 By which process strongly felt but usually repressed emotions are expressed?

a. Optics   b. Overt behavior
c. Catharsis   d. None of these

246 Which of the following is an agent of positive social change?

a) Education   b) Economic development
c) Innovation   d) Calamity Codes:

a. b, c & d   b. c & d
c. a, b & c   d. a & d

247 Mal-adjusted children are mostly found in:

a) Rich families   b) Broken families
c) Joint families   d) Unitary familiesCodes:

a. a & c   b. b & d
c. a & d   d. c & d

248 Decision making for buying/ selling of cattle in rural areas is done by ______

a. Man   b. Woman
c. Children   d. All of these

249 Changes in structure and function of society is called

a. Social change b. Social structure

c. Social integration d None of these

250 Expectation of behaviour from others is known

a. Social Psychology b. Social role

c. Social norms d. None of these

251 Who among the following is associated with 'Rural vacuum theory'

a. A T Mosher b. J P Leagan

c. Willium Ward d. Seaman Knapp

252 Andragogy word derived from

a. Latin b. Greek

c. French d. English

253 Sociogram means

a. Identification of opinion leade

b. To analyse choices or preferences within a group

c. Graphical representation of social links that a person has

d. All of above

254 Motor skill means

a. Movement of (muscles) body b. Movement of finger and toes

c. Movement of arm, legs d. None of these

255 Andragogy term was coined by

a. Alexander Knapp b. Malcolm Knowles

c. Johann Friedrich Herbart d. Eugen Rosenstock Huessy

256 Social learning theory is given by

a. Albert Bandura

b. Aaron Back

c. Sigmund Freud and William James

d. Wolfgang Kohler

257 In groups willing to accept rules to work in group comes under

a. Performing b. Norming

c. Adjoining d. None of these

258 Which quarter of Johari window depicts the Highly Inter group Behaviour?

a Arena b. Blind

c. Façade d. None of these

Answer Key

1. a	2. c	3. d	4. a	5. b	6. a	7. c	8. b	9. a	10. c
11. a	12. c	13. a	14. d	15. a	16. b	17. b	18. a	19. a	20. c
21 c	22. b	23. b	24. a	25. a	26. c	27. a	28. b	29. c	30. a
31. c	32. a	33. b	34. a	35. d	36. b	37. d	38. a	39. c	40. a
41. a	42. c	43. a	44. b	45. c	46. a	47. b	48. a	49. b	50. a
51. b	52. b	53. a	54. d	55. a	56. b	57. a	58. c	59. a	60. a
61. a	62. d	63. b	64. a	65. a	66. c	67. a	68. a	69. c	70. b
71. a	72. c	73. d	74. a	75. c	76. d	77. a	78. a	79. c	80. a
81. c	82. d	83. d	84. c	85. d	86. b	87. d	88. b	89. b	90. a
91. c	92. d	93. b	94. b	95. d	96. a	97. b	98. a	99. b	100. c
101. d	102. a	103. a	104. b	105. a	106. c	107. a	108. b	109. c	110. d
111. d	112. c	113. a	114. b	115. a	116. c	117. a	118. d	119. c	120. a
121. c	122. d	123. a	124. a	125. c	126. b	127. c	128. d	129. c	130. d
131. d	132. c	133. a	134. d	135. c	136. b	137. d	138. d	139. c	140. c
141. a	142. c	143. d	144. b	145. a	146. a	147. c	148. c	149. b	150. d
151. a	152. a	153. b	154. d	155. a	156. a	157. c	158. a	159. b	160. c
161. d	162. c	163. c	164. d	165. c	166. a	167. b	168. d	169. c	170. b
171. b	172. b	173. a	174. c	175. a	176. a	177. c	178. d	179. b	180. d
181. c	182. a	183. d	184. d	185. c	186. d	187. a	188. a	189. d	190. c
191. a	192. c	193. d	194. d	195. b	196. b	197. c	198. a	199. d	200. d
201. a	202. a	203. c	204. d	205. b	206. a	207. c	208. a	209. c	210. a
211. c	212. a	213. b	214. d	215. c	216. c	217. b	218. a	219. b	220. a
221. d	222. a	223. d	224. d	225. d	226. d	227. a	228. b	229. c	230. d
231. d	232. c	233. a	234. a	235. c	236. b	237. d	238. c	239. a	240. a
241. a	242. d	243. a	244. a	245. c	246. c	247. b	248. a	249. a	250. c
251. a	252. b	253. d	254. a	255. a	256. a	257. b	258. a		

4

Research Methodology

1 What is referred as systematic and controlled extension of common sense?

a. Knowledge b. Tradition

c. Science d. Intelligence

2 According to Method of tenacity- men hold firmly to which of the following?

a. Truth b. Lie

c. Misconception d. Superstition

3 Which of the following is the method of established belief?

a. Method of tenacity b. A priori method

c. Method of authority d. None of these

4 Apriori method is also known as which of the following?

a. Method of superstition b. Scientific method

c. Method of authority d. Method of intuition

5 Mil productivity of the six sample households are 8, 11, 9, 7, 13 and 6 liters, respectively. What is the median value of the given data set?

a. 8.5 b. 9

c. 7.5 d. 8

6 What is the basic aim of science?

a. Theory b. Concept

c. Construct d. Practice

7 Who has written the famous book 'How we think'?

a. John Dewey b. Shiv Khera

c. Kerlinger d. Guilford

8 What is a conjectural statement?

a. Theory

b. Connection between two statements

c. Problem

d. A hypothesis

9 Hypothesis can be deduced from which of the followings?

a. Theory b. Other hypothesis

c. Both a & b d. None of these

10 Which of the following usually starts with a problem/ problematic situation?

a. Question b. Research

c. Science d. Philosophy

11 When problem is too general, which of the following is true?

a. Problem can be tested b. Problem cannot be tested

c. Solution can be replicated d. Solution cannot be replicated

12 Which of the following is true about hypothesis?

a. Prediction b. Forecasting

c. Correct interpretation d. Incorrect interpretation

13 Which of the following is correct about construct?

a. Theory b. Plan

c. Concept d. Action

14 Which of the following is true about variable?

a. Imagination b. Symbol

c. Specification d. Assumption

15 What kind of definition defines a construct with other constructs?

a. Intuitive b. Summative

c. Constitutive d. Replicative

16 Which variable is manipulated by the experimenter?

a. Dependent b. Independent

c. Both a & b d. Manipulated

17 How independent variable is related with dependent variable?

a. Presumed Cause b. Presumed effect

c. Presumed result d. None of these

18 Which one of the following is true about dependent variable?

a. Predicted to b. Predicted for
c. Predicted by d. None of these

19 Which one of the following is true about independent variable?

a. Predicted by b. Predicted for
c. Predicted from d. Predicted to

20 X-axis in coordinate geometry is known in which of the following?

a. Abscissa b. Ordinate
c. Both a & b d. None of these

21 Manipulated variables are otherwise known as ________

a. Active variable b. Concurrent variable
c. Research variable d. Experimental variable

22 Which of the following is also referred as Measured variables?

a. Categorical variable b. Attribute variable
c. Concurrent variable d. Manipulated variable

23 In which kind of measurement Categorical variable belong?

a. Nominal b. Ordinal
c. Interval d. Ratio

24 Which among the following concerns about polytomies?

a. Active variable b. Dummy variable
c. Categorical variable d. Continuous variable

25 Which of the following variable can be called as 'in the head' variable?

a. Manipulated variable b. Intervening variable
c. Categorical variable d. Continuous variable

26 Which of the following is mostly used to measure variability?

a. df b. CD
c. Variance d. CV

27 When the student group is very heterogeneous in reading achievement, then what will be the variance in reading score?

a. Large b. Small
c. Less d. Nil

28 In the formula ($V_M = V_S/n_s$) if V_S = Variance of Sample, n_s =Size of sample, then V_M = ?

a. Standard error
b. Standard variance of the mean
c. Standard measure
d. Standard deviation

29 Experimental variance is usually associated with the variance engendered by active manipulation of which type of variable?

a. Independent variables
b. Dependent variable
c. Both a & b
d. None of these

30 The independent variable is the source of which type of variance?

a. Error variance
b. Cumulative variance
c. Extraneous variance
d. Systematic variance

31 Which type of variance is shared by two or more variables?

a. Common factor variance
b. Nominal variance
c. Factorial variance
d. None of these

32 When events are random then which of the following is true?

a, Individually they can be predicted
b. Individually they cannot be predicted
c. By group they cannot be predicted
d. None of these

33 Which of the following individual is associated with randomization?

a. Ronald Fisher
b. Gosset
c. Charles Spearman
d. Kendall

34 Under which principle- every member of a population has an equal chance of being selected?

a. Principle of replication
b. Principle of generalization
c. Principle of randomization
d. Local Control

35 Non-probability samples do not use which of the following?

a. Researcher
b. Data collector
c. Random Sampling
d. Structured procedure

36 Which type of sampling method relates to Quota sampling?

a. Probability
b. Choice
c. Non-Probability
d. Lottery

37 Purposive sampling is a form of which type of sampling?

a. Probability b. Choice

c. Non-Probability d. lottery

38 Which of the following indicates Systematic sampling?

a. Probability b. Choice

c. Non-Probability d. Lottery

39 Which one of the following is true about the omniscient being?

a. There is always randomness b. There is no randomness

c. There is sometimes randomness d. There is occasionally randomness

40 Which one of the following is part of analysis?

a. Categorization b. Ordering

c. Summarizing of data d. All of these

41 Which one of the following is the numbers of objects in sets and subsets?

a. Standard deviation b. Frequencies

c. Variance d. Quartile deviation

42 Which one of the following is considered as the partition or a sub-partition?

a. Distribution b. Category

c. Definition d. Compartmentation

43 Which one of the following is the two dimensional representation of a relation or relations?

a. Picture b. Correlation

c. Graph d. None of these

44 Which measures of central tendency is used in social science research?

a. Mean b. Median

c. Mode d. All of these

45 Which one of the following is the most used average in extension research?

a. Median b. Mode

c. Standard Deviation d. Mean

46 Mode is mostly used for which purposes?

a. Descriptive b. Simplification

c. Calculation d. Generalization

47 Which among the following is the principle measure of variability?

a. Variance b. Standard deviation

c. Both a & b d. CV

48 Which one of the following is the number, that is a composite of two or more numbers?

a. Index b. Composite

c. Scale d. Test

49 Canonical correlation is a logical extension of which of the following?

a. Correlation b. Multiple Regression

c. Variance d. Standard Deviation

50 Which one of the following is the composite of two numbers that relates one number to the other in fractional or decimal form?

a. Ratio b. Multiplication

c. Addition d. Subtraction

51 Which one of the following is a numerical tabular presentation of data, usually presented in frequency or percentage form?

a. Sudoku b. Table

c. Crossbreak d. Sociometry

52 Concept of 'Law of large numbers ' was given by ____________

a. Gosset b. Jacob Bernoulli

c. R.A. Fisher d. Charles Spearman

53 When we divide standard deviation of the population with the square root of sample size which of the following we can get?

a. Standard deviation b. Variance

c. Standard error of mean d. t value

54 A parameter is a associated with which of the following?

a. Population b. Sample

c. Group d. t-vale

55 Bartlett's test is used for which of the following?

a. Test of heterogeneity b. Test of replicate

c. Test of unity d. Test of homogeneity

56 Which test is also called distribution free test?

a. Parametric test b. Nonparametric test

c. t-test d. F-test

57 Probability that the null hypothesis will be rejected when it is actually false is stating which of the following?

a. Energy of a statistical test b. Error of a statistical test

c. Variance of a statistical test d. Power of a statistical test

58 When Parametric tests are powerful than non-parametric tests?

a. Sometimes b. Occasionally

c. Always d. Never

59 For which purpose the Kruskal-Wallis test- is used?

a. One-way analysis of variance b. Two-way analysis of variance

c. Multi-way analysis of variance d. Factor analysis

60 For what purpose the Friedman Test- is used?

a. One-way analysis of variance b. Two-way analysis of variance

c. Multi-way analysis of variance d. Factor analysis

61 'Kendell' Coeeficient of Concordance' is denoted by which letter?

a. A b. B

c. C d. W

62 Which of the following is/ are included in Research design?

a. Plan b. Structure

c. Strategy d. All of these

63 What is the basic purpose of research design?

a. Provide answers to research questions b. Control variance

c. Both a & b d. Extension

64 Which of the following suggest selection of research design?

a. Research problems b. Research output

c. Researcher d. Extension agency

65 What is the main technical function of research design?

a. Control Variance b. Conducting research

c. Giving output d. Formulating objectives

66 Which one of the following is true about the error variance?

a. Predictable b. Unpredictable

c. Supposition d. Assumption

67 Which one of the following is the 'ideal of the science'?

a. Theory b. Knowledge

c. Controlled experiment d. Uncontrolled experiment

68 What is the literal meaning of 'ex post facto'?

a. From what is done afterward b. Posting factors

c. Past experience d. Future plans

69 Which among the following is the important source of extraneous variance?

a. History b. Maturation

c. Both a & b d. Replication

70 Which one of the following is known as data discipline?

a. Design b. Experimentation

c. Solution d. Analysis of data

71 Who among the following has divided field studies into two broad types- 'exploratory' and 'hypothesis testing'?

a. Spearman b. Katz

c. Likert d. Lindquist

72 Variable that can be measured in the smallest degree of fineness is called

a. Discrete variable b. Continuous variable

c. Moderator variable d. Qualitative variable

73 Which type of research is a useful tool for educational fact-finding?

a. Experimental b. Laboratory

c. Survey d. case study

74 Which of the following is true about the rule?

a. Guide
b. Method
c. Command
d. All of these

75 Which of the following means identity or similarity of form?

a. Mesomorphism
b. Polymorphism
c. Isomorphism
d. Telomorphism

76 Which one of the following is an assumption that is essential prerequisite to carrying out some operation?

a. Supposition
b. Enquiry
c. Test
d. Postulate

77 Which one of the following is the lowest level of measurement?

a. Nominal
b. Ordinal
c. Interval
d. Ratio

78 Which of the following test is ordinal in nature?

a. Intelligence test
b. Aptitude test
c. Personality test
d. All of these

79 Which one of the following is the accuracy or precession of a measuring instrument?

a. Reliability
b. Validity
c. Both a & b
d. Accuracy

80 Which one of the following is considered as the most ubiquitous method of obtaining information from people?

a. Observation
b. Questionnaire
c. Interview
d. None of these

81 'F scale' used to measure which of the following?

a. Diplomacy
b. Degree of democracy
c. Authoritarianism
d. Audacity

82 'Rokeach's Value Survey' is which type of scale?

a. Rank Order
b. Nominal
c. Ratio
d. Interval

83 In graphic rating scales lines or bars are combined with which phases?

a. Summary
b. Introductory
c. Descriptive
d. Analytic

84 Which one of the following is used to describe the directed dependencies among a set of variables?

a. Factor analysis b. Correlation
c. Path Analysis d. PCA

85 Which geneticist developed Path analysis around 1918?

a. Gabriel Tarde b. Sewall Wright
c. G J Mendel d. Newcomb

86 'Causal Analysis Framework' was developed by which of the following personality?

a. Judea Pearl b. Gabriel Tarde
c. Newcomb d. G J Mendel

87 Which one of the following is another name for Latent Trait Analysis?

a. Response theory b. Item theory
c. Item Response Theory d. Value addition theory

88 The Rasch model is a psychometric model used for analyzing which type of data?

a. Categorical Data b. Continuous data
c. Omnipresent data d. None of these

89 What is the other name of 'Item Response Theory'?

a. Strong true score theory b. Modern Mental Test Theory
c. Latent trait theory d. All of these

90 Which of the following method was introduced by Harold Hotelling in 1936?

a. Canonical-Correlation Analysis b. Factor analysis
c. PCA d. Correlation analysis

91 Under which situation, Linear Discriminant Analysis can be used?

a. Bankruptcy prediction b. Face recognition
c. Marketing d. All of these

92 Which one of the following is the widely used method for factor extraction?

a. PCA b. Path analysis
c. Group analysis d. Discriminant analysis

93 Common factor analysis, also known in which of the following names?

a. Principal Factor Analysis b. Principal Axis Factoring
c. Both a & b d. None of these

94 What is the full version of MANOVA?

a. Multiple analysis of variance
b. Multivariate analysis of variance
c. Both a & b
d. None of these

95 Analysis of variance (ANOVA) method was developed by which of the following personality?

a. R.A. Fisher
b. Gosset
c. Likert
d. Hotelling

96 Which one of the following can be called as a general linear model which blends ANOVA and regression?

a. Analysis of Covariance
b. Analysis of variance
c. Both a & b
d. None of these

97 Best Linear Unbiased Prediction (BLUP) was developed by which of the following individual?

a. Descartes
b. H Hotteling
c. Charles Roy Henderson
d. Gosset

98 Which one of the following is the most common measure of central tendency in nominal measurement?

a. Mean
b. Median
c. Mode
d. Both a & b

99 Which of the following is not allowed as the measure of central tendency in ordinal type of measurement?

a. Mean
b. Median
c. Mode
d. None of the these

100 Interval type variables are also called ________

a. Scaled Variables
b. Rational Variable
c. Internal variables
d. Interval variables

101 Which of the following is not a measure to correct confounding effect

a. Reliability testing
b. Randomization
c. Elimination
d. Addition

102 The Kelvin temperature scale is an example of which type of measurement?

a. Nominal
b. Ordinal
c. Interval
d. Ratio

103 WIPO stands for

a. World Information and Patents Organization
b. World Intellectual Property Organization
c. World International Property Organization
d. World Information Protection Organization

104 Which type of research contributes to solid foundation of reliable knowledge?

a. Basic research b. Applied research
c. Adaptive research d. Strategic research

105 Which of the following concept denotes that knowledge comes from experience?

a. Empiricism b. Rationalism
c. logic d. Inductive reasoning

106 Which of the following personalities is associated with Rationalism Approach to knowledge generation?

a. Rensis Likert b. Aron Fisher
c. Rene Descartes d. Pablo Neruda

107 Which of the following form of reasoning is the process of finding out specific conclusion from a set of premises?

a. Rationalism b. Deductive reasoning
c. Inductive reasoning d. Probabilistic reasoning

108 Which of the following is true about inductive method?

a. Scientific method b. Bottom-Up
c. Generative approach d. All of these

109 Which of the following is true about deductive method?

a. Top-down b. Bottom-Up
c. Confirmatory approach d. Both a & b

110 ______________ is a bridge between empirical inquiry and theory.

a. Concept b. Idea
c. Hypothesis d. Fact

111 IRB stands for ___________

a. Internal Review Board b. Institutional Review Board
c. International Readers' Board d. Internal Report Bureau

112 Science can answer ______________

a. Ethical questions b. Moral questions

c. Judgmental questions d. None of these

113 'Should' statement is a ____________

a. Value statement b. Hypothetical statement

c. Theoretical statement d. None of these

114 In which of the following 'Systematic error' is associated?

a. Reliability b. Validity

c. Both a & b d. None of these

115 If a researcher calculate average milk yield of different animals which measurement he would use?

a. Nominal b. Interval

c. Ordinal d. Ratio

116 Which of the following is the rank-order scale of measurement?

a. Nominal b. Interval

c. Ordinal d. Ratio

117 Which of the following is not a method of data collection?

a. Interview schedule b. Questionnaire

c. Observation d. Experiment

118 Which of the following is provided by the open ended question?

a. Qualitative data b. Quantitative data

c. Both of these d. Predictive type of data

119 When all the member of a society is having the equal chance of being selected is known as-

a. Quota sampling b. Non-random sampling

c. Snowball sampling d. None of these

120 ______________ is a primary threat to the interrupted time-series design

a. Selection-history b. Selection-maturation

c. History effect d. All of these

121 Which one of the following can be considered as threat to internal validity in the non equivalent comparison-group design?

a. Selection-history effect b. Selection-maturation effect

c. Selection-regression d. All of these

122 Which one of the following is considered as the most frequently used quasi-experimental design?

a. Non equivalent comparison-group

b. Equivalent control group design

c. Time-series design

d. None of these

123 Which one of the following is the purpose of the research when it is done to test hypotheses and theories about how and why phenomena?

a. Explanatory b. Descriptive

c. Historical d. None of these

124 Which of the following can be considered as a systematized knowledge derived through observation, experimentation or any other systematic method or procedure?

a. Theory b. Principle

c. Science d. Concept

125 Rationalistic science includes which of the following?

a. Philosophy b. Theology

c. Both a & b d. None of these

126 Which of the following can be categorized under 'Natural Science'?

a. Physics b. Chemistry

c. Biology d. All of these

127 Which of the following subject does not come under the area of 'Social Science'?

a. Anthropology b. Political Science

c. Psychology d. None of these

128 Metaphysical Explanations- are accepted by ___________

a. Layperson b. Social- Scientists

c. Mathematicians d. Extension specialists

129 Purpose of theory is to generate hypotheses that can be tested – this statement comes under which of the following principles?

a. Principle of Phenomenalism b. Principle of Deductivism

c. Principle of Inductivism d. None of these

130 The word 'Research' was derived from which language?

a. French b. German

c. Italian d. Sanskrit

131 The word Research derived from 'Researche' which means-

a. Argument b. Belief

c. Quest d. Skepticism

132 The main purpose of which type of research is 'Gathering knowledge for knowledge's sake'?

a. Fundamental or basic research b. Applied or practical research

c. Adaptive Research d. Action research

133 Which type of research can gather knowledge that could aid in the betterment of human destiny?

a. Applied or practical research b. Adaptive Research

c. Action research d. Strategic research

134 Which type of research basically describes 'what is'?

a. Historical research b. Experimental research

c. Descriptive research d. None of these

135 Who among the following defined action research as – "method of trying consciously to find out whether or not certain activities actually lead to the results that were anticipated"?

a. Knowles b. Khaparde

c. Axion d. English

136 'Control of variables' is difficult in which of the following researches?

a. Psychological researches b. Sociological researches

c. Educational researches d. All of these

137 Who among the following divided 'Field Studies' in the 'Exploratory field studies' and 'Hypothesis-testing field studies' categories?

a. Katz b. Pearson

c. Ibrahimovic d. Spearman

138 In Exploratory field studies-

a. Hypothesis are formulated

b. Hypothesis are not formulated

c. Relationship of the variables are studied

d. Both a &c

139 Which of the following variables are not manipulable?

a. Home background b. Aptitude

c. Intelligence d. All of these

140 Content analysis is also known as

a. Document analysis b. Content checking

c. Document checking d. Scalogram

141 In 'Case Study' method unit may be -

a. Family b. Social group

c. Social institution d. All of these

142 Which of the following word/s are true for the term 'variable'?

a. Attributes b. Characteristics

c. Can be measured d. All of these

143 Antecedent variable is also known as ___________

a. Independent Variable b. Dependent variable

c. Both a & b d. None of these

144 'Adoption of dairy farming practices' is which type of variable?

a. Independent Variable b. Dependent variable

c. Antecedent variable d. All of these

145 Moderator variables are ___________

a. Independent variables b. Dependent variable

c. Both a & b d. None of these

146 Which of the following variable can be measured in any arbitrary degree of fineness?

a. Moderator b. Discrete

c. Continuous d. None of these

147 Which of the following variable consists only of whole numbers?

a. Continuous b. Discrete

c. Moderator d. Antecedent

148 The stimulus variables is also known as

a. Action Variables b. Antecedent variables

c. Moderator variables d. Discrete variable

149 In the randomized block design the researcher will identify how many extraneous factor?

a. One b. Two

c. Three d. Four

150 Ultimate conclusion of every man shall be the same in ____________

a. Science b. Philosophy

c. Superstitions d. None of the above

151 The simplest research design is ____________

a. Latin-Square Design b. Randomized block designs

c. One-shot Case Study d. Factorial designs

152 Meaning of Ex-post facto is ____________

a. From what is done afterwards b. Retrospectively

c. After the fact d. All of these

153 In which type of sampling method sampling units are groups of elements?

a. Simple Random Sampling b. Cluster sampling

c. Quota sampling d. Snowball sampling

154 In case of how many authors only the surname of the first author is cited followed by et al.?

a. 6 b. 7

c. 8 d. 9

155 Which of following should be used rarely while writing a report?

a. Abbreviation b. Italics

c. Both a & b d. Bold headings

156 Which one of the following is not the major section of thesis?

a. Introduction b. Conclusion

c. Results d. Footnote

157 In which part of thesis the results are fully interpreted?

a. Conclusion b. Summary

c. Implication d. Discussion

158 Qualitative data analysis techniques are relatively ____________

a. Old b. Moderately old

c. New d. None of these

159 Which of the following code means a segment of textual data that has overlapping codes?

a. Co-occurring codes b. Priori code

c. Face sheet code d. Inductive code

160 In which of the following process transformation of qualitative research data from written interviews or field notes into typed text is done?

a. Segmenting b. Coding

c. Transcription d. Memorizing

161 __________ symbols represents a population parameter.

a. σ b. SD

c. r d. O

162 Which of the following is the standard deviation of a sampling distribution?

a. Sampling error b. Sample error

c. Simple error d. Standard error

163 Two key branches of the field of inferential statistics are

a. Hypothesis testing b. Estimation

c. Both a & b d. None of these

164 State which of the following is the good way to get a small standard error?

a. Repeated sampling b. Small sample

c. Large sample d. Large population

165 Cronbach's alpha is a coefficient of__________

a. External consistency b. Readability

c. Internal Consistency d. Difficulty

166 Spearman–Brown prediction formula, also known as __________

a. Spearman–Brown prophecy formula

b. Step up formula

c. Viscosity formula

d. None of these

167 In psychometric analysis Item Response Theory (IRT) also known as

a. Latent Trait Theory b. Strong True Score Theory

c. Modern Mental Test Theory d. All of these

168 Regression equations are also known as ___________

a. Prediction equation
b. Linear equation
c. Parabolic equation
d. All of these

169 Number of pair can be formed by taking 8 statements is ___________

a. 4
b. 28
c. 64
d. 72

170 Which technique allows researcher to group variables into factors?

a. Path analysis
b. Factor analysis
c. Square –root frequency method
d. None of these

171 Empirical inquiry which investigates a contemporary phenomenon within its real - life context is known as ___________

a. Case Study
b. Investigation
c. Scientific research
d. Phenomenon analysis

172 Which one of the following is a non parametric test?

a. Chi-square test
b. t-test
c. z-test
d. All of the above

173 To test the superiority or inferiority of two groups by indicating a direction of difference, which of the following can be used?

a. One tail t-test
b. Two tail t-test
c. F test
d. None of these

174 In which of the following research design the research investigator manipulates one/more independent variables in

a. Ex post facto research design
b. Action research design
c. Participatory research design
d. Experimental research design

175 Research questions and background of the research problem is generally mentioned in which part of thesis?

a. Introduction
b. Review of literature
c. Research Methodology
d. Results and Discussion

176 An interview schedule/ questionnaire should contain which type of question?

a. Multiple choice questions
b. Open-ended questions
c. Double meaning questions
d. Both a & b

177 Cluster sampling is a ______________

a. Probability sampling method
b. Non-Probability sampling method
c. Both a & b
d. Indifferent method

178 Quota sampling is a ______________

a. Probability sampling method
b. Non-Probability sampling method
c. Both a & b
d. Indifferent method

179 Which of the following indicates the homogeneity of the test?

a. Test – retest reliability
b. Internal consistency reliability
c. Scorer reliability
d. Alternate form reliability

180 Which of the following is not a unit of content analysis?

a. Theme
b. Words
c. Attitude
d. Item

181 The last step of hypothesis testing is to accept or reject which of the following?

a. Alternate hypothesis
b. Null hypothesis
c. Both a&b
d. None of these

182 What is IPI?

a. Internal Portfolio Initiative
b. Information Personalization Index
c. Information Percent Index
d. International Public Initiative

183 The concept of Thematic Appreciation Test (TAT) was given by which of the following personality?

a. Henry Fayol
b. Gosset
c. Henry Murray
d. R.A. Fisher

184 R^2 denotes which of the following?

a. Coefficient of correlation
b. Coefficient of determination
c. Coefficient of reproducibility
d. None of these

185 Post test only, equivalent group design the experimental and control group are ______________

a. Matched
b. Equivalent
c. Non-equivalent
d. Non matched

186 Thematic appreciation Test (TAT) is a classical example for which type of projective method?

a. Association
b. Expression
c. Construction
d. Choice ordering

187 In the sampling process, the population is defined in which of the following terms?

a. Element b. Unit

c. Time d. All the Above

188 In interview method chances of getting response is

a. Low b. More

c. Medium d. Nil

189 What is the outcome of action research?

a. Action outcome b. Research outcome

c. Both a & b d. None of the above

190 When the sample size is less than 30 which of the following test is used?

a. t-test b. z-test

c. Both a & b d. None of these

191 The idea of Inkblot test was given by

a. Murray b. Rorschach

c. Taylor d. Fisher

192 Likert scale is which type of scale?

a. Nominal b. Ordinal

c. Interval d. Ratio

193 Which of the following is true?

a. Tests are scales b. All scales are tests

c. Both a & b d. None of these

194 To improve the reliability of Thurstone's scale the method proposed by whom is used?

a. Thorndike b. Fisher

c. Eyesenck and Crown d. Likert

195 History is a threat to which type of Validity?

a. External b. Historical

c. Internal d. None of these

196 Under MAXMINCON principle which variance should be minimized?

a. Systematic b. Error

c. Extraneous d. None of these

197 Arbitrary zero point is observed in which type of measurement?
a. Nominal b. Ordinal
c. Interval d. Ratio

198 If 'Q' value of one item/ statement is more then we have to
a. Accept the item b. Reject the item
c. Change/Modify the item d. None of these

199 Which type of surveys gather data over a period of time?
a. Horizontal b. Longitudinal
c. Geographical d. Substantial

200 The book- Foundation of Behavioral Research- was written by whom?
a. F.N. Kerlinger b. Gosset
c. F. Newcomb d. N. R. Rivera

201 "Rejecting null hypothesis when it is true"- indicate which type of error?
a. Type-I error b. Type-II error
c. Type-III error d. None of the above

202 'Accepting null hypothesis when it is false'- indicate which type of error?
a. Type-II error b. Type-I error
c. Both are true d. None of the above

203 Classifying the variables in terms of their mathematical properties is known as
a. Levels of measurement b. Quantification
c. Categorization d. Demystification

204 In which scale the numbers of any one sub class are equivalent of the property being scaled?
a. Nominal b. Ordinal
c. Ratio d. Interval

205 In which scale it is impossible to determine precisely how far one score is far from another?
a. Nominal b. Ordinal
c. Interval d. Ratio

206 Which type of sampling is commonly used in Journalism?
a. Quota sampling b. Purposive sampling
c. Convenient sampling d. Cluster sampling

207 Psychological and physical isolation are part of which method?

a. PRA b. RRA

c. Role playing d. Non-participant observation

208 The aim of controlled observation is to check any bias due to

a. Faulty perception

b. Incomplete information

c. Effect of external stimuli on the specific situation

d. All of the above

209 Which of the following is the essential of good interview schedule?

a. Accurate communication b. Accurate response

c. Both a & b d. Accurate spelling

210 There is no possibility of prior grouping or classification into which the replies are being received in

a. Open end questions b. Structured questions

c. Semi- structured questions d. Cafeteria questions

211 In which of following, exact wordings of the questions are not preplanned?

a. Structured interview b. Standardized interview

c. Controlled interview d. Undirected interview

212 In which of the following, there is need to create an impression that the other researchers would be welcomed by the villagers?

a. Personal interview b. Observation

c. Training d. All the above

213 Which of the following is true in Random Observation study?

a. No Variable is conceptualised

b. Hypothesis is not formulated

c. No sampling procedure is followed

d. All the above

214 In which study, as many relevant variables as possible are brought in plan of analysis?

a. Diagnostic study b. Descriptive study

c. Observation study d. Explorative study

215 When observation fails to disclose the factors to a given problem, a scientist can resort to

a. Experiment
b. Descriptive study
c. Exploratory study
d. None of the above

216 Who expounded 4 methods of fixing belief?

a. Albert Mayer
b. Charles Peirce
c. F. N. Kerlinger
d. R. Fredrick

217 Without any logic people try to cling to their beliefs even in the face of clearly conflicting facts

a. Method of tenacity
b. Method of authority
c. Method of apriori
d. Method of science

218 Viewing science as a problem solving rather than facts and body of information is a

a. Static view
b. Dynamic view
c. Both a & b
d. None of these

219 ____________ is a logical arrangement in three propositions consisting of two premises and a conclusion that naturally follows from them.

a. Science
b. Syllogism
c. Fact
d. Concept

220 If the premises are untrue, any conclusion drawn from them is also

a. Untrue
b. True
c. Logically correct
d. Largely true

221 Who among the following contributed to inductive process by gathering specific facts and then derive generalization?

a. Francis Fakor
b. Aristotle
c. Roger Beckon
d. J.C. Bose

222 ________________ is an expressive and declarative statement.

a. Definition
b. Fact
c. Concept
d. Grammar

223 The layman builds up theoretical structures in loose fashion is known as

a. Common sense
b. Fact
c. Science
d. Causality

224 Major weakness of ex post facto research is

a. Inability to manipulate independent variables

b. Lack of power to randomise

c. Risk of improper interpretation

d. All of the above

225 Empirical research in extension education started in

a. Late 1960's b. Early 1960's

c. Late 1940's d. Late 1950's

226 Data analysis using single criterion is/ are

a. Multiple regression b. Variance, Covariance

c. Canonical correlation d. All of these

227 Which one of the following can be considered as an extension of KR-20?

a. Cronbach's alpha b. Test-retest

c. Spearman Brown d. Tukey's HSD

228 Cronbach's alpha is used to measure ________________

a. Internal consistency b. Face validity

c. Content validity d. None of these

229 Bayes' Rule applied for which of the following aspect?

a. Situational probability b. Systematic probability

c. Conditional probability d. None of these

230 We can say that one event is certain, if its probability is

a. 100% b. 1%

c. 50% d. 25%

231 If a function only increase or only decreases, then it is known as

a. Poly tone b. Poly chrome

c. Monotone d. Monochrome

232 Which of the following is/are true for discrete variable?

a. Quantitative b. Countable

c. Both a & b d. None of these

233 Which of the following term is used to denote number of Type I errors divided by the number of rejected null hypotheses?

a. False Discovery Rate
b. True Discovery Rate
c. Discovery Rate
d. Invention Rate

234 When the truth of the premises does not guarantee the truth of the conclusion, it is known as

a. Valid argument
b. Invalid logical argument
c. Logical argument
d. Valid logical argument

235 Who has given 'Principle of insufficient reason'?

a. Laplace
b. Fisher
c. Aristotle
d. P. C. Maholanobis

236 The linear association with time is known as

a. Monolithic trend
b. Secular trend
c. Cuboidal trend
d. Linear trend

237 Who is associated with famous quote 'whenever you can, count'?

a. Sir Francis Galton
b. Sir Isaac Newton
c. R.A. Fisher
d. E. Gosset

238 Pattern+ Residual= ?

a. Concept
b. Equation
c. Trend
d. Data

239 Who has introduced the concept of boxplot?

a. F Galton
b. Roger Bacon
c. J.W. Tukey
d. R..A. Fisher

240 The term 'percentile' was introduced by whom?

a. F Galton
b. Roger Bacon
c. J.W. Tukey
d. R.A. Fisher

241 Research methods (set-I) and data collection tools (set-II) are given in the following table.Match the two sets and indicate your answer by selecting the correct code:

Set-I (Research methods)	Set-II (Data collection tools)
a. Experimental method	1. Using primary and secondary sources
b. Ex-post facto method	2. Questionnaire
c. Descriptive survey method	3. Standardized tests
d. Historical method	4. Typical characteristic tests

Codes: a b c d

a. 2 1 3 4 b. 3 4 2 1

c. 2 3 1 4 d. 2 4 3 1

242 The issue of 'research ethics' may be considered pertinent at which stage of research?

a. At the stage of problem formulation and its definition

b. At the stage of defining the population of research

c. At the stage of data collection and interpretation

d. At the stage of reporting the findings

243 In which of the following, reporting format is formally prescribed?

a. Doctoral level thesis

b. Conference of researchers

c. Workshops and seminars

d. Symposia

244 The Dean of an agricultural college conducts an interactive session of teachers and students with a view to explore the possibility of their enhanced participation in college programmes. This endeavour may be related to which type of research?

a. Evaluation research

b. Fundamental research

c. Action research

d. Applied research

245 In doing action research what is the usual sequence of steps?

a. Reflect, observe, plan, act

b. Plan, act, observe, reflect

c. Plan, reflect, observe, act

d. Act, observe, plan, reflect

246 Which sequence of research steps is logical in the list given below?

a. Problem formulation, analysis, development of a research design, hypothesis making, collection of data, arriving at generalization and conclusions.

b. Development of a research design, hypothesis making, Problem formulation, analysis, arriving at generalization and conclusions.

c. Problem formulation, hypothesis making, development of a research design, analysis and formulation of generalizations and conclusions.

d. Problem formulation, deciding about the sample and data collection tools, formulation of hypothesis, collection and interpretation of research evidence.

247 Match the items given in List-I with the items of List-II, use the codes given below:

List-I	List-II
A) Random sampling	i) Population is scattered
B) Cluster sampling	ii) Large scale survey
C) Multistage sampling	iii) Population is infinite
D) Systemic sampling	iv) Law of chance

Codes: (a) (b) (c) (d)

a. IV I II III b. I II III IV

c. II IV III I d. III II IV I

248 Match the items given in List-I with the items of List-II, use the codes given below:

List-I	List-II
A) Perceptual learning	I) Sensory experiences
B) Conceptual learning	II) Connecting different types
C) Associative learning	III) Acquisition abstract
D) Imagination learning	IV) Written, spoken, symbolsCodes:

a. IV III II I b. I II III IV

c. II IV I III d. III I IV II

249 Which of the following are not characteristics of sampling in research?

a. Sample should provide all information about whole of the population.

b. Sample can never be hypothetical.

c. Sample must be adequate enough to represent the entire population.

d. Sample should be biased.

250 Who said that the schedule is nothing more than a list of questions which are answered in order to test the hypothesis?

a. Goode and Hatt b. Thomas Carson McCormick

c. C.M. Moser d. Emory S. Bogardus

251 A research design is

a. The process of making decision before the situation in which the decisions are to be carried out arises.

b. The arrangement of conditions with economy in research procedure.

c. The entire process of planning and carrying out of research study.

d. All of these

252 Which is not important aspect while formulating hypothesis in research?

a. Hypothesis must be clear

b. Hypothesis must be testable

c. Hypothesis should define variables

d. Hypothesis should not be limited

253 The dialogue method of discovering the truth was proposed by

a. Saint Augustin b. Plato

c. Socrates d. Heraclities

254 The most important characteristics of a standardized test area) Objectivityb) Reliabilityc) Practicabilityd) ValidityCodes:

a. a & b b. b & c

c. b & d d. d & a

255 Objectivity refers to:

a. Bias free b. Multiplicity

c. Suggestion d. opinion

256 Scale value of a statement in a Thurstone's Equal Appearing Interval Scaling technique is 2.59. Then, which of the following is true?

a. Median is less than 2.59 b. Median is more than 2.59

c. Median is equal to 2.59 d. None of the above

257 Research which tries to solve an ongoing problem having immediate relevance to the society called as __________

a. Action research b. Exploratory research

c. Descriptive research d. Applied

258 The level of measurement attached to categorical variable is __________

a. Ratio b. Ordinal

c. Nominal d. Interval

259 Most widely used research in extension studies

a. Experimental research b. Historical research

c. Field Experiments d. Descriptive research

260 Define a construct with other construct is called __________

a. Operational definition b. Constitutive definition

c. Both a & b d. Structural

261 __________ is a symbol to which numerals or values are assigned

a. Construct b. Measurement

c. Variables d. concept

262 In a Paired Comparison test with sample size 75, the cell entry of f25 in F-matrix is 34. Then, cell entry of f52 will be __________.

a. 19 b. 41

c. 43 d. 55

263 The variables are not related to the purpose of the study but may affect the dependent variable __________

a. Extraneous variables b. Control variables

c. Intervening variables d. Response variables

264 Which is not a non-parametric test?

a. F-test b. Z-test

c. Chi-square test d. All of the above

265 Which of the following is correct?

a. Communality (h^2) shows how much of each variable is accounted for by the underlying factor taken together.

b. When Eigen values of all factors are totaled, the resulting value is termed as the total sum of squares

c. Eigen value indicates the relative importance of each factor in accounting for the particular set of variables being analysed

d. All of the above

266 Method of selecting fraction of population in such a way that it represent the whole population

a. Census b. Sampling

c. Interpretation d. Representation

267 Which one of the following is true about two group post-test comparison?

a. Randomization is possible

b. Pre-test is conducted

c. Good interaction effect of pre-test and treatment

d. All of these

268 __________ are self administered survey forms that consists of set of questions

a. Interview schedule b. Questionnaire

c. Both a&b d. None of the above

269 Interviewer bias can be eliminated in the following method of research?

a. Observation b. Mail survey

c. Interview d. All the above

270 Non-parametric tests are also called as ________

a. Standard tests b. Distribution-free tests

c. Powerful tests d. None of these

271 Which one of the following is not a method of drawing a random sampling?

a. Population mean b. Computer Program

c. Random number table d. Fish bowl draw

272 Which one of the following is not an ethical issue relating to the researcher?

a. Provision or deprivation of a treatment

b. Restrictions imposed by sponsors

c. Inappropriate research methodology

d. Deliberate attempt to hide

273 In a Likert's methods of Summated Rating scale construction technique, statements having t value equal or greater than ________ are selected for final scale.

a. 1.5 b. 1.75

c. 2.75 d. 3.5

274 Small amount of seed tested in different agro climatic situation comes under

a. On farm testing b. In laboratory testing

c. Minikit trial d. All of above

275 Number of pairs in a Paired Comparison test with 6 stimuli will be

a. 15 b. 10

c. 12 d. None of these

276 The proportion of errors in a Scalogram analysis is 0.25. Then, phi coefficient of analysis is ____.

a. 0.50 b. 0.70

c. 0.75 d. None of these

277 The association between categories of herd size and knowledge scores of farmers could be tested by________________________

a. Chi-square test b. Principal Component Analysis

c. Discriminant analysis d. None of these

278 The research design which is appropriate to educate the farmers about the advantages of colostrums feeding in calves is ____________

a. Field experiments b. Ex-post facto

c. Random Block Design d. None of these

279 Which is not a threat to internal validity of a design?

a. Ecological Representativeness b. Regression effect

c. Attrition d. Maturation

280 In exploratory type of research, the major focus is on

a. Hypothesis testing

b. Hypothesis formulation

c. Profile Development and Description

d. Experimentation

281 Which is active variable ?

a. Quantity of colostrums b. Body weight

c. Farmer perception d. All of the above

282 A constant 5 is subtracted from each observation of a set, the mean of the set is reduced by

a. 25 b. 5

c. 15 d. 10

283 ____________ is an uneasy and dissatisfied state from which individuals struggle to free themselves and pass on to the state of belief

a. Doubt b. Mind set

c. Emotion d. Bias

284 Serendipity Experiment of warfarin is conducted by

a. Lee Roderick b. Ed Carlson

c. Frank Schofield d. K.P. Link

285 'Re- invention' term was coined by

a. Shoemaker b. E.M.Rogers

c. Downs and Mohr d. Charters and Pellegrin

286 During development of a knowledge test, 46 out 60 respondents gave the correct answer of a statement. Then, difficulty index of the said is ____________.

a. 45 b. 76.67

c. 15 d. None of these

287 Dummy coding is called

a. Nominal
b. Ordinal
c. Ratio
d. None of these

288 In a Thrustone's technique of attitude scale construction, Q value and C_{25} value a statement were 1.75 and 0.27. Then, C_{75} of the statement is ________.

a. 2.02
b. 1.5
c. 0.47
d. 1.48

289 Milk productivity of the six sample households are 8, 11, 9, 7, 13 and 6 liters, respectively. What is the median value of the given data set?

a. 8
b. 8.5
c. 7.5
d. 9

290 A developed attitude scale, having 15 statements, was administered before 25 experts to check its reproducibility. Experts were asked to give their response on binary response i.e. agree and disagree on each statement and found 65 errors. Then, co-efficient of reproducibility of the developed scale is ________.

a. 82.67
b. 83.67
c. 81.67
d. 85.50

291 There are 8 statements were selected during a paired comparison test. Then, how many pairs will be prepared?

a. 29
b. 27
c. 32
d. 28

Answer Key

1. c	2. a	3. c	4. d	5. a	6. a	7. a	8. d	9. c	10. b
11. b	12. a	13. c	14. b	15. c	16. b	17. a	18. a	19. c	20. a
21. a	22. b	23. a	24. b	25. b	26. c	27. a	28. b	29. a	30. d
31. a	32. d	33. a	34. c	35. c	36. c	37. c	38. a	39. b	40. d
41. b	42. b	43. c	44. d	45. d	46. a	47. c	48. a	49. b	50. a
51. c	52. b	53. c	54. a	55. d	56. b	57. d	58. c	59. a	60. b
61. d	62. d	63. c	64. a	65. a	66. b	67. c	68. a	69. c	70. a

71. b 72. a 73. c 74. d 75. c 76. d 77. a 78. d 79. a 80. c
81. c 82. a 83. c 84. c 85. b 86. a 87. c 88. a 89. d 90. a
91. d 92. a 93. c 94. b 95. a 96. a 97. c 98. c 99. a 100. a
101. d 102. d 103. b 104. a 105. a 106. c 107. b 108. d 109. d 110. c
111. b 112. d 113. a 114. b 115. d 116. c 117. d 118. a 119. d 120. c
121. d 122. a 123. a 124. c 125. c 126. d 127. d 128. a 129. b 130. a
131. c 132. a 133. a 134. c 135. b 136. d 137. a 138. b 139. d 140. a
141. d 142. d 143. a 144. b 145. a 146. c 147. b 148. a 149. a 150. a
151. c 152. d 153. b 154. a 155. c 156. d 157. d 158. c 159. a 160. c
161. a 162. d 163. c 164. c 165. c 166. a 167. d 168. a 169. b 170. b
171. a 172. a 173. a 174. d 175. a 176. d 177. a 178. b 179. b 180. c
181. b 182. c 183. c 184. b 185. b 186. c 187. d 188. b 189. c 190. a
191. b 192. b 193. a 194. c 195. c 196. b 197. c 198. b 199. b 200. a
201. a 202. a 203. a 204. a 205. b 206. c 207. d 208. d 209. c 210. a
211. d 212. d 213. d 214. a 215. a 216. b 217. a 218. b 219. b 220. a
221. a 222. a 223. a 224. d 225. d 226. d 227. a 228. a 229. c 230. a
231. c 232. c 233. a 234. b 235. a 236. b 237. a 238. d 239. c 240. a
241. b 242. d 243. a 244. c 245. b 246. c 247. a 248. a 249. d 250. b
251. d 252. d 253. c 254. c 255. a 256. c 257. a 258. c 259. d 260. b
261. c 262. b 263. a 264. d 265. d 266. b 267. d 268. b 269. b 270. b
271. a 272. a 273. b 274. c 275. a 276. c 277. a 278. a 279. a 280. a
281. d 282. b 283. a 284. d 285. d 286. b 287. a 288. a 289. b 290. a
291. d

5

Management

1 Who among the following quoted that 'Organizations are social units'?

a. Etzioni b. Max Weber

c. Peter Drucker d. Henry Fayol

2 ___________is network of geographically-distant employees who are linked by electronic communication.

a. A virtual organization b. A distance organization

c. An open organization d. An aerial organization

3 Virtual organizations are _____

a. More flexible b. Have less hierarchy

c. Geographically-distant d. All of these

4 Management term came from French word ' menage' which means ________

a. Housekeeping b. Beekeeping

c. Storekeeping d. System operation

5 ______can be used to analyze the competitive situation.

a. Johari Window b. TOWS matrix

c. SWOT analysis d. All the above

6 The WT strategy aims to minimize which of the following?

a. Internal weaknesses b. External threats

c. Both a & b d. Wireless threats

7 Which one of the following the most gainful situation in a TOWS matrix?

a. SO b. WO

c. ST d. WT

8 Which type of planning is aimed for possible future environments which may or may not occur?

a. Contingency planning b. Situational planning

c. Systematic planning d. Future planning

9 Legal authority is granted by whom?

a. Leaders b. Judges

c. Society d. Law

10 What is the nature of staff function?

a. Advisory b. Autocratic

c. Dictating d. Supportive

11 Nehru Yuva Kendra (NYK) was initiated in India in_________

a. 1970 b. 1972

c. 1992 d. 1969

12 TRYSEM was initiated in the year_________

a. 1979 b. 1989

c. 1971 d. 1983

13 In TRYSEM beneficiaries were within the age group of________

a. 18-35 years b. 21-50 years

c. 21-35 years d. 18-50 years

14 Which one of the following is incorrectly matched?

a. 6 sigma-3.4 defects per million opportunities

b. 5 sigma-233 defects per million opportunities

c. 4 sigma- 6210 defects per million opportunities

d. 3 sigma- 308537 defects per million opportunities

15 Voluntary coordination can be achieved in any organization by which of the following?

a. Arbitration b. Adjustment

c. Mutual Agreement d. Both b & c

16 ______is the input output ratio within a time period with due consideration for quality.

a. Production b. Productivity

c. Labour d. Profit

17 Who among the following is acknowledged as 'the father of scientific management'?

a. Fredrick W. Taylor b. Luther Gulik

c. Elton Mayo d. Henri Fayol

18 Who among the following is considered as 'the father of modern management theory'?

a. Fredrick W. Taylor b. Luther Gulik

c. Elton Mayo d. Henri Fayol

19 Who among the following is known for time and motion studies?

a. Luther Gulik b. Max Weber

c. Frank Gilberth d. Elton Mayo

20 'Theory of bureaucracy' was given by ________.

a. Luther Gulik b. Max Weber

c. Frank Gilberth d. Elton Mayo

21 Who among the following is known as 'the father of social system approach'?

a. Fredrick W. Taylor b. Luther Gulik

c. Vilfredo Pareto d. Henri Fayol

22 Who among the following is associated with 'Hawthorne studies'?

a. Henri Fayol b. Max Weber

c. Frank Gilberth d. Elton Mayo

23 7-S framework for management analysis developed by________

a. The McKinsey & Company b. Peter Drucker

c. The Disney & Company d. Swanson

24 What is statement of expected results expressed in numerical terms?

a. A budget b. Numerology

c. Account d. Finance

25 Who propounded 'Borderless flat world'?

a. Stoner b. Thomas Friedman

c. Vilfredo Pareto d. Peter Drucker

26 ____________is characterized by core cultural values and an ongoing commitment to eliminate social oppression.

a. Multicultural organization b. Mono-cultural organization

c. Semi-cultural organization d. Traditional organization

27 Which one of the following organisation maintains the dominance of one group over all others?

a. Exclusionary organisation b. Multicultural organisation

c. Redefining organisation d. Compliance organisation

28 Empathy is important in managing which of the following?

a. Homogeny
b. Uniformity
c. Diversity
d. All of these

29 Famous book 'The functions of the executive' has been written by which of the following personality?

a. Peter Drucker
b. Chester Barnard
c. Rolling
d. Rogers

30 Six Sigma denotes which of the following aspects?

a. Virtually no defects in any process
b. Virtually significant defects in any process
c. Six significant defects in any process
d. Total quality defects in any process

31 Concept of 'Double loop learning' given by which one of the following personality?

a. Thorndike
b. Argyris
c. J P Leagan
d. Pavlov

32 Horizontal organizations are characterized by which of the following themes?

a. Revolves around process
b. Not revolved around task
c. Customers drive performance
d. All of these

33 Establishing an intentional structure of roles for people to fill in an organization is known as _____

a. Staffing
b. Recruiting
c. Planning
d. Organizing

34 Which one of the following can be called as the essence of the managership?

a. Planning
b. Coordination
c. Staffing
d. Leading

35 'Making known to outside agencies unethical company practices' is generally known as ____

a. Malfunctioning
b. Horn-blowing
c. Whistle- blowing
d. Ear-blowing

36 In which one of the following concept, the foreign subsidiaries are given a great deal of managerial freedom?

a. Polycentric orientation
b. Ethnocentric orientation
c. Geocentric orientation
d. Regiocentric orientation

37 ______is the discipline dealing with what is good and bad and with moral duty and obligation.

a. Psychology
b. Sociology
c. Philosophy
d. Ethics

38 ______is a statement of policies, principles or rules that guide behavior.

a. Ethics
b. Folkways
c. Code
d. Taboos

39 'Chaebol' is characterized by a tight collusion between whom?

a. Government and industrial conglomerates
b. People and industrial conglomerates
c. NGO and industrial conglomerates
d. Government and foreign industrialists

40 'Inhwa' is the concept of harmony prevalent in which of the following country?

a. China
b. Korea
c. Japan
d. Malaysia

41 In which of the following theories selected Japanese managerial practices are adapted to the environment of the United States.

a. Theory A
b. Theory X
c. Theory Y
d. Theory Z

42 ________means that the 'Whole is greater than its parts'.

a. System
b. Energy
c. Synergy
d. Collectivism

43 ______are general statements that guide thinking in decision-making.

a. Policies
b. Plans
c. Ethics
d. Budget

44 Which of the following theory emphasizes Leadership is inherent rather acquired?

a. Trait theory
b. Contingency theory
c. Great man theory
d. Path goal theory

45 ________are the assumptions about the environment in which the plan is to be executed.

a. Promises b. Framework

c. Climate d. Premises

46 Which of the following suggest an area in which the performance is essential for the success of the enterprise?

a. Problematic area b. Probabilistic area

c. Key result area d. Uncertain area

47 Which of the following replies the question 'What is our business'?

a. Mission b. Target

c. Intension d. Vision

48 What indicates the commitment to win in the competitive environment?

a. Strategic intent b. Future intent

c. Conflict intent d. Strategic challenge

49 In TOWS matrix which one of the following can be called as mini-mini strategy?

a. WT b. WO

c. ST d. SO

50 In portfolio matrix weak competitive position and high business growth rate is denoted by-

a. Cash cows b. Question mark

c. Dogs d. Stars

51 Delphi technique was developed by which of the following?

a. Olaf Helmer b. Robert Chamber

c. Ralf Linton d. Alex F. Osborn

52 The headquarter of International Organization for Standardization (ISO), which was established on 23 February 1947 is situated in ____________

a. Geneva b. Dublin

c. Madrid d. Lisbon

53 The selection of a course of action from among alternatives is called as_______

a. Decision Making b. Controlling

c. Planning d. Performing

54 ________ is comparing the additional revenue and the additional cost arising from increasing output.

a. Marginal Analysis b. B-C Ratio
c. Overhead Cost Analysis d. Variable Cost Analysis

55 Cost effectiveness analysis tries to achieve which of the following?

a. The best ratio of benefit and cost
b. Highest profit
c. Lowest cost
d. Zero cost

56 Programmed decisions are used for what purpose?

a. Structured work b. Routine work
c. Both a & b d. None of these

57 Who among the following is considered as father of 'Brainstorming'?

a. Olaf Helmer b. Thurston
c. Alex F. Osborn d. Thorndike

58 ________ is an individual who transforms a dream or an idea into a profitable venture by employing innovation and creativity.

a. Entrepreneur b. Interpruneur
c. Tycoon d. Manager

59 Who was considered as first lady of management?

a. Elizabeth Taylor b. Indira Noyee
c. Lillian Gilbreth d. Margaret Thatcher

60 ______ is a distinct business set up as units to ensure the promotion and handling of certain specific products.

a. Strategic Business Unit b. Core Business Units
c. Detached Business Units d. Independent Business Units

61 Which of the following indicates collective learning, coordination and integration of skills to obtain 'streams of technology'?

a. Core competency b. Ability
c. Power d. Authority

62 ________ is the ability of individuals to influence the beliefs of other person.

a. Energy b. Power
c. Strength d. Authority

63 ________ is the right in a position to exercise discretion in making decisions which affect others.

a. Authority b. Power
c. Charisma d. Competency

64 'The clearer the line of authority, the clearer will be the responsibility for decision making', this principle is known as_____

a. Principle of line of Command b. Principle of Hierarchy

c. Principle of Authority d. Scalar Principle

65 ERG theory was given by_____

a. Clayton Alderfer b. B F Skinner

c. Adams d. Edwin Locke

66 The tendency to disperse decision making authority in an organized structure is known as—

a. Decentralization b. Centralization

c. Departmentalization d. Authorization

67 Centralization of authority that was once decentralized is known as_________

a. Authorization b. Recentralization

c. Departmentalization d. Compartmentalization

68 An organization chart shows which of the following?

a. Formal authority relationships

b. Informal authority relationships

c. Formal inter organisation relationships

d. All of these

69 A good position description informs everyone of the incumbent's__________

a. Authority b. Responsibilities

c. Power d. None of these

70 Opening the vacant position to attract the best qualified persons in an enterprise is referred as __________

a. Principle of open competition b. Principle of closed competition

c. Principle of large competition d. Principle of hard competition

71 'Attracting candidates to fill positions in the organisation structure'- is known as ______

a. Staffing b. Managing

c. Recruiting d. Training

72 'Degree to which the data predict the candidate's success as a manager'- is denoted by which of the following?

a. Validity
b. Reliability
c. Honesty
d. Integrity

73 Which of the following is a technique for selecting and promoting managers?

a. Assessment center
b. Promotion centre
c. Recruitment centre
d. Growth centre

74 Introducing new employees to the organisation is known as__

a. Orientation
b. Attachment
c. Foundation
d. All of these

75 Which of the following gives managers a clear idea of their path of development?

a. Unplanned progression
b. Planned progression
c. Random progression
d. Selective progression

76 According to Field Force theory- which forces are needed to maintain equilibrium in an organisation?

a. Driving forces
b. Restraining forces
c. Both a & b
d. None of these

77 'Treating people with respect, irrespective of their position in the organization'- is referred as

a. Concept of individual dignity
b. Concept of individual personality
c. Concept of individual leadership
d. Concept of individual authority

78 Who gave the Concept of Theory X and Theory Y ?

a. Herzberg
b. Vroom
c. McGregor
d. F Taylor

79 The traditional assumptions about the nature of people were included in which theory?

a. Theory X
b. Theory Y
c. Theory Z
d. None of these

80 According to Herzberg's Two factor theory which of the following is known as Dissatisfies?

a. Maintenance
b. Hygiene
c. Job context factors
d. All of these

81 Force= Valence X Expectancy- this equation can be best explained by whose theory?

a. Herzberg's Two factor theory b. Vroom's Expectancy theory

c. McGregor theory d. Maslow theory

82 According to economist and most managers which parameter is ranked high on the scale of motivators?

a. Money b. Prestige

c. Labour d. Satisfaction

83 Which reward includes a feeling of accomplishment and self- actualization?

a. Intrinsic b. Extrinsic

c. Monitory d. All of these

84 Which of the following refers to enlarging the scope of the job by adding similar tasks without enhancing responsibility?

a. Job degradation b. Job enlargement

c. Job enrichment d. Job transformation

85 Introducing higher sense of challenge and achievement in job is known as

a. Job degradation b. Job enlargement

c. Job enrichment d. Job transformation

86 The concept of 'Managerial Grid ' was given by-

a. Peter Drucker b. Luther Gullick

c. Blake and Mouton d. Max Weber

87 The managerial grid has two dimensions, which are

a. Concern for manager and concern for company

b. Concern for people and concern for production

c. Concern for people and concern for nation

d. Concern for people and concern for organisation

88 Which style refer to managers concern themselves very little with either people or production and have minimum involvement in the jobs.

a. Managerial Grid 1.1 style b. Managerial Grid 9.9 style

c. Managerial Grid 5.5 style d. Managerial Grid 9.1 style

89 Leadership Continuum concept was developed by________

a. Robert Tannenbaum and W.H. Schmidt

b. Luther Gullick

c. Blake and Mouton

d. Max Weber

90 Which theory of leadership emphasizes the goal setting and guiding the best path for the subordinates?

a. Managerial Grid b. Path- goal theory

c. Management By Objective d. None of these

91 The leaders who identify 'what needs to be done' in order to achieve goals are known as

a. Transactional leaders b. Transformational leaders

c. Charismatic leaders d. Local leader

92 Which line committee also carries out managerial function?

a. Plural executive b. Odd executive

c. Lower executive d. Change executive

93 Who is assigned to investigate employee concerns?

a. Middleman b. Manager

c. Counselor d. Ombudsperson

94 'Effective control requires attention to factors critical to evaluating performance against plans' is principle of which of the following?

a. Critical point control b. Scalar

c. Critical path d. Hierarchy

95 Which is an approach for setting goals and productivity measures based on best organisational practices?

a. Priority setting b. Job setting

c. Benchmarking d. Hierarchy

96 Clan control is based on which of the following variables?

a. Norms b. Shared values

c. Expected behavior d. All of these

97 Which chart shows the time relationships between the events of a production program?

a. Bar Chart b. Pie Chart

c. Flow Chart d. Gantt Chart

98 _______is the sequence of events that takes the longest time and that has zero slack time.

a. Critical path b. Dummy activity

c. Parallel path d. Pseudo path

99 Compulsory coordination can be achieved through which of the following?

a. Organizational hierarchy b. Money

c. Staff authority d. None of these

100 What is the name of group, in which people from the same organizational area meet regularly to solve problems they experience at work?

a. Rescue circle b. Spy circle

c. Think Tank d. Quality circle

101 When a manager makes the decision based on his knowledge, he is considered as _____

a. Authoritarian b. Democratic

c. Group d. Both a & c

102 Transactional Analysis concentrates which elements of communication between people?

a. Styles b. Content

c. Both a & b d. None of these

103 Who is associated with 'Human Resource model of Motivation'?

a. Kurt Lewin b. Thorndike

c. Thomson d. Douglas McGregor

104 B=f (P S) the fundamental equation of human behaviour where P= the person and S= the situation. This concept was given by whom?

a. Kurt Lewin b. Thorndike

c. Thomson d. Douglas McGregor

105 Immaturity-Maturity Theory was given by whom?

a. Chris Argyris b. A. Maslow

c. Ivan Pavlov d. Chester Bernard

106 Charismatic Leadership Theory was given by whom?

a. Hersey- Blanchard b. House

c. Mitchell d. Frederick Luthans

107 Path Goal Theory was given by whom?

a. Hersey- Blanchard b. Reddin

c. House and Mitchell d. Frederick Luthans

108 Concept of 'Leadership competencies' given by whom?

a. Hersey- Blanchard b. Reddin

c. Bennis-Nanus d. Frederick Luthans

109 Who among the following gave '3-D management style concept'?

a. Hersey- Blanchard b. Reddin

c. Bennis-Nanus d. Frederick Luthans

110 Tridimensional Leader effectiveness model was given by______

a. Hersey- Blanchard b. Reddin

c. Bennis-Nanus d. Frederick Luthans

111 The concept behind 'Management by Objectives' has given by __________

a. Frederick Taylor b. Peter Drucker

c. Frederick Luthans d. Sir Grancis Galton

112 BARS in performance appraisal stands for _________

a. Biologically Anchored Rating Scale

b. Behaviorally Authorized Rating Scale

c. Behaviorally Anchored Rating Scale

d. Behaviorally Anchored Ratio Scale

113 Peter Drucker first described MBO in 1954 in his book _______

a. The practice of management b. Management By Objective

c. The systems of management d. Objectives in management

114 The subsistence theory of wages is also known as _______

a. Iron law of wages b. Golden law of labour

c. Hand to Mouth theory d. None of these

115 According to the management guru Peter Drucker, the basic task of management includes both marketing and ____________.

a. Selling b. Pricing

c. Innovation d. Packaging

116 Who conducted the study on 'low-efficiency and failures of certain enterprises' in 16th century from which the practice of modern management originates?

a. Sir Thomas More b. Luther Gullick

c. Sir Grancis Galton d. Frederick Luthans

117 'The art of getting things done through people' this definition of management was given by which of the following personality?

a. Richard Parker b. Martin Luther

c. Mary Follett d. Luther Gullick

118 Which of the following is used to perform all the activities by a manager?

a. Human skills b. Material Resources

c. Scientific methods d. All the above

119 In the management of any activity, a manager comes across which of the following conflict?

a. Human Conflict b. Conflict of Goals

c. Conflict of Choice d. All the above

120 Which of the following statement is true about system?

a. The system are subject to entropy

b. Systems try to remain in an equilibrium

c. A system is a comprehensive assembly of parts

d. All the above

121 Who has written the book 'General and Industrial Management'?

a. F W Taylor b. Henri Fayol

c. Peter Drucker d. Willium Gilberth

122 The famous book 'The Principles of Scientific Management' was written by which of the following author?

a. F W Taylor b. Peter Drucker

c. Willium Gilberth d. None of these

123 'Process of determining the goals and objectives and evolving strategies for the achievement of these goals'- the statement explains which of the following?

a. Planning b. Controlling

c. Organising d. Leading

124 'Filling the positions in the organization structure'- coming under which managerial function?

a. Leading b. Organizing

c. Staffing d. None of these

125 Bringing a harmony and smoothness in the various group activities and individual efforts is known as ___________

a. Coordination b. Planning

c. Organizing d. Leading

126 Measurement of an output, comparing it with the goals, the objectives and the target, and taking corrective actions indicates which of the following management function?

a. Staffing b. Controlling

c. Coordinating d. Planning

127 'Achievement of the plan'-is ensured by which of the following?

a. Controlling b. Planning

c. Staffing d. None of these

128 Who among the following gave the definition of management as 'Management is the transformation of resources into utility'?

a. Henry Fayol b. Peter Drucker

c. Fredmund Malik d. Max Weber

129 Which one of the following is considered as the first 'Principle of organization'?

a. Planning b. Budgeting

c. Coordination d. Staffing

130 People who are directly responsible for achieving organizational goals are coming under which type of authority?

a. Staff b. Horizontal

c. Diagonal d. Line

131 According to Henry Fayol management consists of how many functions?

a. Three b. Four

c. Five d. Six

132 The famous book 'The wealth of nations' written by whom?

a. Amartya Sen b. Karl Marx

c. Adam Smith d. Manmohan Singh

133 The book 'Science of management' was written by

a. Henry R. Towne b. Philip Kotler

c. Tom Peters d. Robert C. Merton

134 Harvard Business School introduced the first MBA degree in the year

a. 1905 b. 1914

c. 1945 d. 1921

135 Scientific management is also known as-

a. Taylorism b. Fayolism

c. Inventorism d. None of the above

136 Six sigma concept was developed by

a. Motorola b. Nokia

c. Sony d. Onida

137 Who among the following has given the concept of POSDCORB as the function of management?

a. F Taylor b. Max Weber

c. Luther Gullick d. Henri Fayol

138 Maximax principle stands for maximizing which of the following?

a. Maximum b. Minimum

c. Lowest d. Meager

139 Which one of the following does not determine the span of control?

a. Supervisors' personality b. Element of space

c. Organizations' age d. Managers' salary

140 According to system approach to planning which of the following elements come in the system?

a. Input b. Process

c. Output d. All of these

141 Identify the organisation which is one of the first organizations to get general consultative status with the United Nations Economic and Social Council?

a. ISO b. ICAR

c. SBI d. PNB

142 Coordination is needed to avoid which of the following?

a. Conflicts b. Monotony

c. Independence d. Injustice

143 According to management principle equality also means________

a. Injustice b. Empowerment

c. Stability d. Fairness

144 Which one of the following is considered as the key to system control?

a. Sub systems b. System boundary

c. Flow d. Feedback

145 Who among the following has described 'usefulness of properly defined policies'?

a. M V Higginson b. Max Weber

c. Thomson d. F Taylor

146 Peter Drucker used the concept of MBO as an approach to which managerial function?

a. Organizing b. Staffing

c. Planning d. Controlling

147 Which one of the following is not the element of MBO system?

a. Participation

b. Individual goals

c. Top level goal setting

d. Dictatorship in implementation of plan

148 The capacity to control others is known as__________

a. Energy b. Authority

c. Power d. Autocracy

149 When the span of control is increased the results will be ______

a. Inefficient supervision b. Slow communication

c. Long travel of messages d. All of these

150 Who introduced quality control in Japan?

a. Peter Drucker b. Hugo Munsterberg

c. Edwards Deming d. Henry Fayol

151 When permission is granted to some one to act one's own behalf, this type of authority is known as_______

a. Legal b. Technical

c. Ultimate d. Operational

152 Which type of authority is achieved by competence of an individual?

a. Legal b. Technical

c. Ultimate d. Operational

153 Set of characteristics that describe an organisation and which distinguish an organisation from other organisation is known as_________

a. Organizational climate b. Organizational culture

c. Organizational setting d. Organizational environment

154 Financial account and anticipated results of some actions is known as__________

a. Auditing b. Banking

c. Budgeting d. Money lending

155 Which one of the following is the aspect of budgeting?

a. Revenue b. Profit

c. Expenditure d. All of these

156 Which one of the following is not a function of budget?

a. Allocation of funds b. Prediction of unanticipated results

c. Reflecting the actual plan d. Specification of what is to be done

157 Which of the following comes under contingency long term plan?

a. Dearness Allowance b. House Rent Allowance

c. Stationary items d. All of these

158 Which one of the following is tool of TQM?

a. Benchmarking b. Quality control

c. Both a & b d. PERT

159 Which one of the following is not true about extension management?

a. Involuntary participation b. Software activity

c. Widespread activity d. Professional activity

160 Which model helps to know about the awareness in interpersonal relations?

a. Sociometry b. Transactional analysis

c. Johari window d. SWOT analysis

161 In 'Johari window' quadrant- 1 is also known as________

a. Area of free activity b. Blind area

c. Hidden area d. Area of unknown activity

162 In Johari window, 'not known to others but known to us' is coming under which quadrant?

a. First b. Second

c. Third d. Fourth

163 In Johari window quadrant- 4 is also known as________

a. Area of free activity
b. Blind area
c. Hidden area
d. Area of unknown activity

164 Who gave the 'Five mode model of resolution of conflict'?

a. Kenneth W Thomas
b. Ralph H Kilmann
c. Both a & b
d. Swanson

165 Which one of the following is result of insensitively managed conflict?

a. Bickering
b. Bruised feeling
c. Wasted time
d. All of these

166 Which one of the following does not indicate theory X?

a. Work is inherently distasteful
b. Most people are not ambitious
c. Work is as natural as play
d. Most people has little capacity for creativity

167 Hygiene factors are also known as ________

a. Maintenance factor
b. Survival factor
c. Job factor
d. Motivating factor

168 Which one of the following is a hygiene factor of motivation?

a. Supervision
b. Policies and administration
c. Working condition
d. All of these

169 Which of the following motivators does not belong to the two factor theory of motivation?

a. Achievement
b. Growth
c. Challenging work
d. Supervision

170 Which of the following situation indicates "If you win I must loose"?

a. Zero sum power game
b. Motivation game
c. Frustration game
d. Challenging game

171 Which of the following denotes Collaborative behaviour of an individual?

a. High need of power
b. High need of affiliation
c. Low need of power
d. Low need of affiliation

172 Which among the following facilitates Competitive behaviour?

a. Need for power
b. Need for affiliation
c. Need for achievement
d. None of these

173 According to ERG theory Maslow's fundamental needs are coming under which category?

a. Growth b. Relatedness

c. Existence d. Readiness

174 Need for personal creativity is coming under which category of needs under ERG theory?

a. Growth b. Relatedness

c. Existence d. Readiness

175 Under which category, 'Need for inter-personal relation' is coming as per ERG theory?

a. Growth b. Relatedness

c. Existence d. Readiness

176 Forced Choice method of performance appraisal was developed to eliminate which of the following?

a. Distrust b. Mistakes

c. Bias d. Dominance

177 The ability to coordinate and integrating all in an organizations' interest is coming under which type of skill?

a. Human skill b. Conceptual skill

c. Technical skill d. None of these

178 Under human skill which one of the following is included?

a. Working with other people b. Understanding other people

c. Motivating other people d. All of these

179 Who among the following has given three basic kinds of skills?

a. Robert L. Katz b. F Taylor

c. Henry Fayol d. Peter Drucker

180 Who among the following was associated with classical school of management?

a. F W Taylor b. H L Gantt

c. V. Gilberth d. M P Follet

181 If a system interacts it environment is known as __________

a. Closed system b. Open system

c. Moderate system d. Synergistic system

182 Which one of the following is true about system boundary?

a. Rigid in closed system
b. Flexible in open system
c. Both a & b
d. Rigid in closed system

183 Which among the following is considered as the input of a plan?

a. Past experience
b. Felt needs
c. Funds availability
d. All of these

184 Which one of the following is considered as the guide of administrative action?

a. Policy
b. Plan
c. Calendar of work
d. Profile

185 When the output is re-channelized as inputs it is known as______

a. Process
b. Approach
c. Feedback
d. Method

186 Which among the following is true about system?

a. Unorganized
b. Simple
c. Combination of parts
d. Static

187 Which of the following phases are coming under the system approach to planning?

a. Policies
b. Procedures
c. Plans
d. All of these

188 Who among the following has described the concept of physiological organisation theory?

a. Simon
b. March
c. Both a & b
d. Mouton

189 Who among the following is associated with TQM?

a. E Deming
b. Swanson
c. E Fleming
d. F Taylor

190 When the group size in an organisation is increased then complexity of relationship will be ________

a. Decreased
b. Same
c. Increased
d. Double

191 Who focused on application of Psychology to industry and management?

a. Walter D. Scott
b. Hugo Munsterberg
c. Vilfredo Pareto
d. Chester Barnard

192 The word Supervision derived from Latin word______

a. Super + Videre b. Super + Visum

c. Both a & b d. None of these

193 Drawing a general impression about an individual, on the basis of a 'single characteristic' is called as

a. Prejudice b. Halo effect

c. Stereotype d. Avoidance

194 Promoting team spirit vis-a-vis management principles is also referred to as

a. Esprit di cops b. Sprit be corps

c. Esprit de corps d. None of these

195 Reduction of costs through a system, wherein 'Production Quantities' are equal to 'Delivery Quantities' happens in the case of

a. KANGAN b. KANBAN

c. KAIZEN d. KIEZEN

196 The technique concerned with a "never-ending search for perfection' through 'continuous improvement' happens to be

a. KANGAN b. KANBAN

c. KAIZEN d. KIEZEN

197 In which type of organisation virtual supervision will be more effective?

a. MNC b. TNC

c. Both a & b d. None of these

198 Which one of the following is correct about non-manager?

a. Has no one under him

b. Supervised by managers

c. Has less responsibility than managers

d. All of these

199 Which one of the following arises from inner state of disequilibrium which gets crystallized into wants or expectation?

a. Needs b. Action

c. Tension d. Satisfaction

200 Which one of the following is false?

a. Cost is important in CPM

b. Time is vital in CPM

c. Uncertainty is allowed in PERT

d. While PERT is event oriented, CPM is activity oriented

201 Which one of the following is a barrier to motivation?

a. Negative self Image
b. Cultural models
c. Self-doubt
d. All of these

202 Which instititute developed Activity Slack Bar Chart?

a. NAARM, Hyderabad
b. NIRD, Hyderabad
c. IIM, Ahmadabad
d. IIT, Mumbai

203 Orientations of people to perceive contingency relationships between their actions and outcomes is known as

a. Strategic planning
b. Emergency management
c. Locus of control
d. Perceptual learning

204 Costs for controlling environmental language are technically known as

a. Abatement costs
b. Reductionist cost
c. Environmental cost
d. None of the above

205 Design skill of manager refers to

a. Solving problems that benefit the enterprise

b. Understanding the relationship among the elements

c. Possessing technical knowledge

d. Maintaining human relationship with all

206 Who suggested 4 groups of adopter categories as Pioneers, Professional, Imitators and skeptics?

a. Nityashree and Siddaramaiah
b. S.N. Singh
c. K.N. Singh
d. K. Vijayaraghavan

207 Which one of the following is a Management Pad?

a. Quality circle
b. Demassing
c. Strategic alliance
d. All of these

208 Which theory says 'Despite the emphasis on group decision making, responsibility remains with the individual'?

a. Social learning theory
b. Theory Z
c. Bureaucracy theory
d. Executive theory

209 Action plans through which strategies are executed is referred to as

a. Tactics
b. Haptics
c. Idealist
d. Policies

210 Which of the following characterize 'Mechanistic Management System'?

a. Specialized differentiation of tasks
b. Hierarchical structure
c. Vertical interactions
d. All of these

211 When a country can produce any item cheaply than any other country, then it can be said that the country has

a. Absolute advantage
b. Relative advantage
c. Progressive advantage
d. Tentative advangae

212 When marketing and advertising is done by using mass media (T.V., Radio, Newspaper etc.), then this is known as ____________ marketing.

a. Below the line
b. Above the line
c. Up the line
d. Down the line

213 Which type of bonus is paid to an employee who agrees to perform a difficult task?

a. Difficulty bonus
b. Risk bonus
c. Acceptance Bonus
d. None of these

214 The first stage to test new products is known as

a. Alpha test
b. Beta test
c. Gamma test
d. Delta test

215 Which of the following term is used to assign responsibility for failure?

a. Blame game
b. Blaming
c. Blamestorming
d. None of these

216 The place where actual physical work is get done in a Industry is known as

a. Workstation
b. Power station
c. Coalface
d. Sub station

217 Who has written one of the bestselling books on management 'The Age of Paradox'?

a. Max Weber
b. Henry Fayol
c. Elton Mayo
d. Handy Charles

218 Legacy systems based on

a. Outdated technology
b. State of art technology
c. High end technology
d. Simple technology

219 Which of the following theory states that 20% of effort produces 80% of results?

a. Pareto principle
b. 80/20 rule
c. Both a & b
d. None of these

220 When discrimination on the basis of age is done, it is known as

a. Ageism
b. Volatility
c. Injustice
d. Dogmatism

221 An obsolete, old fashioned product can be called

a. Antediluvian
b. Orthodox
c. Both a & b
d. None of these

222 Which of the following term can be used to denote small period of rapid growth in trade and economy?

a. Hamlet
b. Boomlet
c. Drumlet
d. Bear run

223 When a economy face a rapid unstable growth the situation can be termed as

a. Boom economy
b. Bull run
c. Bubble economy
d. None of these

224 When a business house runs a business on internet as well as in traditional outlets, it is known as

a. Clicks and mortar
b. Clicks and bricks
c. Both a & b
d. None of these

225 The unauthorized copy of a product/ output is known as ________

a. Copycat
b. Tampering
c. Knock-off
d. Photocopy

226 Effectiveness is measured in

a. Problem solving ability
b Doing things right
c. Producing results
d All of these

227 Working Capital for a farm business comprises of

a. Current Assets + Current Liabilities
b. Current Assets / Current Liabilities
c. Current Assets - Current Liabilities
d. None of these

228 The tool used to assess whether an institution's activities are correlated with its vision and objectives is

a. Scorecard b. Balanced scorecard
c. Situation analysis d. SWOT analysis

229 Objectives are _______________ of management action

a. Design b. Starting point
c. Planning d. All of the above

230 *In the term 'BOSCARD' D stands for*

a. Deliverables b. Disenchantment
c. Development d. Disinvestment

231 17th century mercury plant entrepreneur is related to

a. Robert F. Hebert b. James A. Watkins
c. Richard Parker d. None of these

232 In network diagram when multiple successor activities originate from a common predecessor activity then the point is known as

a. Divergent point b. Burst point
c. Convergent point d. None of these

233 The study of how likely a project is to be completed effectively is known as

a. Efficiency study b. Evaluative study
c. Feasibility study d. Monitoring

234 'HERMES' is a project management method created by

a. USA government b. Swiss government
c. German Government d. British Government

235 Which is not capital good?

a. Building b. Gold in Locker
c. Machines d. Equipment

236 HRD originated in

a. George Washington University b. Pune University

c. Cambridge university d. Oxford University

237 ____________ is a technique to forecast possible outcomes for decision making.

a. Puerto Rico simulation b. Gibraltar simulation

c. San Diego simulation d. Monte Carlo simulation

238 Which of the following term is used for aggressive advertising, marketing, promotion and selling of a product/ commodity?

a. Hard sell b. Wrestling sell

c. Boxing sell d. Soft sell

239 What is the bad characteristic of Leadership Behaviour?

a. Being grounded in ethics and integrity

b. Making decision

c. Poor communication skill

d. Inspiring those around you

240 Total Quality Management is a part of

a. HRD b. MBO

c. PERT d. CPM

241 The 360^0 performance appraisal was first developed by

a. Wipro b. General Electric (USA)

c. TATA motors d. Hindustan Unilever

242 Measurement of opinion leadership given by

a. Rogers b. Katz and Lazerfeid

c. Wiemann d. None of these

243 Behaviour Anchored Rating scale (BARS) is related to

a. Performance appraisal b. Sociometry

c. Psychological disorder d. None of these

Answer Key

1.	a	2.	a	3.	d	4.	a	5.	b	6.	c	7.	a	8.	a	9.	d	10.	a
11.	b	12.	a	13.	a	14.	d	15.	d	16.	b	17.	a	18.	d	19.	c	20.	b
21.	c	22.	d	23.	a	24.	a	25.	b	26.	a	27.	a	28.	c	29.	b	30.	a
31.	b	32.	d	33.	d	34.	b	35.	c	36.	a	37.	d	38.	c	39.	a	40.	b
41.	d	42.	c	43.	a	44.	c	45.	d	46.	c	47.	a	48.	a	49.	a	50.	b
51.	a	52.	a	53.	a	54.	a	55.	a	56.	c	57.	c	58.	a	59.	c	60.	a
61.	a	62.	b	63.	a	64.	d	65.	a	66.	a	67.	b	68.	a	69.	b	70.	a
71.	c	72.	a	73.	a	74.	a	75.	b	76.	c	77.	a	78.	c	79.	a	80.	d
81.	b	82.	a	83.	a	84.	b	85.	c	86.	c	87.	b	88.	a	89.	a	90.	b
91.	a	92.	a	93.	d	94.	a	95.	c	96.	d	97.	d	98.	a	99.	a	100.	d
101.	a	102.	c	103.	d	104.	a	105.	a	106.	b	107.	c	108.	c	109.	b	110.	a
111.	b	112.	c	113.	a	114.	a	115.	c	116.	a	117.	c	118.	d	119.	d	120.	d
121.	b	122.	a	123.	a	124.	c	125.	a	126.	b	127.	a	128.	c	129.	c	130.	d
131.	d	132.	c	133.	a	134.	d	135.	a	136.	a	137.	c	138.	a	139.	d	140.	d
141.	a	142.	a	143.	d	144.	d	145.	a	146.	c	147.	d	148.	c	149.	d	150.	c
151.	d	152.	b	153.	a	154.	c	155.	d	156.	b	157.	d	158.	c	159.	a	160.	c
161.	a	162.	c	163.	d	164.	c	165.	d	166.	c	167.	a	168.	d	169.	d	170.	a
171.	b	172.	a	173.	c	174.	a	175.	b	176.	c	177.	b	178.	d	179.	a	180.	d
181.	b	182.	c	183.	d	184.	a	185.	c	186.	c	187.	d	188.	c	189.	a	190.	c
191.	b	192.	c	193.	b	194.	c	195.	b	196.	c	197.	c	198.	d	199.	a	200.	b
201.	d	202.	a	203.	c	204.	a	205.	a	206.	a	207.	d	208.	b	209.	a	210.	d
211.	a	212.	b	213.	c	214.	a	215.	c	216.	c	217.	d	218.	a	219.	c	220.	a
221.	a	222.	b	223.	c	224.	c	225.	c	226.	d	227.	c	228.	b	229.	b	230.	a
231.	c	232.	b	233.	c	234.	b	235.	b	236.	a	237.	d	238.	a	239.	c	240.	b
241.	b	242.	a	243.	a														

6

Programme Planning and Evaluation

1 Which of the following is a statement of situation, objectives, problems and solutions?

a. An extension programme b. An extension plan
c. An extension project d. An extension report

2 Which of the following is predetermined course of action?

a. Project b. Plan
c. Evaluation d. Budget

3 What is a plan of activities to be undertaken in a particular time sequence?

a. Plan b. Programme
c. A calendar of work d. Budget

4 What implies a gap between the existing and desirable situation?

a. Need b. Desire
c. Wish d. All the above

5 Which needs are consciously recognized needs?

a. Unfelt b. Felt
c. Both a & b d. None of the above

6 Japanese concept of harmony is represented by which of the following word?

a. Ba b. Ha
c. Ya d. Wa

7 Which type of change is aimed in Programme planning?

a. Planned change b. Sudden change
c. Unplanned change d. Slow change

8 Designing a course of action to achieve ends is referred as______

a. Management b. Planning
c. Modeling d. Architecture

9 What is an outline of procedure and pertains only to some phase of extension work?

a. Project b. Plan

c. Calendar of work d. Programme

10 The condition when people decide to change is known as______

a. Solution b. Situation

c. Target d. Problem

11 Principles of Programme Planning were given by________.

a. Kelsey and Hearne b. Linton and Pareek

c. G L Ray d. Koontz and Weihrich

12 Sound programme planning selects problems based on which aspect?

a. Situation b. Objectives

c. Needs d. Choice

13 A good programme has 'Permanence with __________

a. Flexibility b. Rigidity

c. Inflexibility d. None of the above

14 Programme building is a ______.

a. Continuous process b. One step process

c. Static process d. None of the above

15 Programme is a ______.

a. Coordinating process b. Independent process

c. Isolated process d. None of the above

16 Analyzing progress of ongoing project with predetermined indicators and objectives is referred as________

a. Evaluation b. Monitoring

c. Assessment d. All of these

17 Which of the followings is/are monitoring indicator/s?

a. Process indicators b. Impact indicators

c. Both a & b d. Product indicators

18 Which evaluation type gathers data to formulate an effective extension programme?

a. Formative b. Summative

c. Receptive d. Deceptive

19 Which evaluation type would measure output of a programme to decide its continuity?

a. Formative b. Summative

c. Receptive d. Deceptive

20 ________ monitoring is the systematic recording and periodic analysis of information by villagers with the help of development agents.

a. Participatory b. Scientific

c. Anticipatory d. Ex-Ante

21 Programme means ____________

a. A proclamation b. A prospectus

c. A list of events d. All the above

22 Which one of the following is a modern tool for analysis of situation?

a. Factor analysis b. PERT

c. TOWS Matrix d. CPM

23 'An extension programme is a statement of situation, objectives, problems and solution' who gave this important definition?

a. Rogers b. R S Sandhu

c. Kelsey and Hearne d. Leagans

24 Which of the following characteristics is/are true for planning?

a. A simple process

b. Process of making decision

c. Progressive step-by-step process

d. All the above

25 Which of the following is the basic part of planning?

a. Defining goals b. Analysis of results

c. Evaluation d. Synthesis

26 In social planning which of the following is/are involved?

a. Individual b. Societal value

c. Both a & b d. None of these

27 Who among the following author described the assumptions about the extension planning?

a. Uday Pareek b. Peter Drucker

c. Lynton d. Boyle

28 Which is a necessary prerequisite of effective social process in extension planning?

a. Planned change b. Unplanned change

c. Forced change d. Static change

29 Extension programme planning is a______

a. Social action process b. Individual action process

c. Leader's action process d. Extension action process

30 Which of the following is the end-product of extension programme planning?

a. Report b. Extension programme

c. Evaluation d. Overall development

31 Action is preceded by which of the following?

a. Planning b. Implementation

c. Evaluation d. Monitoring

32 Who among the following said that an extension programme must meet the felt needs of the people?

a. Sumner b. Thomson

c. Brunner d. Leagans

33 Extension programme planning has permanence with____________

a. Time limit b. Rigidity

c. Flexibility d. All of these

34 Which of the following is true about extension programme planning?

a. An educational process b. Coordinating process

c. Continuous process d. All the these

35 How many phases are there in the model for planning extension and rural development programme developed by R.S. Sandhu?

a. Six b. Seven

c. Five d. Two

36 Quick approach to analyse a situation for assessing farmer's need by a multidisciplinary team is

a. Rapid Rural Analysis b. Participatory Rural Analysis

c. Rapid Rural Appraisal d. Participatory Rural Appraisal

37 Which one of the following is true about the RRA?

a. Formal

b. Non-structured

c. Midway between formal and Non-structured

d. None of these

38 Which of the following is/are the characteristics of RRA?

a. Rapid b. Eclectic

c. Holistic d. All of these

39 Who among the following identified three levels of educational objective?

a. Thompson b. Thorndike

c. Leagan d. Max Weber

40 Which of the following characteristics is associated with a good objective?

a. Dynamic

b. Static

c. Midway between dynamic and static

d. Fraudulent

41 Which of the following can be considered as the expanded concept of extension programme planning?

a. Programme Projection b. Programme Setting

c. Programme Evaluation d. Programme Monitoring

42 Which of the following can be considered as the alternative approaches for planning an extension programme?

a. Farming System Approach b. PPBS

c. PERT d. All of these

43 Which characteristic is associated with Planning, Programming and Budgeting System (PPBS)?

a. Emphasis on output b. Emphasis on input

c. Emphasis on resources d. None of these

44 Which of the following is true in case of Critical Path Method?

a. Have no slack time

b. Have float

c. Difference between EST and LST is more than zero

d. None of these

45 In PERT variability is __________ of difference between pessimistic time and optimistic time.

a. One-sixth b. One-fourth

c. One-fifth d. Half

46 Concept of CPM was developed by whom?

a. Polaris weapon system b. US navy

c. Du Pont company d. Robert Chamber

47 Which one of the following is basic orientation of CPM?

a. Probabilistic b. Deterministic

c. Summative d. Opportunistic

48 The arrows on CPM indicate which of the following?

a. Activity b. Event

c. Slack Time d. Float

49 In CPM, events are denoted by which of the following?

a. Square b. Triangle

c. Rectangle d. Circle

50 Dummy activity does not require_______

a. Time b. Resources

c. Material d. Both a & b

51 Difference between LST and EST is known as _______

a. Float b. Slack time

c. Both a & b d. Event

52 Which one of the following is true about critical activity?

a. Have no slack period b. Have no float

c. Falls on critical path d. All of these

53 Dummy activity is denoted by which of the following?

a. Broken arrows b. Circle

c. Bold arrows d. Coloured arrows

54 The activity which is having preceding activity but no succeeding activity is called _____

a. Bumper b. Dangler

c. Dumper d. Ocular

55 Which one of the following is true about PERT?

a. Probabilistic
b. Deterministic
c. Summative
d. Opportunistic

56 The concept of PERT is given by________

a. Polaris weapon system
b. US navy
c. Du Pont company
d. Both a & b

57 PERT technique is developed in which year?

a. 1947-48
b. 1953-54
c. 1919-20
d. 1958-59

58 Who among the following has developed the concept of CPM in 1957?

a. M.R. Walker
b. J.E.Walker
c. Both a & b
d. S.K. Wadkar

59 The word 'evaluation' has its origin in which language?

a. German
b. Greek
c. Latin
d. French

60 Which of the following evaluation type is a matter of routine?

a. Self- evaluation
b. Internal evaluation
c. Scientific research
d. External evaluation

61 Objective + activities + resources + change =?

a. Goal
b. Target
c. Project
d. Programme

62 Which one of the following is element of programme planning?

a. Analysis
b. Evaluation
c. Resetting objectives
d. All of these

63 Which one of the following is considered as blue print for action?

a. Plan
b. Goal
c. Solution
d. Target

64 Which one of the following is true about programme planning?

a. Educational Process
b. Coordinating Process
c. Evaluating Process
d. All of These

65 Who among the following was associated with RRA?

a. Robert Chambers
b. Peter Hildebrand
c. Robert Rhoades
d. All of these

66 Which situation is suitable for RRA?
a. Evaluating rural situation b. Identifying rural situation
c. Diagnosing rural situation d. All of these

67 Which one of the following is not an objective of RRA?
a. Appraising needs b. Prioritizing areas
c. Management d. Implementing action plan

68 Which one of the following is not an objective of PRA?
a. Less involvement of villagers b. Generate information
c. Initiate research studies d. Estimate trends

69 Which one of the following is principle of PRA?
a. Optimal ignorance b. Offsetting biases
c. Seeking diversity d. All of these

70 PRA was developed during which year?
a. 1970-71 b. 1975-76
c. 1988-89 d. 1995-96

71 Which one of the following is not the insider's role in PRA?
a. Respondent b. Presenter
c. Analyst d. Planner

72 Whose role is more facilitative in nature?
a. RRA b. PRA
c. Both a & b d. PERT

73 Semi-structured interview used in which of the following?
a. RRA b. PRA
c. Both a & b d. PERT

74 Which one of the following is coming under participatory mapping?
a. Social map b. Resource map
c. Agro ecological map d. All of these

75 Under resource map which of the following will come?
a. Forest areas b. Water resources
c. Agricultural land d. All of these

76 'Transact walk' is which type in nature?
a. Exploratory b. Adventurous
c. Derogatory d. Artistic

77 To get a cross sectional view of one village which of the following PRA tool can be used?

a. Venn diagram b. Consequence diagram

c. Transect walk d. Livelihood analysis

78 To know about pest attack incidences, crop rotation and rainfall pattern, which PRA tool can be used?

a. Venn diagram b. Seasonality analysis

c. Time line d. Transect walk

79 Which of the following PRA tool is used to show the historical events in the village?

a. Venn diagram b. Seasonality analysis

c. Time line d. Transect walk

80 Which one of the following is basic principle of PANR?

a. Seeking diversity b. Offsetting Biases

c. Listening and learning d. All of these

81 Correct expansion of PANR is ___

a. Participatory Assessment of Natural Resources

b. Participatory Analysis of Natural Resources

c. Participatory Analysis of National Resources

d. Participatory Analysis of Normal Rainfall

82 What is the full form of PLA?

a. Participatory Learning and Action

b. Programmed Learning and Action

c. Process of Learning and Assessment

d. Participatory Learning and Analysis

83 Which one of the following is not a principle of PLA?

a. Changing behavior b. Sharing Information

c. Increase income d. Selecting appropriate method

84 Which one of the following is final outcome of PRA technique?

a. Maps b. Village Plan

c. Baseline information d. All of these

85 Which one of the following shows the movement of villagers outside of the village?

a. Venn diagram b. Mobility map
c. Trend analysis d. Seasonal analysis

86 To know the possession of assets by villagers which of the following method can be used?

a. Wealth ranking b. Social Map
c. Resource map d. Matrix ranking

87 Which of the following PRA tool shows important village institutions, groups as well as the villagers' view of their importance in the community?

a. Venn Diagram b. Mobility map
c. Wealth ranking d. Transect walk

88 Second five year plan of India was given by______

a. P C Maholanobis b. Harrod Domar
c. Planning commission d. Jawahar lal Neharu

89 First five year plan was based on______

a. Harrod-Domar Model b. P C Maholanobis Model
c. Gandhi Plan d. Nehru Plan

90 The First Five-year Plan was launched in which of the following year?

a. 1951 b. 1950
c. 1947 d. 1952

91 Abolition of Planning Commission was announced by which Prime Minister of India?

a. Deva Gowda b. Manmohan Singh
c. Rajiv Gandhi d. Narendra Modi

92 Who was the first chairman of Planning Commission of India?

a. Jawahar Lal Nehru b. Indira Gandhi
c. Lal Bahadur Shastri d. Rajendra Prasad

93 Planning Commission was established in accordance with which article of the Indian constitution?

a. Article 42 b. Article 45
c. Article 39 d. Article 37

94 Which of the following was proposed by ICAR during twelfth five year plan?

a. ARYA
b. STUDENT READY
c. FARMERS FIRST
d. All of these

95 Who is the ex-officio chairman of Planning Commission and National Development Council?

a. Finance Minister
b. President of India
c. Prime Minister
d. Home Minister

96 When was the Planning Commission established?

a. 23rd March 1951
b. 23rd March 1950
c. 23rd March 1949
d. 23rd March 1947

97 Sarvodaya Plan in 1950 was the brain child of ________

a. Jaiprakash Narayan
b. Sardar Vallabhbhai Patel
c. Mahatma Gandhi
d. Acharya Vinoba Bhave

98 First five year plan of India was focused on________

a. Cottage Industry
b. Service
c. Manufacturing
d. Agriculture

99 Which plan was focused on "Growth With Social Justice & Equality"?

a. Ninth Plan
b. Tenth Plan
c. Eleventh Plan
d. Eighth Plan

100 'Removal of poverty' (Garibi Hatao) was the slogan of which five year plan?

a. Fifth Plan
b. Tenth Plan
c. Fourth Plan
d. Eighth Plan

101 Which of the following needs resources like labour, time, material and money for accomplishment?

a. Event
b. Dummy Activity
c. Activity
d. EST

102 The procedure by which LST values are computed is known as______

a. Forward pass
b. Backward pass
c. Activity slack
d. Critical event

103 Which of the following is the procedure by which EST values are computed?

a. Forward pass
b. Backward pass
c. Activity slack
d. Critical event

104 Which one of the following is true about critical path?

a. Longest path b. Smallest path

c. Narrow path d. Broad path

105 Which one of the following is main thrust of CPM?

a. Analysis of budget b. Shortening project time

c. Controlling project time d. Analysis on time-cost relationship

106 In which type of programme PERT analysis is mainly used?

a. Construction programme b. Defense programme

c. Research programme d. Both b & c

107 In which type of programme CPM analysis is mainly used?

a. Construction programme b. Defense programme

c. Research programme d. Both b&c

108 Who among the following first attempted economic planning in India?

a. M. Visvesvaraya b. P C Mahalanobis

c. Harod Dumar d. Jack Roosevelt

109 Which of the following was not given due importance in the ICAR classification of 20 Agro-Ecological regions and 60 sub regions?

a. Socio-economic endowment

b. Market support

c. Service sector in agricultural development

d. All of these

110 ______________________ is a standard against which results are measured.

a. Benchmark b. Baseline

c. Base level d. None of these

111 Which of the following comment/s are true about logical framework (logframe)?

a. A management tool b. Type of logic model

c. Improves evaluation d. All of these

112 Which of the following expressed by a value of an indicator?

a. Target b. Goal

c. Objective d. Aim

113 Which of the following type of evaluation focuses on a specific cross cutting area?

a. Process Evaluation
b. Thematic Evaluation
c. Participatory Evaluation
d. Outcome Evaluation

114 Which of the following evaluation is done during the implementation of programme to determine if the programme is likely to reach its objective?

a. Process Evaluation
b. Thematic Evaluation
c. Participatory Evaluation
d. Outcome Evaluation

115 Which of the following is a LFA tool used for consolidating cause-effect hierarchy?

a. Solution tree
b. Objective tree
c. Problem tree
d. Feedback tree

116 What is the term used to denote situation prior to the project intervention?

a. Initial data
b. Introductory information
c. Baseline
d. Ground reality

117 Which of the following is synonym of 'Development Objective'?

a. Overall objective
b. Specific objective
c. Both a & b
d. None of these

118 Which of the following is true for 'monitoring'?

a. Continuous function
b. Needed for project management
c. Systematic collection and analysis of data
d. All of these

119 Which of the following denote a strategic planning tool, used for giving Terms of reference for new projects?

a. BCWP
b. BOSCARD
c. BCWS
d. None of these

120 When the 'Extreme Project Management' (XPM) can be used?

a. Very complex project
b. Uncertain project
c. Both a & b
d. None of these

121 National Institute for Transforming India (NITI) Aayog was formed on ________

a. 1st January 2015
b. 1st January 2014
c. 15th August 2014
d. 2nd October 2014

122 Krishi Gyan Kendra (KGK) is functioning only in

a. Haryana b. Himachal Pradesh

c. Punjab d. Gujarat

123 Arrange the stages of evaluation of social development programme as per their sequence in adoption. Use the codes given below: a) Development of instrument b) Analysisc) Determining the parametersd) Administering the toolscodes:

a. a, b, c, d b. b, c, d, a

c. c, d, a, b d. c, a, d, b

124 ____________ improves performance of workers and helps to plan new strategies.

a. Research b. Evaluation

c. Motivation d. Planning

125 Indian Council of Food and Agriculture is a ____________

a. Think- Tank in Agriculture

b. Farmers dispute settlement body

c. Agriculture programmes evaluation body

d. Agricultural Policy execution body

126 Condition that the people after study, with or without outside help, have decided need changing is called ________

a. Solution b. Planning

c. Problem d. Situation analysis

127 Specification of work to be done/ procedure to be followed in order to accomplish a particular objective is called __________

a. Project b. Programme

c. Scheme d. Planning

128 __________is a predetermined course of action

a. Work b. Event

c. Plan d. Goal

129 Which is not a principle of programmepanning ________

a. Programme planning is educational process

b. Programme planning is continuous process

c. Programme planning is co-ordinating process

d. Programme planning is permanent with rigidity

130 ________________involves collection, compilation and analysis of facts in a given situation in order to identify local needs, interests, problems and priorities

a. Situational analysis b. Need analysis

c. Problem analysis d. Planned analysis

131 The participatory approach is rapid and quick in assessing the situation with the help of multidisciplinary team is ____________

a. PLA b. FSR/E

c. PRA d. RRA

132 "Handing over the stick to the insider" relates to ____________.

a. PLA b. FSR/E

c. PRA d. RRA

133 Which among the following is not a PRA principle ____________

a. Offsetting bias b. Optimal ignorance

c. Seeking diversity d. Wild catch

134 In a Cause and effect diagram (problem tree) consequences are indicated by ____________

a. Trunk b. Roots

c. Branches d. Leaves

135 The PRA tool used for temporal analysis across annual cycles with month season as a basic unit of analysis ____________

a. Seasonal calendar b. Ishikawa diagram

c. Fishbone diagram d. Both b and c

136 'Affinity Diagram' which is used to organize brainstorming data was developed by

a. Edward Knapsack b. Uttam Singh

c. Kawakita Jiro d. Robert Taylor

137 'Plan-Do-Check-Act cycle' which is a four-stage approach of problem-solving is also known as

a. Deming cycle b. Shewhart cycle

c. Omnibus cycle d. Both a & b

138 Which statement is correct

a. PERT used for routine projects

b. PERT gives exact time for each activity

c. PERT is Activity oriented

d. None of the above

139 Purpose of evaluation is ___________

a. To locate strong and weak points of project

b. To establish benchmark for further programme

c. To determine extent of our objectives achieved

d. All the above

140 ___________ is the second look of the proposed plan

a. Monitoring b. Evaluation

c. Appraisal d. Planning

141 Evaluation of evaluation is called ___________

a. Re-evaluation b. Repeated evaluation

c. Meta-evaluation d. Secondary evaluation

142 Direction of movement refers to ___________

a. Aim b. Objective

c. Goal d. Mission

143 'Fishbone diagram' which is also known as cause & effect diagram, has been developed by

a. Alexander Deming b. Kaoru Ishikawa

c. Mc Gregor d. Daniel Katz

144 Which of the following is a method of strategic planning for quality?

a. Hoshin planning b. Ikebana planning

c. Strategic planning d. None of these

145 The chart which indicates the number of defective units in a given sample is known as

a. np chart b. pp chart

c. pq chart d. qq chart

146 Investment requirement for medium enterprise is

a. Rs 5 to 10 crore b. Rs 1to5 crore

c. Rs 1to 10 crore d. Above Rs 10 crore

147 Routine decisions are

a. Programmed b. non-programmed

c. Both d. None of these

148 The 3rd phase of Entrepreneurship Development process is known as

a. Sustaining
b. Training phase
c. Post training phase
d. None of these

149 Which is successful cooperative movement in India

a. Credit cooperatives
b. Input cooperatives
c. Milk cooperatives
d. All the above

150 First step of decision-making process is

a. Make your decision
b. Gather information for weighing your options
c. Identify your goal
d. Consider the consequences

151 1st four stage in planning known as

a. Programme planning
b. Evaluation
c. Accountability
d. Implementation

152 The evaluation done at implementation stage of progarmme is known as

a. Ex- ante evaluation
b. Formative evaluation
c. In-ante evaluation
d. Planning evaluation

153 Farmers Back to Farmer approach is related to

a. Rhodes and Booth
b. J P Leagans
c. K N Singh
d. Narendra Modi

154 RAWE (Rural Agricultural Work Experience) stipend is near about

a. Rs. 2500
b. Rs.3000
c. Rs.4000
d. Rs.5000

155 Who is the best for providing service in Anganwadi?

a. Men
b. Women
c. Youth
d. All of the above

156 Which step are not comes under programme planning

a. Identification of problem
b. Formulating supporting plans
c. Determination of objectives and goals
d. Collection of facts

157 Which agency initiated one stop solutions to farmers,

a. C-DAC
b. Service Tata Kisan Sanchar
c. Apple
d. Reliance

158 A PRA technique for current situation analysis or immediate solution to particular topic objective is

a. Exploratory PRA b. Topical PRA

c. Problem Solving d. None of these

159 Who has given the theory of 'zero defects'?

a. Mc Callaghan b. Philip Crosby

c. Rupert Mc Lloyd d. None of these

Answer Key

1. a	2. b	3. c	4. a	5. b	6. d	7. a	8. b	9. a	10. d
11. a	12. c	13. a	14. a	15. a	16. b	17. c	18. a	19. b	20. a
21. d	22. c	23. c	24. d	25. a	26. c	27. d	28. a	29. a	30. b
31. a	32. c	33. c	34. d	35. a	36. c	37. c	38. d	39. a	40. a
41. a	42. d	43. a	44. a	45. a	46. c	47. b	48. a	49. d	50. d
51. c	52. d	53. a	54. b	55. a	56. d	57. d	58. c	59. c	60. a
61. d	62. d	63. a	64. d	65. d	66. d	67. c	68. a	69. d	70. c
71. a	72. b	73. b	74. d	75. d	76. a	77. c	78. b	79. c	80. d
81. b	82. a	83. c	84. d	85. b	86. a	87. a	88. a	89. a	90. a
91. d	92. a	93. c	94. d	95. c	96. b	97. a	98. d	99. a	100. a
101. c	102. b	103. a	104. a	105. d	106. d	107. a	108. a	109. d	110. a
111. d	112. a	113. b	114. a	115. b	116. c	117. a	118. d	119. b	120. c
121. a	122. a	123. d	124. b	125. a	126. c	127. a	128. c	129. d	130. a
131. d	132. c	133. d	134. d	135. a	136. c	137. d	138. d	139. d	140. c
141. c	142. b	143. b	144. a	145. a	146. a	147. a	148. a	149. c	150. c
151. a	152. b	153. a	154. b	155. b	156. b	157. b	158. a	159. b	

7

Process of Communication

1 Which element of speech is often used to refer to as 'Paralanguage'?

a. Non-verbal b. Verbal

c. Vocal d. None of these

2 Which of the followings is a kind of paralinguistic respiration in the form of a sudden and sharp inhalation of air through the mouth?

a. A gasp b. Blow

c. Puff d. Sigh

3 Written communication first emerged through the use of which of the followings?

a. Monograph b. Pictographs

c. Cartograph d. both a & b

4 Which shows relations among signs in formal structures?

a. Semantic b. Synthetic

c. Simulates d. Syntactic

5 Which of the following relates to different interpretations of the meanings of certain words?

a. Syntactic noise b. Synonyms

c. Semantic noise d. None of the above

6 'Mistakes in grammar can disrupt communication' is related to which of the followings?

a. Syntactical noise b. Structural noise

c. Semantic noise d. Contextual noise

7 Which is the most important element in the communication process?

a. Receiver b. Communicator

c. Message d. Channel

8 All communication takes place around a__________.

a. Receiver b. Communicator
c. Message d. Channel

9 The word communication comes from the Lain *Communis* meaning_______.

a. Community b. common
c. Communality d. Speech

10 Communication involves______.

a. Interdependence b. Independence
c. Isolation d. None of these

11 Aristotle implied that prime goal of communication is______

a. Order b. Influence
c. Persuasion d. Direct

12 According to Berlo- sole purpose of communication is to_________

a. Order b. Influence
c. Persuasion d. Direct

13 Festinger described the purpose of communication as________

a. Consumatory b. Instrumental
c. Influence d. Both a & b

14 Who among the following identified 4 levels of communication?

a. Thayer b. Aristotle
c. Berlo d. Festinger

15 Who among the following quoted that 'Living is largely a matter of communicating'?

a. Smith b. Aristotle
c. Berlo d. Festinger

16 Comprehension + Validity + Utility =?

a. Communication credibility b. Communication effectiveness
c. Communication reliability d. Communication fidelity

17 ____refers to the extent the message conveyed by the source which is clear to the receiver.

a. Reliability b. Fidelity
c. Comprehension d. Utility

18 The basic persuasive communication model was given by_____

a. Aristotle
b. Schramm
c. Shannon and Weaver
d. Berlo

19 Role of 'Field of Experience' was described in whose model of communication?

a. Aristotle
b. Schramm
c. Shannon and Weaver
d. Berlo

20 Mathematical Theory of Communication was given by _____

a. Aristotle
b. Schramm
c. Shannon and Weaver
d. Berlo

21 Who developed Information theory related to accurate communication of information?

a. Aristotle
b. Schramm
c. Shannon
d. Berlo

22 Which communication model has Noise as an important component?

a. Aristotle model
b. Schramm model
c. Berlo model
d. Shannon and Weaver model

23 _______is degree of randomness or choices or one's degree of freedom of choice to select a message.

a. Entropy
b. Empathy
c. Fidelity
d. Canopy

24 Information can be measured by which of the following?

a. Entropy
b. Redundancy
c. Fidelity
d. Canopy

25 Which of the following term refers to the amount of information which can be added or omitted in a noiseless channel?

a. Redundancy
b. Entropy
c. Empathy
d. Fidelity

26 __________refers to the amount of information that can be transmitted per unit of time.

a. Fidelity
b. Channel capacity
c. Credibility
d. Redundancy

27 ______refers to any sound, or distortion that may be added into the channel which are not intended by the sender.

a. Fecundity b. Fidelity
c. Noise d. Effects

28 If attitude affect the communication process of two individuals then the type of communication barrier acted here is

a. Psychological barrier b. Semantic barrier
c. Environmental barrier d. Cultural barrier

29 SMCR indicates whose model of communication?

a. Schramm's Model b. Leagan's Model
c. Berlo's Model d. New Comb's Model

30 Concept of mass- media model of communication was given by________

a. Westley and McLean b. Aristotle
c. New Comb d. Shannon and Weaver

31 Hovland designed a persuasion model of communication by following whose idea?

a. Aristotle b. New Comb
c. Leagans d. Berlo

32 Words are basically linear, but when they are printed become________

a. One dimensional b. Two dimensional
c. Three dimensional d. Circular

33 Which of the following author authored the book 'Theory of Mass Communication'?

a. McLuhan b. DeFleur
c. Shanon and Weaver d. New Comb

34 Who introduced the concept that 'Medium is message'?

a. DeFleur b. McLuhan
c. Shanon and Weaver d. Aristotle

35 Who initiates the communication process?

a. The communicator b. Receiver
c. Medium d. Message

36 The term that denotes ability to convey accuracy in meaning is________

a. Communication IQ
b. Communication redundancy
c. Communication competence
d. Communication entropy

37 Which of the following individual is associated with Communication I.Q. ?

a. Chattopadhyay
b. Defleur
c. McLuhan
d. Paul Preston

38 Which of the following is a Code?

a. Language
b. Book
c. Letter
d. Sentence

39 Hypodermic needle model (Magic bullet theory) is based on which of the following principle?

a. M-S principle
b. T-S principle
c. Q-A principle
d. S-R principle

40 Which of the following model associated with mass media communication channel?

a. Hypodermic needle model
b. Two step flow model
c. Multi step flow model
d. One step flow model

41 Which of the following is a characteristic of 'Fog distortion'?

a. Information is lost
b. Information is masked
c. Information is fogged over
d. All of these

42 In which type of distortion no information is lost?

a. Fog
b. Mirage
c. Systematic
d. None of these

43 Which distortion gives extra unwanted information?

a. Fog
b. Mirage
c. Systematic
d. None of these

44 Which of the following refers to perceived trustworthiness and expertise accorded to a source by its audience?

a. Fidelity
b. Fuzziness
c. Credibility
d. Redundancy

45 Which of the following is the combination of mass media channel with interpersonal channels?

a. Media forums b. Group discussion

c. Symposium d. Colloquium

46 Media forum concept was originally started in which country?

a. Indonesia b. Philippines

c. India d. Canada

47 Which of the following refers to the degree to which a farmer exposes himself to various information sources?

a. Communication I Q b. Communication Skill

c. Communication behavior d. Communication Knowledge

48 Which of the following network provides the greatest amount of member satisfaction?

a. Star b. Circle

c. Slash d. Comcon

49 Feedback is basically _______ .

a. Message oriented b. Receiver oriented

c. Source oriented d. Medium oriented

50 Who developed Role taking theory?

a. New Comb b. Mead

c. Westley d. Mclean

51 Inference theory is associated with which of the following concept?

a. Empathy b. Fidelity

c. Sympathy d. Credibility

52 Relationship between size of a group and empathetic accuracy is_____________

a. Inverse b. Positive

c. Both a & b d. Not related

53 In which year Satellite television broadcasting was initiated in India with the launching of Satellite Instructional Television Experiment (SITE)?

a. 1975-76 b. 1982-83

c. 1985-86 d. 1978-79

54 The concept of 'Key-communicator' was first developed by________

a. Hovland
b. Mead
c. Knowles
d. Lazersfeld

55 ________is the quick reading of the text to get overall meaning or gist of the text.

a. Kinesics
b. Skimming
c. Deciphering
d. Conciseness

56 Television was introduced in India in which year?

a. 1927
b. 1959
c. 1965
d. 1955

57 Key-communicator's exposure to mass media is ________ than their follower.

a. Greater
b. Lesser
c. Equal
d. Not specific

58 Wilson and Gallup classified extension teaching methods according to which category?

a. Form
b. Use
c. Relative importance
d. Both a & b

59 4-s formula of personal letters has been given by________

a. McGregor
b. McDonald
c. McClelland
d. McCormick

60 'Flag method' is which type of method?

a. Individual contact method
b. Group Contact Method
c. Mass Method
d. Mass Media Method

61 Famous theory of instinct or imitation was given by__________

a. McDonald
b. Gabriel de Tarde
c. McCormick
d. Hovland

62 Exhibition is classified in which type of method?

a. Mass contact
b. Individual contact
c. Group contact
d. Both b & c

63 Circular letter is written by______

a. Extension functionary
b. Joint Secretary
c. Lay leader
d. Both b & c

64 Which among the followings refers to the perceived degree of expertise and trustworthiness accorded to a source by its audience at a given time?

a. Source credibility b. Source personality
c. Source excellence d. All the above

65 Television belongs to which generation of media?

a. Fourth generation b. Second generation
c. Third generation d. first generation

66 Who introduced the modern poster in the year 1867?

a. Jules Cheret b. James Rowling
c. Rogers d. Walt Disney

67 Which screen is suitable for three dimensional projections?

a. Aluminium screen b. Silver screen
c. Both a & b d. Black screen

68 Who has given the concept of two step flow of communication?

a. James Rowling b. Lazersfeld
c. McDonald d. Gabriel de Tarde

69 Information exists in the mind of whom?

a. Receiver b. Follower
c. The Sender d. Supporter

70 The process by which people and other animals communicate via touching is known as__________

a. Haptic communication b. Chronemics
c. Monochronic d. Polychronic

71 Which one of the following is the study of the use of time in nonverbal communication?

a. Haptic b. Chronemics
c. Monochronic d. Polychronic

72 The United States is considered which type of society?

a. Haptic b. Chronemics
c. Monochronic d. Polychronic

73 Indian culture can be considered as __________

a. Haptic b. Chronemics
c. Monochronic d. Polychronic

74 Which time system suggests that things are done one at a time and time is segmented into precise, small units?

a. Haptic b. Chronemics

c. Monochronic d. Polychronic

75 Which of the following studies the eye contact ?

a. Oculesics b. Proxemics

c. Chronemics d. Haptic

76 Which of the following studies measurable distances between people as they interact with one another?

a. Oculesics b. Proxemics

c. Chronemics d. Haptic

77 The concept of Proxemics was given by which of the following individual?

a. Edward T. Hall b. Bogardus

c. Thorndike d. James Buffet

78 According to Proxemics Social distance ranges between

a. 4 to 8 feet b. 5-10 feet

c. 8-14 feet d. 2-4 feet

79 Baa of sheep, moo of cow, quack of duck are the examples of

a. Semiotics b. Onomatopoeia

c. Semantopeia d. Myopia

80 Which of the following is the study of meaning-making?

a. Semiotics b. Epistemology

c. Neolexia d. Myopia

81 'Communication is first accepted as propaganda and latter accepted as fact' this concept is known as______

a. Rumour b. Craze

c. Sleeper effect d. Fashion

82 Lexicology is the part of linguistics which studies ________

a. Words b. Letters

c. Sentence d. Verbs

83 Theory of knowledge- is also known by which name?

a. Epistemology b. Semiotics

c. Lexicology d. Semantopeia

84 The term “epistemology” was introduced by which of the following individual?

a. J K Hollande b. James Frederick Ferrier

c. Adams d. Gabriel Tarde

85 The act of creating a new word is also known as ___________

a. Neology b. Neolexia

c. Lexicology d. Semantopeia

86 New usage of an existing word- is best known as

a. Neolexia b. Lexicology

c. Neologism d. Epistemology

87 Which of the following studies the ways in which context contributes to meaning?

a. Pragmatics b. Biosemiotic

c. Semeiotics d. Zoosemiotics

88 The term “biosemiotic” was first used by which of the following?

a. Friedrich S. Rothschild b. Rutherford

c. Maslow d. Robert Redfield

89 Tactile perception- refers to which of the following?

a. Speech b. Smell

c. Touch d. Vision

90 Interpretation of signs- related to which of the following?

a. Pragmatic b. Biosemiotic

c. Semeiotics d. Zoosemiotics

91 Which among the following means ability to understand another speaker’s intended meaning?

a. Pragmatic Competence b. Verbal Competence

c. Telepathic Competence d. Comic Competence

92 The study of animal communication is also known as________

a. Pragmatic b. Biosemiotic

c. Semeiotics d. Zoosemiotics

93 No time for students to read printouts, reports, projections and forecast is known as_________

a. Information indigestion b. Information overlooked

c. Information overload d. Worn out behavior

94 Which one of the following is associated with literal meaning?

a. Connotation b. Structural

c. Contextual d. Denotation

95 The direction, purpose, kind and method of communication collectively can be referred as ________

a. Pattern of communication b. Communication system

c. Source of communication d. Role of communication

96 Who among the following proposed a transactional model of communication?

a. Barnlund b. Berlo

c. New Comb d. Aristotle

97 Which of the following interfere with effective transmission and reception of a message?

a. Sound b. Vibration

c. Noise d. Pollution

98 Who among the following is called as the "father of communication studies"?

a. Leagans b. Wilbur Lang Schramm

c. Berlo d. Aristotle

99 Who among the following wrote the book 'Mass Media and National Development'?

a. Berlo b. Mead

c. Wilbur Lang Schramm d. Sumner

100 Walter Lippmann's barriers to effective communication include which of the following aspect(s)?

a. Artificial censorship b. Gatekeepers in the media

c. Shrinking news holes d. All the above

101 ________ is finding out by the degree of trustworthiness and expertness with which a source has been viewed by a receiver.

a. Communication credibility b. Fidelity

c. Empathy d. Sympathy

102 The communication that flows from subordinate to the superiors or superiors to the subordinate is called as ________

a. Horizontal communication b. Mass communication

c. Vertical communication d. Diagonal communication

103 The communication that occurs among the colleagues or co-workers is called as ________

a. Horizontal communication
b. Mass communication
c. Vertical communication
d. Intra-personal communication

104 Communication that follows official chain of command and can move upward, downward or horizontally for performing various tasks is known as____________

a. Informal communication
b. Formal communication
c. Non - official communication
d. None of these

105 The organizational communication that is not defined by the organisation's structural hierarchy is called as

a. Informal communication
b. Non - official communication
c. Both a & b
d. Formal communication

106 The faithful performance of all the elements of communication process in an organization is called as_______

a. Organizational communication pattern
b. Organizational communication effectiveness
c. Organizational communication system
d. Organizational communication ability

107 Any loss/ change in the original form of communication in terms of its meaning, intent and understanding when reproduced by the intended receiver is called as_______.

a. Communication distortion
b. Communication brake
c. Information fatigue
d. None of these

108 The internal or external factors which block the process of communication or prevent effective exchange of ideas or thoughts are known as__________

a. Communication disturbance
b. Communication stress
c. Communication barriers
d. Communication hurdle

109 Key communicators are also known as_______________

a. Gate keepers
b. Spark plugs
c. Style-setters
d. All of these

110 Which among the following method is useful to the extension workers in finding out the natural or local or informal leaders in the villages?

a. Sociometric method
b. Self-designating method
c. Information ratings
d. All of these

111 Which of the following is not the characteristic of a key communicator?

a. High social status
b. More cosmopolitan
c. Innovativeness
d. Stick to tradition

112 Which of the following is not the communication barrier?

a. Lack of empathy
b. Information overload
c. Insufficient information
d. Audible speech

113 Grapevine Communication is also known as__________

a. Informal Communications
b. Official Communication
c. Formal Communication
d. Mass Communication

114 Which among the following is not the aspect related to non verbal communication?

a. Appearance
b. Body language
c. Silence
d. Speech clarity

115 Study of body language is called as

a. Proximics
b. Kinesics
c. Conciseness
d. Deciphering

116 The space around the speaker is called__________

a. Proximics
b. Kinesics
c. Conciseness
d. Deciphering

117 To say more in less words or fewer words is called as______

a. Proximics
b. Kinesics
c. Conciseness
d. Deciphering

118 Which of the following means assigning of meanings to voices.

a. Kinesics
b. Skimming
c. Deciphering
d. Conciseness

119 Which of the following is incorrectly matched with respect to message distortion?

a. Fog distortion-Information is marked
b. Systemic distortion-No information is lost
c. Mirage distortion- Unwanted information comes in
d. Stretch distortion- Full information is lost

120 Which one of the following is incorrectly matched with respect to message flow model?

a. Hypodermic model- Direct audience effects

b. One step flow model- Different effects

c. Two step flow model- Indirect audience effect

d. Multistep flow model- Same effect

121 Which of the following is incorrectly matched?

a. Aristotle- Persuasion

b. Berlo- Influencing

c. Festinger- Consummatory and instrumental award

d. Schramm- Inorganic nature of communication

122 Which one of the following in not correctly matched?

a. Patting of hands- Approval b. Hugging- Affection

c. Smiling- A welcome d. Shouting- Anger

123 'Mind, self and society'- this book has been written by-

a. E.L. Thorndike b. Mildred Horton

c. George H. Mead d. None of these

124 'The origin of language'- this book has been written by-

a. E.L. Thorndike b. O.H. Benson

c. George H. Mead d. Paul Hoffman

125 Who wrote the famous book 'The process and effects of mass communication'?

a. Wilbar Schramm b. O. Cooley

c. G.H. Mead d. P. Chidambar

126 Ornament or possession that communicates information about a person, is known as

a. Museum b. Artifact

c. Collection d. Vault

127 A set of rules which is used to translate a message from one form to another is known as

a. Code b. Encryption

c. Description d. Solving mystery

128 Which of the following media is incomplete and requires human involvement and participation?

a. Hot Media b. Cool media

c. Direct media d. None of these

129 Arguments which do not follow the rules of logic is known as

a. Doctrine b. Dominancy

c. Fallacy d. Illogical

130 ________________ helps a communicator in evaluating the success of previous message.

a. Feedback b. Response

c. Decoding d. Encoding

131 According to whom the function of communication is to entertain, inform, persuade and stimulate?

a. Aristotle b. Cicero

c. J.P. Leagans d. Coombs and Ahmed

132 When officials of same rank from Agriculture and Animal Husbandry department communicates with each other, it is known as

a. Vertical communication

b. Inter-departmental communication

c. Gangplank

d. Intra-departmental communication

133 Which branch of philosophy investigates the interpretation of texts?

a. Hepatics b. Citadel

c. Phonemics d. Hermeneutics

134 Who developed the concept 'Mcworld'?

a. Adam Amith b. McDonald

c. Benjamin Barber d. Richmond Greggory

135 Which of the following theory suggests that 'Communication is Story Telling'?

a. Novel Theory b. Narrative Theory

c. Creative Theory d. Reinforcement Theory

136 ________________ is the emotive aspects of the speech and audience.

a. Sympathy
b. Pathos
c. Emotional outburst
d. Ethos

137 ________________ is the irrelevant information which is used to divert attention away from the real issue.

a. Red herring
b. Sword fish
c. Camouflage
d. Vail

138 Rumors travels through which of the following channels?

a. Informal channels
b. Formal channels
c. Official orders
d. None of these

139 Impersonal and superficial casual talk is known as

a. Hard talk
b. Small talk
c. Balanced talk
d. Absurd talk

140 Which of the following suggests the role reversal between source and receiver during conversation?

a. Turn talking
b. Role taking
c. Role reversal
d. Small talking

141 Expressive communication is driven by

a. Passive aggression
b. Encoder's personal characteristics
c. External clues
d. Encoder-decoder contract

142 Positive classroom communication leads to

a. Coercion
b. Submission
c. Confrontation
d. Persuasion

143 Classroom communication is the basis of

a. Social identity
b. External inanities
c. Biased passivity
d. Group aggression

144 Effective communication pre-supposes

a. Non-alignment
b. Domination
c. Passivity
d. Understanding

145 When verbal and non-verbal messages are contradictory, it is said that most people believe in

a. Indeterminate message b. Verbal message

c. Non-verbal message d. Aggressive message

146 The typical feature of an information-rich classroom lecture is in the nature of being

a. Sedentary b. Staggered

c. Factual d. Sectoral

147 Among the following, identify the continuous type of data :

a. Number of languages a person speaks

b. Number of children in a household

c. Population of cities

d. Weight of students in a class

148 Given below are two premises ((a) and (b)). From those two premises four conclusions (i), (ii), (iii), (iv) are drawn. Select the code that states the conclusions validly drawn from the premises (taking singly or jointly.)

Premises: a) Untouchability is a curse..

b) All hot pans are untouchable

Conclusions: i) All hot pans are curse

ii) Some untouchable things are hot pans

iii) All curses are untouchability

iv) Some curses are untouchability

a. (i) and (ii) b. (ii) and (iii)

c. (iii) and (iv) d. (ii) and (iv)

149 If the statement 'none but the brave wins the race' is false which of the following statements can be claimed to be true?

a. All brave persons win the race

b. Some persons who win the race are not brave

c. Some persons who win the race are brave

d. No person who wins the race is braves

150 If two standard form categorical propositions with the same subject and predicate are related in such a manner that if one is undetermined the other must be undetermined, what is that relation?

a. Contrary b. Sub contrary

c. Contradictory d. Subaltern

151 Men and women may have different reproductive strategies but neither can considered inferior or superior to the other, any more than a bird's wings can be considered superior or inferior to a fish's fines. What type of argument it is?

a. Biological b. Physiological
c. Analogical d. Hypothetical

152 Among the following propositions two are related in such a way that they cannot both be true but can both be false. Select the code that states those two propositions.

Propositions:

(a) Every student is attentive
(b) Some students are attentive
(c) Students are never attentive
(d) Some students are not attentive

Codes:

a. a and b b. a and c
c. b and c d. c and d

153 In which teaching method learner's participation is made optimal and proactive ?

a. Discussion method b. Buzz section method
c. Brainstorming session method d. Project method

154 The book entitled 'pedagogy of the oppressed' is written by

a. Paulo Freire b. R.N. Tagore
c. Paterson d. S. Waghmare, V. Waghmare

155 "Reflection without Action is mere verbalism, action without reflection is pure activism" who made the above statement?

a. McKenzie b. Knowles
c. Freire d. Goodman

156 Assertion (A): An oral message is more dynamic and makes direct impact than a written message.

Reason (R): An oral message is always better than a written message.

Codes:

a. (A) is correct and (R) is wrong b. (R) is correct and (A) is wrong
c. Both (A) and (R) are wrong d. Both (A) and (R) are correct

157 Assertion (A): One of the greatest attributes of a successful leader is the ability to communicate simply and effectively.

Reason (R): Knowledge alone is adequate for a successful leader.

Codes:

a. (A) is correct and (R) is wrong b. (R) is correct and (A) is wrong

c. Both (A) and (R) are correct d. Both (A) and (R) are wrong

158 Match the items given in List-I with the items of List-II, use the codes given below:

List-I	List-II
a) Teaching technology	i) Use of media
b) Behaviour technology	ii) System analysis
c) Instructional technology	iii) Social skill training
d) Management technology	iv) Realizing certain objectives

Codes: (a) (b) (c) (d)

a. IV III I II b. I II III IV

c. II IV III II d. III II IV I

159 Agricultural Communication: Process and methods Book written by____________

a. G L Ray b. A S Sandhu

c. Adavireddy d. K N Singh

160 ______________refers to communicating one self

a. Intrapersonal communication b. Interpersonal communication

c. Organizational communication d. Intrapersonal communication

161 ___________is the actual physical product of the source-encoder

a. Channel b. Treatment

c. Message d. Receiver

162 'Emotive aspects of the speech and audience' as conceptualized by Aristotle is known as

a. Pathos b. Emotions

c. Hepatics d. Semitics

163 Encoding skills includes ______________

a. Writing b. Painting

c. Reading d. Both a & b

164 Decoding skill includes ___________

a. Reading b. Drawing

c. Writing d. Both a & b

165 The best example for impersonal cosmopolite channel is ___________

a. Extension agent b. Opinion leader

c. Newspaper d. Sale agent

166 According to Berlo, communication is

a. Continuous process b. Dynamic process

c. Ongoing process d. All of these

167 Noise is the most important communication element of model ___________

a. Berlo model b. Schramm model

c. Shannon and weaver's model d. Leagans model

168 According to the role taking theory which statement is correct

a. Concept of self is developed through communication

b. Concept of self can't developed through communication

c. He develop concept of self then communicate with others

d. None of the above

169 If attitude affect the communication process of two individuals then the type of communication barrier acted here is ___________

a. Environmental barrier b. Cultural barrier

c. Psychological barrier d. Semantic barrier

170 Which statement is correct

a. Both noise and fidelity are same

b. There is no relation between noise and fidelity

c. Other name of fidelity is noise

d. None of the above

171 When irrelevant information is used to divert attention away from the real issue is known as

a. Salmon b. Red herring

c. Trout d. None of these

172 'Name calling' fallacy which suggests the attack on a person rather than the argument itself; is also known as

a. Ad hominem b. Ad bohenem

c. Ad fallacy d. None of these

173 Fidelity in communication is associated with ________

a. Effectiveness b. Noise

c. Faithfulness d. None of these

174 Which one of the following is a sign system that is used for deaf children who have additional disabilities

a. Makaton b. Humming

c. Signalling d. None of these

175 The hearing that a deaf child has is known as

a. Subsistence hearing b. Zero hearing

c. Residual Hearing d. Blind hearing

176 Which of the following term is used to denote the situation when words are pronounced clearly but without sound?

a. Soundless voice b. Lip speaking

c. Monologue d. Lip sync

177 Which approach of communication mainly focuses on listening skills?

a. Auralism b. Hearing

c. Listening d. Audacity

178 Who developed Media Dependency Theory?

a. Kartz b. McCOMBS

c. Ball-Rokeach and DeFluer d. Shaw

179 SPRING Network works in collaboration with

a. DFID and Nike Foundation b. USAID and DFAT

c. Both a & b d. None of these

180 Flesch-Kincaid reading ease formula is

a. 206.835(0.826wl x 0.015 sl)

b. 206.835 - 1.015 x (words/sentences) - 84.6 x (syllables/words).

c. 0.39 x (words/sentences) + 11.8 x (syllables/words) - 15.59.

d. None of these

181 In expectancy motivation theory, motivation is

a. Motivation (force) = "Valence x Expectancy

b. Motivation (force) = " Life x Expectancy

c. Motivation (force) = " Hygiene x Expectancy

d Motivation (force) = "Valence x Strength

182 X having 20 marks in knowledge and Y having 40 marks then which of following is correct?

a. X having half knowledge of Y

b. Y having 100% more knowledge than X

c. Y having more knowledge of X

d. None of these

183 If one measure has a reliability of 0.80 and the reliability of another measure is 0.30, what is the correlation between this

a. 0.55 b. 0.24

c. 0.49 d. 0.99

184 Syntax means

a. Rules order of sign or words

b. Proper order of sentence in paragraph

c. Contextual meaning of sentence

d. None of these

185 Synergy means

a. Working in isolation

b. The whole in greater than it is parts

c. Individual is superior than team

d. None of these

186 Approaches in language teaching involves

a. Design b. Backward design

c. Central design d. All of these

187 The writing style KISS 'K' denotes to

a. Keep b. Kept

c. Knights d. None of these

188 Any group of symbols that can structured in a way that is meaningful to some person called as__________

a. Model b. Code

c. Specimen d. Elements

189 __________refers to the manner in which a message is handled to get information across to an audience

a. Credibility b. Treatment

c. Movement d. Feedback

190 Which of the following term indicates the study of origins of a particular word?

a. Phonetics b. Etymology

c. Grammaticus d. Refractive

191 Eliminate the odd one out __________

a. Campaign b. Exhibition

c. Farmers fair d. Result demonstration

192 A technology transferred from one person to another person who are closely interacted with each other is called

a. System effect b. Peer effect

c. Neighbourhood effect d. None of these

193 Which have continuous contact which farmer?

a. Leaflet b. Folder

c. Bulletin d Pamphlet

194 Which one of the following is text analysis software developed by Lexical Computing Limited?

a. Text Engine b. Search Engine

c. Sketch Engine d Lexical Analytica

195 Which does not loose personal touch?

a. Newsletter b. Leaflets

c. Magazines d None of these

Answer Key

1. a	2. a	3. b	4. d	5. c	6. a	7. a	8. c	9. b	10. a
11. c	12. b	13. d	14. a	15. a	16. b	17. c	18. a	19. b	20. c
21. c	22. d	23. a	24. a	25. a	26. b	27. c	28. a	29. c	30. a
31. a	32. a	33. b	34. b	35. a	36. c	37. d	38. a	39. d	40. a
41. d	42. c	43. b	44. c	45. a	46. d	47. c	48. a	49. c	50. b
51. a	52. a	53. a	54. d	55. b	56. b	57. a	58. b	59. d	60. a
61. b	62. a	63. a	64. a	65. a	66. a	67. c	68. b	69. c	70. a
71. b	72. c	73. d	74. c	75. a	76. b	77. a	78. a	79. b	80. a
81. c	82. a	83. a	84. b	85. b	86. c	87. a	88. a	89. c	90. c
91. a	92. d	93. a	94. d	95. a	96. a	97. c	98. b	99. c	100. d
101. a	102. c	103. a	104. b	105. c	106. b	107. a	108. c	109. d	110. d
111. d	112. d	113. a	114. d	115. b	116. a	117. c	118. c	119. d	120. d
121. d	122. d	123. c	124. a	125. a	126. b	127. a	128. b	129. c	130. a
131. b	132. c	133. d	134. c	135. b	136. b	137. a	138. a	139. b	140. a
141. b	142. d	143. a	144. d	145. c	146. c	147. d	148. a	149. b	150. c
151. c	152. b	153. a	154. a	155. c	156. a	157. a	158. a	159. b	160. a
161. c	162. a	163. d	164. a	165. c	166. d	167. c	168. a	169. c	170. d
171. b	172. a	173. a	174. a	175. c	176. b	177. a	178. c	179. a	180. b
181. a	182. c	183. c	184. a	185. b	186. d	187. a	188. b	189. b	190. b
191. d	192. b	193. c	194. c	195. a					

8

Information and Communication Technology

1 Which of the following are considered as drivers of ICT in Agriculture?

a. Low-cost connectivity
b. Advances in data storage and exchange
c. Democratization of information
d. All the above

2 'Telephone lady' concept was introduced in________

a. USA b. China
c. Bangladesh d. India

3 'Bhoomi Project' is implemented in________

a. Karnataka b. Andra Pradesh
c. Madya Pradesh d. Rajasthan

4 Kisan Call Centres (KCC) started in India during________

a. 2001 b. 2004
c. 2010 d. 2005

5 Kisan Call Centres (KCC) helpline number is __________

a. 1555 b. 5115
c. 1551 d. 1515

6 Which one of the following is an internet based network of public and private agricultural libraries and information centers, coordinated by the National Agriculture Library (NAL), USA?

a. AgMARK b. AgLIB
c. AgNAL d. AgNIC

7 The Agricultural Libraries Network coordinated by ________

a. FAO b. CYMMIT
c. ICRISAT d. ILRI

8 FAO of the United Nations initiated agricultural information networking through AGRIS which was established in____

a. 1974 b. 1990

c. 1975 d. 1980

9 CSIRO stands for______

a. Commonwealth Scientific and Industrial Research Organization

b. Centre of Scientific and Industrial Research Organization

c. Central Scientific and Information Research Organization

d. Commonwealth Social and Industrial Research Organization

10 Agrigate-Coordinated by the __________

a. National Library of India b. National Library of USA

c. National Library of Australia d. National Library of Africa

11 ______has been established by organizations and individuals involved in agricultural and rural development in Central and Eastern Europe.

a. AgrisNET b. AGROPEDIA

c. Honey bee network d. AGROWEB CEE network

12 IAALD- stands for

a. International Association of Agricultural Information Specialists

b. International Agency of Agricultural Information Specialists

c. International Association of Agricultural Information Scientists

d. Indian Association of Agricultural Information Society

13 APARIS- stands for

a. Andhra-Pradesh Agricultural Research Information System

b. Asia-Pacific Agricultural Research Information Society

c. Asia-Pacific Agricultural Research Information System

d. Asia-Pacific Agricultural Reference Information System

14 The German Agricultural Information Network is

a. DAINet b. GAINet

c. GARNet d. AgrisNET

15 Entomology Library and Information Network ELIN project hosted by_______

a. The Natural History Museum, London

b. The Natural Agricultural Museum, New Delhi

c. The Natural Library, London

d. The Natural Library, India

16 Virtual Extension and Research Communication Network (VERCON) established by ___

a. FAO b. ILRI

c. ICRISAT d. IARI

17 The official publication wing of the ICAR is

a. Division of Agricultural Education, New Delhi

b. The Directorate of Knowledge Management in Agriculture, New Delhi

c. NCAP, New Delhi

d. NAARM, Hyderabad

18 When journals provide Open Access to their articles, it is referred as_______

a. Golden Road b. Diamond Road

c. Open Road d. Closed Road

19 When authors provide Open Access to their own published articles, by making their own e-prints free for all, it is referred as_______

a. Publicity b. Green Road

c. Philanthropy d. Egalitarian

20 The Partnership on Measuring ICT for Development was launched in _______

a. Beijing China in July 2004 b. Hyderabad in June, 2006

c. Sao Paulo, Brazil in June, 2004 d. New Delhi in June, 2004

21 The Department of Information Technology has initiated a programme for e-governance to establish ___________

a. State Wide Area Network (SWAN)

b. Agri Wide Area Network (AWAN)

c. District Wide Area Network (DWAN)

d. State Wide Agriculture Network (SWAN)

22 A blog is a fusion of words _______

a. "web" and "google" b. "web" and "log"

c. "WAN" and "LAN" d. "glob" and "log"

23 RSS Feed- is

a. Really Simple Syndication b. Really Smart Syndication

c. Rational Simple Syndication d. Really Simple Sympputer

24 The term "Computer" is derived from the word

a. Sympputer b. Comprehension

c. Compute d. Calculate

25 The world's oldest computing device is

a. Chinese devised Abacus b. Calculator

c. PARAM d. None of the above

26 During 1943-46, the world's first electronic computer was built named as

a. Electronic Numerical Integrated Computer (ENIAC)

b. Electronic Numerical Integrated Calculator (ENIAC)

c. Electronic Numerical Information Calculator (ENIAC)

d. Electronic Number & Information Calculator (ENIAC)

27 PARAM by CDAC, Pune is an example of

a. Super computer b. Mini computer

c. Micro computer d. Basic computer

28 HTML stands for

a. Hypertext Monitoring Language b. Hypertext Microsoft Language

c. Hypertext Makeup Language d. Hypertext Markup Language

29 IP stands for _____

a. Information Protocol b. Internet Protection

c. Internet Protocol d. Internet Performance

30 Rice-Crop Doctor- an expert system has been developed by which Institute?

a. MANAGE b. IARI

c. IRRI d. NRRI

31 World's first true operational GIS was developed by the federal Department of Forestry and Rural Development in Ottawa, Canada by whom?

a. Evelyn Pruitt b. Roger Tomlinson

c. Tim Berners-Lee d. Berlo

32 Commercial GIS software includes which of the following?

a. ArcGIS b. GeoMedia

c. Geomatica MapInfo d. All of these

33 The term "remote sensing" was coined by ______

a. Evelyn Pruitt b. Roger Tomlinson

c. Mark Zuckerberg d. Tim Berners-Lee

34 "e-Seva" project is run by Government of______

a. Maharashtra b. Madhya Pradesh

c. Andhra Pradesh d. Haryana

35 Professor Sangeeta Sharma (2002) has suggested concept of ____________

a. Ecology of E-Governance b. Sociology of E-Governance

c. Psychology of E-Governance d. Philosophy of E-Governance

36 _______is the imaginary or virtual space of computers connected with each other on networks, across the globe.

a. Net Space b. Cyber Space

c. Inter space d. Air Space

37 ___________is an important cyber extension tool.

a. Kisan Call Centre b. ATIC

c. ATMA d. KVK

38 Total TV channels increased from 130 in 2004 to _______ in 2018

a. 866 b. 650

c. 701 d. 514

39 Kerala Government runs which of the following project to connect all village panchayats?

a. Akshaya project b. FRIENDS

c. e-Sagu d. Akashaganga

40 Information Villages Project in Puducherry run by whom?

a. Puducherry government

b. Indian Agribusiness Systems Pvt. Ltd

c. MSSRF Chennai

d. Nagaarjuna group

41 __________is India's First E-literate District.

a. Malappuram b. Kottayam

c. Ernakulum d. Chemaravattom

42 The "Wired Village" project was initiated by

a. Vinay Kore b. A K Gupta

c. Sharad Pawar d. Narendra Modi

43 Which of the following is a super computer used in the field of Agro-meteorology?

a. PARAM b. Super Com-Agro

c. CRAY XMP-14 d. RAIN

44 Janmithra project is an ICT initiative by which state?

a. Rajasthan b. Madhya Pradesh

c. Gujarat d. Haryana

45 Gyandoot project is an ICT initiative by which state?

a. Rajasthan b. Madhya Pradesh

c. Gujarat d. Haryana

46 Rasi project is an ICT initiative by which state?

a. Rajasthan b. Tamil Nadu

c. Gujarat d. Haryana

47 Village Knowledge Centre was established by MSSRF in which year?

a. 1999 b. 2004

c. 1998 d. 2001

48 Indian Institute of Information Technology is situated at__________

a. Bangalore b. Hyderabad

c. Pune d. New Delhi

49 The concept of Gyan choupal was given by which of the following personality?

a. M S Swaminathan b. Sam Pitroda

c. Jayant Naralikar d. ManMohan Singh

50 Who Among the following has invented Television?

a. J L Baird b. Mark Zuckerberg

c. Jim Timberline d. None of these

51 Which of the following refers to gigabyte?

a. 1024 bytes b. 1024 kilobytes

c. 1024 megabytes d. 1024 gigabytes

52 What is the full form of http?

a. Hyper Text Transfer Protocol b. Hyper Text Transfer Programme

c. Hyper Text Typing Protocol d. Hypo Text Transfer Protocol

53 RAM stands for

a. Read Access Memory b. Randomly Available Memory

c. Ready Access Memory d. Random Access Memory

54 ROM stands for

a. Random Only Memory b. Ready Only Memory

c. Read Only Memory d. Random Other Memory

55 What is the full form of URL?

a. Uniform Resource Locator b. Universal Reading Library

c. Universal Resource Locator d. None of the above

56 Which one of the following is not machine level language?

a. FORTRAN b. COBOL

c. C++ d. SPANISH

57 Computers understand which of the following number?

a. 1 b. 0

c. 2 d. Both a & b

58 Community radio stations increased from 64 in 2009 to _______ in 2018

a. 247 b. 100

c. 125 d. 143

59 Who invented WWW?

a. Mark Zuckerberg b. Albert Hofmann

c. Tim Berners-Lee d. David Adams

60 Who is called as father of modern information theory?

a. Claude Shannon b. Tim Berners-Lee

c. Charles M. Herzfeld d. Douglas Engelbart

61 Who is the founder of facebook?

a. Mark Zuckerberg b. Albert Hofmann

c. Tim Berners-Lee d. David Adams

62 Google was founded by whom?

a. Larry Page
b. Sergey Brin
c. Both a & b
d. Mark Zuckerberg

63 Who is the CEO of Twitter?

a. Dick Costolo
b. Sergey Brin
c. Evan Williams
d. Mark Zuckerberg

64 Who among the following founded Whatsapp?

a. Brian Acton and Jan Koum
b. Larry Page & Sergey Brin
c. Evan Williams
d. Robert Cailliau

65 Who among the following founded 'hike messaging app'?

a. Bharti Airtel
b. Reliance communication
c. Tata world
d. Bharti SoftBank Innovation Pvt. Ltd

66 Orkut is a social networking website founded by whom?

a. Orkut Büyükkökten
b. Orkut Babilion
c. Orkut Zuckerberg
d. Harold Orkut

67 Which company first introduced mobile phone?

a. Nokia
b. Samsung
c. Apple
d. Motorola

68 __________ is the social interaction among people in which information and ideas are created, shared or exchanged in virtual communities and networks.

a. Media forum
b. E-paper
c. Social media
d. Cyber crime

69 Which country in the world ranks first in terms of internet usage?

a. America
b. India
c. UK
d. China

70 What is the rank of India in terms of internet users in the world?

a. 2nd
b. 3rd
c. 4th
d. 10th

71 What is the rank of India in terms of number of mobile phones in use in the world?

a. 2nd b. 3rd

c. 4th d. 10th

72 mKRISHI is the ICT based initiative through mobile technology to cater to the absolute needs of the rural sector was started by________

a. Tata Consultancy Servises b. Reliance communication

c. Nokia d. IFFCO&Airtel

73 What is the full form of CeRA?

a. The Collection of e-Resources in Agriculture

b. The Consortium for e-Resources in Aquaculture

c. The Consortium for e-Resources in Agriculture

d. The Consortium for e-Readers in Agriculture

74 _________is an initiative to provide market price information across the agricultural markets in India.

a. AGMARKNET b. MARKETNET

c. eMARKETNEWS d. eAGMARK

75 aAQUA - an online expert Question and Answer based community forum, developed by________

a. Media Lab Asia b. IIT Mumbai

c. Both a & b d. IIT Hyderabad

76 vKVK stands for____________

a. Voice (Virtual) Krishi Vigyan Kendra

b. Veterinary Krishi Vigyan Kendra

c. Vocational Krishi Vigyan Kendra

d. Visual Krishi Vigyan Kendra

77 NABG -an ICAR initiative is associated with

a. Agronomy b. Soil Science

c. Extension d. Bioinformatics

78 nLogue was developed to connect every village in a district using terrestrial wireless and provide village kiosks by which Institute?

a. IIT, Kanpur b. IIT Mumbai

c. IIT, Chennai d. IIT Hyderabad

79 Agriwatch.com which is a portal developed for farmers, traders, processors of agricultural outputs, suppliers of agricultural inputs etc. in 2001 by whom?

a. IIT Mumbai

b. Indian Agribusiness Systems Pvt. Ltd

c. IIT Hyderabad

d. Nagaarjuna group

80 iKisan.com which is an agri portal developed by which of the following organisation?

a. Media Lab Asia

b. IIT Mumbai

c. Nagarjuna group of private companies

d. Indian Agribusiness Systems Pvt. Ltd

81 Drishtee.com – is associated with________

a. Rural supply-chain b. Eye-Care

c. Health Care d. Investigation

82 ________is an Union Catalog of Library Resources of Indian National Agricultural Research & Education System (NARES).

a. Agriwatch b. Agrilib

c. AgriCat d. Agries

83 ______is a digital repository of Indian National Agricultural Research System to preserve and provide open access to institutional intellectual assets.

a. KrishiGranth b. KrishiShodh

c. eKrishi d. KrishiKosh

84 ________is an information highway for sharing rice knowledge through latest ICT tools including mobile telephony.

a. Rice Knowledge Management Portal

b. Rice Knowledge Messaging Portal

c. Rice Knowledge Management Platform

d. Research Knowledge Management Portal

85 VASAT is an initiative by which of the CGIAR institute?

a. ICARDA b. ICRISAT

c. ILRI d. IRRI

86 Which of the following is knowledge management initiative of IARI?

a. PUSA agricom

b. Weather based agro-advisory services

c. Cyber extension services in villages

d. All of these

87 AKASHGANGA- an ICT initiative for automatic milk collection solution was initiated in Gujarat in which year?

a. 1999 b. 2001

c. 1996 d. 2006

88 Dairy information and services kiosks (DISKs) initiative was taken by Gujarat cooperative milk market federation ltd. with the help of which institute?

a. IIM, Ahmadabad b. NDRI, Karnal

c. NDDB, Anand d. IIT, New Delhi

89 Village Research Centre (VRC) initiative was launched by which of the following research organisation?

a. ISRO b. ICAR

c. ICMR d. IIHR

90 VRC project was launched via INSAT link on which date?

a. 2nd October 2001 b. 18th October 2005

c. 18th October 2004 d. 18th October 2010

91 National Knowledge Network was launched on which date?

a. 18th October 2005 b. 9th April 2009

c. 2nd October 2001 d. 9th April 2010

92 The word sagu of e-Sagu project comes from which o the following Indian language?

a. Marathi b. Tamil

c. Telugu d. Bengali

93 ekrishi kiran project is run in which of the following state?

a. Gujarat b. Maharashtra

c. Haryana d. Madhya Pradesh

94 Which of the following ICT initiative is run in Kerala state?

a. e-Krishi b. KISSAN

c. Akshaya d. All of these

95 MAHAAGRI SMS is an ICT initiative in which of the following state?

a. Gujarat b. Maharashtra

c. Manipur d. Madhya Pradesh

96 Warna project was launched in which year?

a. 1988 b. 1998

c. 2001 d. 1990

97 Who is the Chairman of National Knowledge Commission?

a. Ashok Ganguly b. P. Balaram

c. Sam Pitroda d. Nandan Nilekani

98 NICNET based Agricultural Extension Informatics Network in India is known as

a. VISTARNET b. PRASRNET

c. eEXTENSION d. Agrisnet

99 ICT term became popular by the use of it in the report made by which of the following?

a. M.S.Swaminathan b. Dennis Stevenson

c. Robert Chamber d. Sam Pitroda

100 Which of the following country topped in the 'ICT Development Index in 2011'?

a. South Korea b. China

c. UK d. India

101 The key concerns in employing ICT in farming is/are

a. Connectivity b. Content Adequacy

c. Accessibility d. All of the above

102 Phablet is a smartphone with screen sizes ranging between

a. 5 and 7 inches b. 3 and 5 inches

c. 9 and 12 inches d. 7 and 9 inches

103 International Telecommunication Union is headquartered at which city?

a. Paris b. Washington

c. London d. Geneva

104 One-piece mobile computer, operated by touch screen is often referred as

a. Capsule b. Tablet

c. Pill d. Pad

105 In which year, computers are first sold commercially?

a. 1951 b. 1969

c. 1961 d. 1975

106 Where first cellular phone communication network started in 1979?

a. Japan b. USA

c. Canada d. Switzerland

107 In which year, American government releases control of internet and WWW was born?

a. 1994 b. 2004

c. 2008 d. 2012

108 Which one of the following is not LAN technology?

a. Ethernet b. Token ring

c. ATM d. None of these

109 A graphical representation of a real person is known as

a. Cartoon b. Graphiti

c. Characterization d. Avatar

110 In which year 'Netscape' web browser introduced?

a. 1994 b. 1995

c. 1997 d. 1999

111 Which of the following in computer screen is set aside for special purpose?

a. Pillar b. Window

c. Door d. Board

112 What is the full form of 'Blog'?

a. Viblog b. Blogger

c. Weblog d. None of these

113 Which of the following is/ are operating system?

a. Unix b. Linux

c. Windows d. All of these

114 What is the full form of USB?

a. United Selection Builder b. Universal Serial Bass

c. Unifying Selection Board d. User Specific Benefit

115 Full form of 'TBT',one of the important terms in ICT is

a. Technology Bound Transmission b. Task Based Tethering

c. Task Based Teaching d. None of these

116 Which of the following is used in web based learning system?

a. SCORM
b. DACOTA
c. BILL
d. None of these

117 The country which is/are following 'FAO-ITU E-agriculture Strategy Guide'-

a. Sri Lanka
b. Philippines
c. Bhutan
d. All of these

118 Who among the following has given the term 'cyberspace'?

a. Sergei Brin
b. William Gibson
c. Larry Page
d. Mark Talbot

119 'Ethernet' technology has been developed by

a. TCS Ltd.
b. WIPRO
c. Xerox corporation
d. Microsoft

120 When a magazine is published on internet or circulated through email it is known as

a. E-zine
b. Internet-zine
c. E-magazine
d. Net-zine

121 'Cyber Dhaba' concept was started by which organization?

a. ICAR
b. UNESCO
c. IFFCO
d. ITC

122 Green SIM card for farmers started in 2008 is a joint venture of________________

a. IFFCO and AIRTEL
b. DRDO-ICAR
c. ICAR and C-DAC
d. ITC-Apple

123 Full form of mobile 'App' is

a. Application
b. Appropriate
c. Apprehension
d. Approved

124 To provide descriptive information regarding different breeds developed by your institute to livestock farmers having Smartphone, which modern communication tool is more appropriate and cost effective?

a. Phone calls
b. Email
c. Mobile Apps
d. Messages

125 Android is based on which of the following operating system?

a. Windows b. UNIX

c. Linux d. macOS

126 In the term 'QR Code' QR stands for

a. Quick Response b. Quality response

c. Quantitative Response d. Qualitative Response

127 Who coined the term 'Internet'?

a. Charles babbage b. Vinton Cerf

c. Mark Zuckerberg d. Dr. John O'sullivan

128 Expand CAAM

a. Centre for Alternative Agriculture Media

b. Cloud Computing Adoption Assessment Model

c. China Association of Automobile Manufactures

d. Centre for Asian American Media

129 Which of the following is data base management system?

a. MS Access b. dBase

c. MySQL d. All of the above

130 What is the major disadvantage of information kiosk?

a. Need continues power supply b. Need e-literacy

c. Need physical set-up d. All of these

131 Cascading Style Sheets are a feature of which of the following?

a. HTML b. RTML

c. QTML d. NMTL

132 Which part of the pages in a word file that cannot be used for printing because of the binding?

a. Gutter b. Free space

c. Blank space d. Both a & b

133 Agriculture information network system

a. AGMARKNET b. VISTARNET

c. AgNIC d HORTNET

134 e- Learning help in exchange of

a. Virtual information b. Offline information

c. Classroom teaching d. None of these

135 " WiKi" word derived from

a. Hawaiian b. English

c. French d. Italian

136 AGRISNET provide infrastructure set up at

a. State level b. District level

c. Village level d. Block level

137 e-HAAT is a subsidiary company of

a. Dhampur Sugar Mill Ltd (2012) b. ITC

c. ICAR d. C-DAC

138 Akash Ganga is an

a. Automatic Milk Collection Systems

b. Satellite

c. NGO

d. None of these

Answer Key

1. d	2. c	3. a	4. b	5. c	6. d	7. a	8. a	9. a	10. c
11. d	12. a	13. c	14. a	15. a	16. a	17. b	18. a	19. b	20. c
21. a	22. b	23. a	24. c	25. a	26. b	27. a	28. d	29. c	30. a
31. b	32. d	33. a	34. c	35. a	36. b	37. a	38. a	39. a	40. c
41. a	42. a	43. c	44. a	45. b	46. b	47. c	48. b	49. a	50. a
51. c	52. a	53. d	54. c	55. a	56. d	57. d	58. a	59. c	60. a
61. a	62. c	63. a	64. a	65. d	66. a	67. d	68. c	69. d	70. b
71. a	72. a	73. c	74. a	75. c	76. a	77. d	78. c	79. b	80. c
81. a	82. c	83. d	84. a	85. b	86. d	87. c	88. a	89. a	90. c
91. b	92. c	93. a	94. d	95. b	96. a	97. c	98. a	99. b	100. a
101. d	102. a	103. d	104. b	105. a	106. a	107. a	108. d	109. d	110. a
111. b	112. c	113. d	114. b	115. c	116. a	117. d	118. b	119. c	120. a
121. c	122. a	123. a	124. c	125. c	126. a	127. b	128. a	129. d	130. d
131. a	132. a	133. b	134. a	135. a	136. d	137. a	138. a		

9

Diffusion of Innovation

1 Extension officer's efficiency can be measured by which of the following parameters?

a. The speed of reducing knowledge gap

b. Number of farmers adopting new practices

c. Productivity increase due to adoption of new practices

d. All the above

2 ________ is the process of communication of an innovation through certain channels over time among the members of a social system.

a. Diffusion | b. Adoption
c. Innovation | d. Communication

3 _____is a special type of communication, wherein the messages are concerned with new ideas.

a. Diffusion of innovation | b. Development communication
c. Both a & b | d. None of these

4 '______' of the idea in the message content of communication that gives diffusion its special character.

a. Credibility | b. Popularity
c. Newness | d. None of these

5 ________is a social process in which subjectively perceived information about a new idea is communicated.

a. Diffusion of innovations | b. Adoption
c. Communication | d. Development communication

6 The spread of a new idea from its source of invention or creation to its ultimate use of adopters is called as ____________

a. Diffusion process | b. Communication
c. Innovation | d. None of these

7 ______is a decision to make full use of an innovation as the best course of action available.

a. Diffusion b. Adoption

c. Transmission d. Management

8 _______ is an idea, practice or object that is perceived as new by a unit of social system.

a. Falkways b. Diffusion

c. An innovation d. Mores

9 _______is an activity through which an individual becomes aware of objects around oneself and of events taking place

a. Behaviour b. Attitude

c. Prejudices d. Perception

10 First few adopters of an innovation who influence the other members of a community to adopt the innovation as they interact with them. This is referred to as the

a. Interaction effect b. Diffusion effect

c. Fusion effect d. Mass effect

11 A few farmers try out and adopt the innovation after its introduction in a village. They can be called as_____

a. Early majority b. Early adopters

c. Innovators d. Laggards

12 A small majority of farmers is influenced by the innovators to adopt the recommended practice, referred as

a. Early adopters b. Late majority

c. Early majority d. Laggards

13 The small group of farmers who take the longest time to adopt an innovation is called as

a. Early adopters b. Late majority

c. Early majority d. Laggards

14 The four main elements involved in diffusion are the innovation, communication channels, time and______

a. The social system b. Message

c. Extension system d. Innovators

15 New varieties of crops and plants, new breeds of livestock, new chemicals and medicines, new technique of doing things etc are known as

a. Innovations
b. Ideas
c. Products
d. Farm inputs

16 Irrespective of the time period the idea or practice was originally developed, when a person first become aware of it, it is ______ to that person.

a. Mere product
b. Luxury good
c. Innovation
d. None of these

17 This group of farmers needs solid proof of benefit and convenience before using a new farm technology

a. Early majority
b. Laggards
c. Late majority
d. Skeptical

18 The S-shaped growth curve in the adopter categories is also known as______

a. Diffusion curve
b. Adoption curve
c. Innovation curve
d. Normal curve

19 The book 'Diffusion of innovation' is written by__________

a. Rogers and Shoemaker
b. M G Ross
c. Rogers
d. Ryan and Gross

20 The design that reduces the uncertainty in the cause-effect relationships involved in advising farmers and desired outcome is referred as __________

a. A technology
b. Folkways
c. Norms
d. Idea

21 ______consists of one or more distinguishable elements of technology that are perceived as being closely related.

a. A technology cluster
b. Propaganda
c. Innovation
d. Package

22 ________ is the means by which messages get from one individual to another.

a. Social system
b. A communication channel
c. Community
d. Feedback

23 Who among the following made significant contribution to the study of diffusion theory?

a. D K Berlo b. Everett Rogers

c. J P Leagans d. Maslow

24 Heart of diffusion process is

a. Advertisement b. Selling

c. Imitation d. Farmer

25 More effective communication occurs in ________ condition

a. Homophilous b. Heterophilous

c. Heterogeneous d. Homozygous

26 ________ is the mental process leading to a decision to adopt or reject, to implement the new idea, and to confirmation of this decision.

a. Communication

b. Diffusion

c. The innovation – decision process

d. Management

27 Which curve shows distribution of adopters over time within a social system?

a. Bell-Shaped Curve b. Upward curve

c. Concave curve d. S shaped curve

28 Which parameters used to partition the curve into five areas of adopter categories?

a. The mean and the standard deviation

b. The mode and the standard deviation

c. The mean and the standard error

d. The variance and the standard deviation

29 ________ is the degree to which an individual or other unit of adoption is relatively earlier in adopting new ideas than other members of a social system.

a. Rate of adoption b. Leadership

c. Entrepreneurship d. Innovativeness

30 ________ is the relative speed with which an innovation is adopted by members of a social system.

a. Innovativeness b. Rate of adoption

c. Both a & b d. Enthusiasm

31 ________ is usually measured by the length of time requirement to adoption of innovation by a certain percentage of the members of a system.

a. The rate of adoption | b. Innovativeness
c. Adoption quotient | d. Diffusion

32 ________ is defined as a set of interrelated units that are engaged in joint problem solving to accomplish a common goal.

a. A social system | b. Community
c. Religion | d. Caste

33 Individual innovativeness is affected by which of the following?

a. Individuals' characteristics | b. The nature of the social system
c. Both a and b | d. None of These

34 If innovations had been promoted equally in two villages by a government agency, the rate of adoption will be

a. High in both villages | b. Different in both villages
c. Equal in both villages | d. Low in both villages

35 ________ is the degree to which an individual is able to influence attitudes or overt behavior of other individual informally with relative frequency.

a. Opinion leadership | b. Innovativeness
c. Rate of diffusion | d. Autocracy

36 Innovators in the social system are often perceived as ________.

a. Deviant | b. Cooperative
c. Friends | d. Outsider

37 Which of the following is/are characteristics of opinion leader?

a. More cosmopoliteness | b. More innovativeness
c. Greater social participation | d. All the above

38 ________ is the degree to which a technology is changed or modified by a user in the process of its adoption and implementation.

a. Reinvention | b. Innovation
c. Re-adoption | d. Modification

39 Which reasons facilitate re-invention?

a. Technologies that are complex and difficult to understand
b. When a technology try to address a wide range of user's problems
c. Lack of knowledge about the technology
d. All the above

40 The technology itself is banned by the government due to several reasons is called as_____

a. Forced discontinuance b. Replacement discontinuance

c. Disenchantment discontinuance d. None of these

41 DDT, BHC and milk adulterants were banned by the government due to their deleterious effects. This is called as

a. Forced discontinuance b. Replacement discontinuance

c. Disenchantment discontinuance d. None of these

42 The farmers who accepts only a few of the recommended practices or uses them at adjusted or modified levels are called as

a. Partial adopters b. Potential adopter

c. Full adopter d. Non adopter

43 Choices to adopt or reject an innovation are made by an individual, independent of the decisions of other members of the system are called as________

a. Optional innovation – decisions

b. Collective innovation – decisions

c. Authoritative innovation – decisions

d. Forced innovation – decisions

44 Choices to adopt or reject an innovation are made by consensus among the members of a system are called as _______

a. Optional innovation – decisions

b. Collective innovation – decisions

c. Authoritative innovation – decisions

d. Forced innovation – decisions

45 Choices to adopt or reject an innovation are made by relatively few individuals in a system who possess power, status, or technical expertise is known as

a. Optional innovation – decisions

b. Collective innovation – decisions

c. Authoritative innovation – decisions

d. Contingent innovation – decisions

46 Choices to adopt or reject can be made only after a prior innovation – decision are called as-_____

a. Optional innovation – decisions

b. Collective innovation – decisions

c. Contingent innovation – decisions

d. Authoritative innovation – decisions

47 Consequences are the changes that occur to an individual or to a social system as a result of_____________

a. The adoption of an innovation b. The rejection of an innovation

c. Either a or b d. None of these

48 Which is the element of diffusion?

a. Innovation b. Communication channels

c. Time d. All of these

49 Types of consequence of innovation are

a. Desirable versus undesirable consequences

b. Anticipated versus unanticipated consequences

c. Direct versus indirect consequences

d. All the above

50 Who has given the five stages of adoption process?

a. E.M. Rogers

b. The North Central Rural Sociology Sub Committee

c. Shoemaker

d. Robert Chamber

51 In which adoption stage a farmer comes to know about the new idea but he lacks full information about it?

a. Interest b. Awareness

c. Trial d. Adoption

52 If the farmers have heard about sugarcane harvester but do not know how it will work, this fits in which of the following stage?

a. Interest b. Trial

c. Awareness d. Evaluation

53 In which adoption stage farmer seeks additional information about the technology from any source?

a. Interest b. Trial

c. Awareness d. Evaluation

54 In which stage farmer makes mental application of the new idea in the contemporary situations and decides whether or not to try it?

a. Trial b. Interest

c. Evaluation d. Awareness

55 In which stage, farmer applies the new idea on a small scale in order to determine its utility in his own situation?

a. Trial b. Interest

c. Evaluation d. Awareness

56 Which of the following may be considered as the practical evaluation of an innovation?

a. Adoption b. Trial

c. Evaluation d. Rejection

57 Who has said that the stages of adoption are dynamic and not static?

a. Y.P. Singh b. E.M. Rogers

c. E.A. Wilkening d. J.P. Leagans

58 In which of the stage the farmer takes the decision to extend the use of the innovation on a continued basis?

a. Adoption b. Trial

c. Evaluation d. Rejection

59 Who postulated that acceptance of innovations may be viewed as a function of social relations in an ideological systems ideas, values and sentiments of farmer?

a. Rogers b. Ryan and Gross

c. Wilkening d. Shoemaker

60 Who stated the paradigm of the adoption of innovation by an individual contains three major divisions: 1. antecedents, 2. process and 3 results?

a. Rogers b. Ryan and Gross

c. Wilkening d. Shoemaker

61 According to Lewin what are the stages of adoption of innovation?

a. Unfreezing - Moving -Freezing b. Moving - Unfreezing - Freezing

c. Freezing - Moving - Unfreezing d. Refreezing - Moving -Freezing

62 Awareness, information, trial and adoption; these four stages of adoption of innovation are given by which of the following?

a. Rahim b. Rogers

c. Wilson and Gallup d. Wilkening

63 Who among the following have suggested five stages of adoption of innovation process- awareness, interest, trial, evaluation and adoption?

a. Bose and Dasgupta b. Rogers

c. Wilson and Gallup d. Wilkening

64 Who had suggested six steps; attention, interest, desire, conviction, action and satisfaction?

a. Bose and Dasgupta b. Rogers

c. Wilson and Gallup d. Wilkening

65 The seven stages of adoption namely Need, Awareness, Interest, Deliberation, Trial, Evaluation and Adoption were suggested by

a. Bose and Dasgupta b. Rogers

c. Singh and Pareek d. Wilkening

66 What is the time taken to pass from the awareness of an innovation to its adoption?

a. Innovation period b. Gestation period

c. Development period d. Adoption period

67 What is the role of agricultural extension workers in diffusion process?

a. Increase the adoption period b. Shorten the adoption period

c. Stabilize the adoption period d. None of these.

68 Which one of the following lacks personal touch?

a. Documentary b. Telephone

c. Advisory letter d. All of the above

69 The social system's norms serve as ______ on the individual's decisions.

a. Incentives b. Restraints

c. Either a or b d. None of these

70 Which sources are important during the awareness stage?

a. Cosmopolite and mass media channels

b. Localite and interpersonal channels

c. Both of these

d. None of these

71 Which sources are important during the persuasion stage?

a. Cosmopolite and mass media channels

b. Localite and interpersonal channels

c. Both of these

d. None of these

72 Which of the following is the first stage in the Innovation Decision Process?

a. Awareness b. Knowledge

c. Interest d. Persuasion

73 What is a state of dissatisfaction or frustration that occurs when one's desires outweigh one's actualities?

a. Need b. Wish

c. Motives d. All the above

74 According to Rogers how many stages are involved in the Innovation-Decision Process?

a. Three b. Seven

c. Five d. Nine

75 At which stage in the innovation-decision process the individual forms a favourable or unfavourable attitude towards an innovation?

a. Confirmation b. Knowledge

c. Persuasion d. Decision

76 At which stage the individual becomes more psychologically involved with an innovation?

a. Confirmation b. Knowledge

c. Persuasion d. Decision

77 Which one of the following is not the perceived attributes of an innovation?

a. Relative advantage b. Compatibility

c. Complexity d. Innovativeness

78 At which stage of innovation decision process, an individual engages in activities which lead to a choice to adopt or reject an innovation?

a. Confirmation
b. Knowledge
c. Persuasion
d. Decision

79 ______occurs when an individual or other decision making unit puts an innovation into use.

a. Implementation
b. Persuasion
c. Confirmation
d. Knowledge

80 At which stage re-invention often occurs?

a. Implementation
b. Persuasion
c. Confirmation
d. Knowledge

81 What kind of effect of re-invention often occurs to the adopters of an innovation?

a. Harmful
b. Beneficial
c. Neutral
d. None of these

82 What is rejection of an innovation?

a. Decision not to adopt an innovation
b. Decision to adopt an innovation
c. Can't say
d. None of these

83 When a farmer rejects after adopting the innovation after its trial is called ______.

a. Active rejection
b. Passive rejection
c. Can't say
d. None of these

84 When a farmer rejects without adopting the innovation including even its trial is called ___.

a. Active rejection
b. Passive rejection
c. Can't say
d. None of these

85 ______is a decision to reject as innovation after having previously adopted it.

a. Direct rejection
b. Indirect rejection
c. Discontinuance
d. None of these

86 ________ is a decision to reject an idea in order to adopt a better idea that supersedes.

a. Replacement discontinuance b. Disenchantment discontinuance

c. Forced discontinuance d. None of the above

87 ________ is a decision to reject an idea as a result of dissatisfaction with the performance.

a. Disenchantment discontinuance b. Replacement discontinuance

c. Forced discontinuance d. None of the above

88 Some farmers continue to adopt an innovation, vigorously, when experts feel that it should not be so done. This is called as________.

a. Over adoption b. Under adoption

c. Active adoption d. Passive adoption

89 Excessive use of pesticides is an example of which of the following term?

a. Over adoption b. Under adoption

c. Active adoption d. Passive adoption

90 What among the following are the causes of over adoption?

a. In sufficient knowledge about an innovation

b. Inability to predict its consequences

c. Prestige- conferring aspect of adopting an innovation

d. All the above

91 ________ is the process by which the farmer who takes up an innovation influences other farmers to do so.

a. Passive adoption b. Active adoption

c. Over adoption d. Under adoption

92 When a farmer who adopts the practice do not influence the other farmers to do the practice is called as __________

a. Passive adoption b. Active adoption

c. Over adoption d. Under adoption

93 Which of the following regarding innovation is more beneficial to the society?

a. Passive adoption b. Active adoption

c. Over adoption d. Under adoption

94 _______is the length of time required to pass through the innovation–decision process.

a. The innovation – decision period b. Gestation period

c. Dormancy period d. Adoption period

95 Who among the followings have a shorter innovation decision period?

a. Innovators b. Early majority

c. Early adopters d. Lagards

96 Which of the following method an extension agents use to increase the rate of adoption?

a. Shortening innovation decision period

b. Increase the rate of awareness-knowledge

c. Both a and b

d. None of these

97 Which of the following term is related to Innovators?

a. Venturesome b. Respectable

c. Deliberate d. Skeptical

98 Which of the following term is related to Early adopters?

a. Venturesome b. Respectable

c. Deliberate d. Skeptical

99 Which of the following is related to Early majority?

a. Venturesome b. Respectable

c. Deliberate d. Skeptical

100 Which of the following is related to Late majority?

a. Venturesome b. Respectable

c. Deliberate d. Skeptical

101 Which of the following is related to Laggards?

a. Venturesome b. Traditional

c. Deliberate d. Skeptical

102 The adoption of an innovation over time follows which type of curve, when plotted over time on frequency basis?

a. Bell-shaped curve b. S-shaped curve

c. U-shaped d. L-shaped

103 If the cumulative number of adopters is plotted, what will be the shape of curve?

a. S-shaped curve b. Bell-shaped curve

c. U-shaped d. L-shaped

104 Which category has greatest degree of opinion leadership in most social systems?

a. Innovators b. Early Adopters

c. Early Majority d. Laggards

105 Who is considered by many as "the man to check with" before using a new idea?

a. Early adopter b. Innovator

c. Laggard d. Early Majority

106 Which adopter category is generally preferred by change agents to speed up the diffusion process?

a. Early adopters b. Innovators

c. Laggards d. Early Majorities

107 Who tends to adopt new ideas just before the average member of a social system?

a. Early adopters b. Innovators

c. Laggards d. Early Majorities

108 Who among the following adopt new ideas just after the average member of a social system?

a. Late majority b. Innovators

c. Laggards d. Early Majorities

109 Who are the traditional and last to adopt an innovation?

a. Late majority b. Innovators

c. Laggards d. Early Majorities

110 What is the sequence of the adopter categories according to innovativeness?

a. Innovators- Early adopters- Early majorities- Late majorities -Laggards

b. Laggards- Late majorities - Early majorities- Early adopters- Innovators

c. Innovators- Early majorities- Early adopters- Late majorities -Laggards

d. Innovators - Early majorities- Late majorities - Early adopters - Laggards

111 The area lying to the left of the mean time of adoption minus two standard deviations includes 2.5 per cent of the individuals, who are they?

a. Late majority | b. Innovators
c. Laggards | d. Early Majorities

112 Who are the lying between the mean minus one standard deviation and the mean minus two standard deviations in adopter category curve?

a. Late majority | b. Innovators
c. Early Adopters | d. Early Majorities

113 The 34 per cent of the adopters between the mean date of adoption and minus one standard deviation are known as______.

a. Late majority | b. Innovators
c. Early Adopters | d. Early Majorities

114 Between the mean and one standard deviation to the right of the mean are located the 34 per cent to adopt the new idea, these are_____________.

a. Late majority | b. Innovators
c. Early Adopters | d. Early Majorities

115 The 16 per cent adopters to the right of mean plus one standard deviation are the last to adopt the innovation are______.

a. Laggards | b. Innovators
c. Early Adopters | d. Early Majorities

116 Which of the following attributes related to the degree to which an innovation is perceived as better than the idea it supersedes?

a. Relative advantage | b. Compatibility
c. Complexity | d. Observability

117 If a new technology or practice gives more yield or income or saves time, labour and cost: or has less risk than the existing one; it has more ____________.

a. Relative advantage | b. Compatibility
c. Complexity | d. Observability

118 Multiple use of an innovation may be a form of __________.

a. Relative advantage | b. Compatibility
c. Complexity | d. Observability

119 _______ indicates the benefits and the costs resulting from adoption of an innovation.

a. Relative advantage
b. Compatibility
c. Complexity
d. Observability

120 What is called as the degree to which an innovation is perceived consistent with the existing values, past experiences and needs of the receivers?

a. Compatibility
b. Relative advantage
c. Complexity
d. Observability

121 For adoption of an innovation, it should be compatible with which of the following?

a. With socio-cultural values and beliefs
b. With previously introduced ideas
c. With client needs for innovations
d. All the above

122 ________refers to the degree to which a new idea or practice is consistent with existing practices relating to economic activities.

a. Physical compatibility
b. Cultural compatibility
c. Social compatibility
d. All the above

123 ________refers to the degree to which an innovation is consistent with the existing values, beliefs, habits and tradition in a social system.

a. Cultural compatibility
b. Physical compatibility
c. Economic compatibility
d. Psychological compatibility

124 The failure of the improved poultry programme in the village having the vegetarian population is related to which of the following?

a. Cultural compatibility
b. Physical compatibility
c. Economic compatibility
d. Psychological compatibility

125 Which of the following attributes is having negative relationship with rate of adoption?

a. Compatibility
b. Complexity
c. Observability
d. Relative Advantage

126 Which of the following attributes is having positive relationship with rate of adoption?

a. Compatibility
b. Relative Advantage
c. Observability
d. All the above

127 What is the term related to the degree to which an innovation is perceived as relatively difficult to understand and use?

a. Compatibility b. Complexity
c. Observability d. Relative Advantage

128 Complexity of an innovation may not prevent its adoption, if it has one of the following attribute?

a. Trialability b. Predictability
c. Observability d. Relative Advantage

129 ________ is the degree to which an innovation may be experimented with on a limited basis before deciding to adopt.

a. Trialability b. Predictability
c. Observability d. Relative Advantage

130 The minikit demonstrations have helped in spreading the cultivation of high yielding variety crops because of the following attribute?

a. Trialability b. Predictability
c. Observability d. Relative Advantage

131 ________ is the degree to which the results of an innovation are visible/ observable, demonstrable and communicable to farmers.

a. Trialability b. Predictability
c. Observability d. Relative Advantage

132 ________ refers to the degree or certainty of receiving expected benefits from the adoption of an innovation.

a. Trialability b. Observability
c. Predictability d. Relative Advantage

133 ________ is an idea that an individual adopts at one point in time in order to lower the probability that some future unwanted event will occur.

a. Preventive innovation b. Predictability
c. Trialability d. Relative Advantage

134 ________ has particularly slow rate of adoption because of individuals have difficulties in perceiving its relative advantage.

a. Preventive innovation b. Predictability
c. Trialability d. Relative Advantage

135 ________ is one who adopts the entire package at recommended levels.

a. Full Adopter b. Partial adopter
c. Non Adopter d. None of the above

136 Who among the followings accepts only a few of the recommended practices?

a. Adopters
b. Partial adopters
c. Non Adopter
d. None of the above

137 What includes in criticism of the of Roger's theory of diffusion?

a. Pro-Innovation Bias
b. Individual-Blame Bias
c. Bias in Favour of Larger and Wealthier Farmers
d. All the above

138 Which factors affect on the diffusion of innovation?

a. The type of innovation-decision,
b. Nature of communication channels
c. The extent of change agents' promotion efforts
d. All the above

139 Who is the forefather of the diffusion theory?

a. E.M. Rogers
b. C. M. Rogers
c. David Bell
d. Gabriel Tarde

140 According to Rogers, Take off point occurs in diffusion curve when _____ percent people adopt the technology.

a. 40-50
b. 2-5
c. 10-20
d. 30-40

141 __________is the point when adoption of an innovation takes-off, when the greatest numbers of people begin to adopt it, and the dramatic upward line on the S-shaped curve begins its ascent.

a. The critical stage
b. The critical mass
c. The trade-off stage
d. All the above

142 Through which element we can easily differentiate diffusion and communication?

a. Innovativeness
b. Message
c. Channel
d. Time

143 The first study of diffusion was conducted on hybrid seed corn in 1943 by_____

a. Rogers
b. Ryan and Gross
c. Gabrial Tarde
d. Lasswell

144 Opinion leaders belong to which of the following category?

a. Laggards
b. Early Majority
c. Early adopters
d. Innovators

145 The average time of adoption by the members of a social system will follow which of the following?

a. Always vary
b. Sometime vary
c. Same for all
d. None of these

146 ___________ refers to diffusion that does not reach or approach 100 percent adoption.

a. Rejection
b. Adverse diffusion
c. Failed diffusion
d. None of these

147 Which one of the following is example of covert behaviour?

a. Replacement Discontinuance
b. Disenchantment Discontinuance
c. Rejection
d. Symbolic adoption

148 Which of the following variable is considered to develop intention as per the theory of planned behaviour (TPB) developed by Ajzen (1991)?

a. Attitude
b. Subjective norms
c. Control
d. All of the above

149 The book 'Communication of Innovation' was written by_________

a. Rogers
b. M G Ross
c. Rogers and Shoemaker
d. Ryan and Gross

150 Crop insurance is the example of which of the following attributes?

a. Preventive innovation
b. Predictability
c. Trialability
d. Relative Advantage

151 Which of the following is not a consequences of adoption of innovation?

a. Desirable or undesirable
b. Direct or indirect
c. Anticipated or non anticipated
d. All are true

152 Modification over an existing product is denoted by

a. Discrete innovation
b. Modified innovation
c. Continuous innovation
d. Modification innovation

153 Accessing email through mobile phone by using 4G network, instead of using computer or laptop is an example of

a. Discontinuous innovation
b. Upgraded innovation
c. Discrete innovation
d. Up gradation innovation

154 Which of the following model describes the steps in the adoption process?

a. Heirarchy of Effects' Model b. Robertson's model

c. Roger's model d. All of these

155 In simple linear model of innovation who is the source of innovation?

a. Manufacturer b. Innovator

c. Early majority d. Late majority

156 Who has given the 'Chain linked model' of innovation?

a. J. W. Hawkins b. Stephen J. Kline

c. E.H. Rudolph d. K.E. Sumner

157 For ranking countries on the basis of innovativeness which of the following index is used?

a. Universal Innovation Index b. Bloomberg Innovation Index

c. UN Innovation Index d. None of these

158 Who among the following is associated with 'concept of diffusion'?

a. Gabriel Tarde b. Friedrich Ratzel

c. Leo Frobenius d. All of them

159 During the period 2010 to 2015, European Innovation Scoreboard (EIS) was published under which of the following title? Innovation Union Scoreboard

a. Innovation Union Scoreboard b. European Scorecard

c. Innovation Scorecard d. European Union Scorecard

160 According to Global Innovation Index (2016), which of the following country rank first in the list?

a. Denmark b. Switzerland

c. Ireland d. USA

161 Match the following list-I with list- II and answer using the codes below:

List - I	List - II
Factors affecting adoption of innovation	Component
i) Social factor	a) Age
ii) Cultural factor	b) Income
iii) Personal factor	c) Family
iv) Economic factor	d) Value system

Codes: iii iii iv

a. c d a b b. c a b d

c. d c a b d. d a c b

162 Match the following list-I with list- II and answer using the codes below:

List-I	List-II
a. Village group action	i. Result demonstration
b. To prove the worth of new practice	ii. Campaign
c. To discuss individual or village problems	iii. Method demonstration
d. To teach a new skill	iv. Farm and home visits

Codes: a b c d

a. i ii iv iii b. ii i iv iii

c. i ii iii iv d. iii ii iv i

163 Which elements do not come under diffusion

a. Innovation b. Channels of communication

c. Social system d. Evaluation

Answer Key

1. d	2. a	3. a	4. c	5. a	6. a	7. b	8. c	9. d	10. a
11. c	12. a	13. d	14. a	15. a	16. c	17. a	18. a	19. c	20. a
21. a	22. b	23. b	24. c	25. a	26. c	27. a	28. a	29. d	30. b
31. a	32. a	33. c	34. b	35. a	36. a	37. d	38. a	39. d	40. a
41. a	42. a	43. a	44. b	45. c	46. c	47. c	48. d	49. d	50. b
51. b	52. c	53. a	54. c	55. a	56. b	57. a	58. a	59. c	60. a
61. a	62. a	63. a	64. c	65. c	66. d	67. b	68. a	69. c	70. a
71. b	72. b	73. a	74. c	75. c	76. c	77. d	78. d	79. a	80. a
81. b	82. a	83. a	84. b	85. c	86. a	87. a	88. a	89. a	90. d
91. b	92. a	93. b	94. a	95. a	96. c	97. a	98. b	99. c	100. d
101. b	102. a	103. a	104. b	105. a	106. a	107. d	108. a	109. c	110. a
111. b	112. c	113. d	114. a	115. a	116. a	117. a	118. a	119. a	120. a
121. d	122. a	123. a	124. a	125. b	126. d	127. b	128. d	129. a	130. a
131. c	132. c	133. a	134. a	135. a	136. b	137. d	138. d	139. d	140. c
141. b	142. a	143. b	144. c	145. a	146. c	147. d	148. d	149. c	150. a
151. d	152. c	153. a	154. d	155. a	156. b	157. b	158. d	159. a	160. b
161. a	162. b	163. d							

10 Training for Development

1. Who developed the simple model of training process?

   a. Rolf P. Lynton and Udai Pareek b. C.R. Kay

   c. Daniel Benor d. R. Pete

2. Which one of the following is not a part of

3. Which of the following would help build team

   a. Role playing b. Seminar

   c. Brainstorming d. T-group

4. What is the purpose of training and development?

   a. Remove performance deficiencies

   b. Improve skill of the employee

   c. Change the attitude of the employee

   d. All the above

5. Sensory stimulation theory is associated with?

   a. Laird b. ...

   c. Training d. None

10

Training for Development

1 Who developed the Simple model of training process?

a. Rolf P. Lynton and Udai Pareek b. C.R. Kay

c. Danial Benor d. R. Pike

2 How many stages of the learning cycle were suggested by David Kolb?

a. Five b. Four

c. Seven d. Nine

3 Which one of the following is not a part of Kolb's learning cycle?

a. Concrete experience b. Reflective observation

c. Abstract conceptualization d. Active participation

4 Who developed Instructional Design Grid?

a. C.R. Kay b. S.K. Peyton

c. R. Pike d. All the above

5 Which of the following would help participants experience what something sounds or feels like?

a. Role playing b. Seminar

c. Brain storming d. T-group

6 What is the purpose of training and development programmes?

a. Remove performance deficiencies in employees

b. Improve skill of the employees

c. Change the attitude of the employee

d. All the above

7 Sensory stimulation theory is associated with which of the followings?

a. Learning b. Teaching

c. Training d. None of these

8 What is the sequence of three phases of the training cycle?

a. Implementation, planning and evaluation

b. Evaluation, planning and implementation

c. Planning, evaluation and implementation

d. Planning, implementation and evaluation

9 In which method the trainer is active and the trainee is passive?

a. Lecture b. Sensitivity training

c. Role playing d. Brainstorming

10 Through which of the following method, practical work is done by the participants who are actively involved in the same?

a. T-group b. Fish bowl exercise

c. Workshop d. Seminar

11 Which training method suits top and middle level officials only and do not help that much to the junior staff?

a. Workshop method b. Sensitivity Training

c. Fishbowl technique d. All the above

12 Seminar through discussions attempts at developing higher______.

a. Cognitive attributes b. Conflicting attributes

c. Both a and b d. None of these

13 Which of the following training method started when the US space scientists at NASA were working on the design of a spacesuit for astronauts?

a. Brainstorming b. Seminar

c. Workshop d. Symposium

14 Which of the following word literally means it is a large group of delegates that confer?

a. Conference b. Seminar

c. Workshop d. Symposium

15 Which programme emphasized the regular and continuous training of extension worker?

a. NES b. CDP

c. T&V d. IADP

16 Which of the following expert gave the catalogue of shortcomings in training in developing countries?

a. Kerrigan and Luke b. Danial Benor

c. Lynton and Pareek d. None of these

17 Which one of the following is true about training?

a. Negligible return b. Low return on investment

c. No return of investment d. High returns on investment

18 Which of the following fact is true about training?

a. Covert process b. Inert process

c. Overt process d. None of these

19 DTCD of United Nations stands for

a. Department of Technical Cooperation for Development

b. Department of Training, Cooperation and Development

c. Department of Testing Cooperation for Development

d. Department of Technology Creation for Development

20 If T is training the Os stands for which of the following option in the equation T=f(K,S,A,Os)

a. Personality traits b. Conduct

c. Empathy d. All of these

21 In which year, Advanced Centers of Training (ACT) in India was launched?

a. March, 1988 b. January, 1992

c. March, 1998 d. January, 1982

22 In the 'Discrete phases approach to training' how many phases are there?

a. 2 b. 3

c. 7 d. 5

23 A standard training curriculum shouldn't contain which of the following component?

a. Course objectives b. Achievement targets

c. Course structure d. Reward and punishment

24 Which of the following training method can be considered as modified version of Panel?

a. Colloquy b. Seminar

c. Conference d. Lecture

25 'Task Force' type of training method was borrowed from which field?

a. Military
b. Industry
c. Politics
d. Religion

26 Which area of Johari window model is good for interpersonal relations?

a. Facade
b. Unknown self
c. Arena
d. Blind spot

27 Which of the following is the other name of T-Group?

a. Technology Group
b. Teachers Group
c. Trainers Group
d. Diagnostic Training Group

28 Which can be considered as distinct contribution of T&V System?

a. Seminar
b. Conference
c. Inter-Disciplinary Team(IDT)
d. Task force

29 From where 'Round Table' name came?

a. Experts sit around round table
b. Discussions take place in several rounds
c. Audience ask question after completion of round
d. None of these

30 Which of the following training method is used for diagnosing, analyzing and seeking solutions?

a. Conference
b. Seminar
c. Symposium
d. Clinic

31 Which formula is appropriate to calculate Training Effectiveness Index (TEI) where no. of trainees attended the course (T_S) and found it useful (T_e)?

a. $TEI = T_e X T_s$
b. $TEI = T_e / T_s$
c. $TEI = T_e X T_s X100$
d. $TEI = T_e / T_s X100$

32 Which formula is appropriate to calculate Training Utility Index (TUI) where T_e = Number of trainee who found training course useful and T_a = Number of trainees?

a. $TUI = T_e X T_a$
b. $TUI = T_e / T_a$
c. $TUI = T_e X T_a X100$
d. $TUI = T_e / T_a X100$

33 Video-text can be considered of which of the following?

a. Tele-text
b. View- data
c. Both a & b
d. None of these

34 In the ABCDEF of Training for Extension Personnel D stands for

a. Delivery b. Diligence

c. Diversion d. Disillusion

35 Who has given the idea of meta-evaluation?

a. Michel Scriven b. Lynton and Pareek

c. Iceberg d. Charles Darwin

36 Which of the following uses the concept of empathy?

a. Buzz session b. Seminar

c. Symposium d. Role playing

37 Which of the following cannot be a duration of training plan?

a. Short term b. Long term

c. Both a & b d. Medium term

38 Territorial training plans include ______

a. National level b. State level

c. District level d. All of these

39 How many different levels of training needs can be possible?

a. 6 b. 7

c. 8 d. 9

40 The levels of training needs includes________

a. Individual b. Sectoral

c. National d. All of these

41 According to York, the term 'Systems Approach' derived from which of the following concept?

a. Engineering b. Agriculture

c. Medical d. Linguistic

42 The Discrete Phases Approach to training is also known as_________

a. Traditional Model b. Modern Model

c. Medieval Model d. Historical Model

43 Who among the following undergo Orientation training?

a. Outside organizational personnel b. Serving personnel

c. Newly appointed personnel d. None of these

44 The training process involves how many phases?

a. 3 b. 4

c. 5 d. 6

45 A good training plan should have which of the following elements?

a. Training policy b. Training results

c. Training tasks d. All of these

46 Which one of the following is known as heart of training programme?

a. Trainer b. Trainee

c. Curriculum d. Training institute

47 Which of the following is known as arteries and veins of training system?

a. Training Methods b. Curriculum

c. Trainer d. Trainee

48 Fish bowl exercise can be used in which of the following situation?

a. Class Room b. Business meeting

c. Both a & b d. Soli-lo-quay

49 Who among the following has laid the foundation of sensitivity training?

a. Peter Drucker b. Robert Chamber

c. Henry Ford d. Kurt Lewin

50 Which among the following is fourth phase of Experiential Learning Cycle?

a. Experience phase b. Process phase

c. Application phase d. Generalization phase

51 Seven step model of presentation is having how many more steps than ELC?

a. 4 b. 5

c. 3 d. 2

52 Which of the following added to ELC to get seven step model of presentation?

a. Climate setting b. Learning objectives

c. Closure d. All of these

53 Which among the following are the aspects of Training Programme Implementation (TPI)?

a. Training infrastructure b. Actual implementation

c. Both a & b d. None of these

54 Which one of the following is last phase of training process?

a. Post training

b. Training Programme Implementation

c. Training Monitoring and Evaluation

d. None of these

55 TME system consists of which of the following sub-systems?

a. Training monitoring b. Training Evaluation

c. Both a & b d. None of these

56 Which of the following are/is the essential of training objective?

a. Simple b. Measurable

c. Attainable d. All of these

57 Which one of the following is not the purpose of training objective?

a. Creating awareness b. Distributing incentives

c. Generate interest d. Impart skills

58 Which one of the following is not the step of SATNA?

a. Problem identification b. Identification of funding agency

c. Job description d. People identification

59 Which of the following are considered as essentials of training reporting?

a. Timely b. Brief

c. Involve minimum paper work d. All of these

60 Which one of the following is not a training monitoring indicator?

a. Valid b. Reliable

c. Non specific d. Relevant

61 Which of the following is considered as domains of concern in training monitoring?

a. Domain of top management b. Domain of trainer

c. Domain of trainee d. All of these

62 Composite Training Organisation Index (CTOI) is which type of index?

a. Weighted index b. Simple index

c. Judgmental index d. Arbitary index

63 In which type of training, evaluation approach was developed as an alternative to the objective approach?

a. Goal free training evaluation

b. Transactional training evaluation

c. Decision oriented training evaluation

d. Illuminative training evaluation

64 Decision oriented training evaluation is also known as______

a. ZIPP Approach b. CIPP Approach

c. DIDP Approach d. BIBP approach

65 Which one of the following training evaluation approach is based on full description and judgment of a programme?

a. Goal free training evaluation

b. Transactional training evaluation

c. Decision oriented training evaluation

d. Illuminative training evaluation

66 Which of the following training evaluation approach was developed as an alternative to all other approaches?

a. Goal free training evaluation

b. Transactional training evaluation

c. Decision oriented training evaluation

d. Illuminative training evaluation

67 A microlab is organized in a programme at which time?

a. Beginning b. Middle

c. Closure d. After

68 The major purpose of microlab is_______

a. Incentivize participant

b. Train the participants

c. Promoting communication

d. To evaluate the training programme

69 The term curriculum is derived from Latin word which means______

a. To participate b. To motivate

c. Syllabus d. To keep running

70 Which one of the following is true about training?

a. Process b. Product

c. End d. Means

71 Which one of the following is also known as long and dirty method of TNA?

a. Experiment method b. Observation method

c. Survey method d. All of these

72 In which type of evaluation programme runs and simultaneously the evaluation is done?

a. Internal evaluation b. External evaluation

c. Ex-post facto evaluation d. Concurrent evaluation

73 Which type of evaluation is done when the programme is finished totally?

a. Internal evaluation b. External evaluation

c. Ex-post facto evaluation d. Concurrent evaluation

74 Which of the following provides the bench mark for evaluation?

a. Training monitoring b. Training objective

c. Training methods d. Training curriculum

75 The concept 'Experiential Learning Cycle' (ELC) was given by______

a. James A Mc Caffery b. Anita Jhamtani

c. Linton and Pareek d. James Iceberg

76 Where the first microlab was conducted?

a. Extension Education Institute, Nilokheri

b. National Science laboratory, New Delhi

c. MANAGE, Hyderabad

d. National Training Laboratories, USA

77 Training given to freshly recruited ARS scientists of ICAR at NAARM Hyderabad falls under which type of training?

a. Foundation training b. In-service training

c. Refresher training d. Management training

78 For what purpose in basket exercise is used?

a. Promoting employees b. Hiring employees

c. Both a & b d. Firing employees

79 Which one of the following is considered as the normal pace of delivery of lecture?

a. 120 words per minute
b. 100 words per minute
c. 160 words per minute
d. 180 words per minute

80 Which one of the following is conducted after lecture?

a. Workshop
b. Forum
c. Buzz session
d. Colloquium

81 Laboratory training is also known as_____

a. T Group
b. Encounter group
c. Sensitivity training
d. All of these

82 Red session and green session are the characteristics of which of the following?

a. Lecture
b. Group discussion
c. Buzz session
d. Brainstorming

83 In which method Trainer : Trainee ratio is minimum?

a. Lecture
b. Group discussion
c. Buzz session
d. Brainstorming

84 Who has given the concept of Delphi Technique?

a. Olaf Helmer
b. Robert Chamber
c. Uday Pareek
d. R K Singh

85 Phillip 66 is also known as _______

a. Huddle system
b. Buzz session
c. Red session
d. Both a & b

86 The duration of sensitivity training is normally______

a. 2-3 days
b. 3-4 days
c. 5-10 days
d. 15-21 days

87 Controlled experience method is also known as__________

a. Simulation method
b. Buzz session
c. Huddle system
d. Phillip 66

88 Which one of the following is included in simulation method?

a. Role playing
b. Behaviour simulation games
c. In-basket exercise
d. All of these

89 When an extension worker trains a farmer at his doorstep it is known as_________

a. Peripatetic training
b. Overseas training
c. Inductive training
d. Orientation training

90 When the training is conducted in the village or farm, it is called as _____

a. On campus training
b. Off campus training
c. Short term training
d. Experimental training

91 When the training is conducted in the training institute, it is called as _______

a. On campus training
b. Off campus training
c. Short term training
d. Experimental training

92 What is the shape of learning curve in a training process?

a. S shape
b. Z shape
c. U shape
d. O shape

93 Who has given the concept of Brainstorming?

a. A F Osborn
b. Olaf Helmer
c. Otis Gibson
d. Rand company

94 Which of the following is the role of a trainer in experiential approach of training?

a. Teacher
b. Preacher
c. Advisor
d. Facilitator

95 Who among the following has written the book 'Handbook of Structural Experiences'?

a. Koontz and Weihrish
b. Anita Jhamtani
c. Pfeiffer and Jones
d. Stoner

96 Which of the following institute follows the covardale methodology of training?

a. NAARM
b. NIRD
c. EEI
d. MANAGE

97 The concept of showing, doing and telling classification of training methods was developed by whom?

a. Reay D G
b. U Pareek
c. Lynton
d. Olaf Helmer

98 Who among the following has given the concept of Objective Training Evaluation model?

a. Fredrick Tyler b. Swanson

c. Ralph W Tyler d. Pfeiffer and Jones

99 In which method Trainer: Trainee ratio is maximum?

a. Lecture b. Group discussion

c. Workshop d. Brainstorming

100 Who among the following is known as the father of 'Transactional Analysis'?

a. Eric Berne b. Ralph W Tyler

c. Fredrick Tyler d. Simon Joule

101 Which of the following term is used when students learn by doing without relying only on the instructor?

a. Discovery Learning b. Adventure learning

c. Both a & b d. None of these

102 ____________________ is a structured experience in which the participants are involved

a. Game b. Descriptive training

c. Exercise d. None of these

103 Which of the following is true about fishbowl exercise?

a. Group process b. Has an discussion group

c. Has an observer group d. All of these

104 Which of the following term is used to know other participants in a training programme and learning from them?

a. Networking b. Ice-breaking

c. Storming d. Norming

105 In which type of learning no feedback is provided to a learner's response?

a. Authoritative learning b. Passive learning

c. Active learning d. Leisez – faire learning

106 The process of determining a trainee's achievement in relation to other trainees is known as ____________________

a. Performance b. Competition

c. Norm referenced measurement d. Progress

107 Metalearning is

a. Learning how to learn
b. Extra learning
c. Situational learning
d. Learning by doing

108 Social learning theory was propounded by

a. Kirkpatrick
b. Albert Bandura
c. Malcom Knowles
d. Sigmund Freud

109 4-phase training evaluation model developed by Kirkpatrick consists of

a. Reaction-Learning-Behaviour-Result
b. Result-Learning-Behaviour-Reaction
c. Behaviour -Learning- Result -Reaction
d. Learning - Behaviour - Result -Reaction

110 Practice beyond what is necessary for retention is known as

a. Over learning
b. Over training
c. Both a & b
d. Over exercise

111 When a trainee progress as a group at a rate equal to that of the slowest learner, it is known as

a. Group paced instruction
b. Lockstep
c. Both a & b
d. None of these

112 Which of the following training can be used to reduce 'learning decay'?

a. Decay training
b. Rebuilding traing
c. Just –time - training
d. Optional training

113 Which of the following term is used to denote the amount of time required for learners to forget what they have learned in training?

a. Forget rate
b. Decay rate
c. Retention rate
d. Foggy rate

114 Which of the following is true about 'Heuristic Routine'?

a. Problem solving approach
b. Trial and error approach
c. Involves act of learning
d. All of these

115 When a separate work area is set up for a learner so that the actual work situation does not pressure the learner, that type of training is known as

a. Capsule training
b. Work training
c. Vestibule training
d. Job training

116 Training evaluation helps in

a. Discovery of training gaps

b. Identifying opportunities in training employees

c. Improvements on training programs

d. All of these

117 CIPP (context, input, process and product) also known as

a. Decision oriented training evaluation

b. Programme evaluation model

c. Critical Infrastructure Protection Project

d. None of these

118 How many number of elements involved in training?

a. 4 b. 5

c. 6 d. 7

119 In a training programme, cost of resource, number of trainees and tasks are important at______

a. Training productivity b. Training planning

c. Programme implementation d. All of the above

120 In DWCRA, skill training was part of ________

a. TRYSEM b. PMKVY

c. Both d. ICDS

121 Vocational training related to

a. Knowledge and attitude b. Knowledge and skill

c. Skill and adoption d. Attitude and adoption

122 Which of the following is true for 'Asynchronous learning'?

a. Instructional design

b. Allows students to access content outside of the classroom

c. Independent of the instructor

d. All of the above

123 Brainstorming includes

a. Red and Green session b. Red and Blue session

c. Red and Yellow session d. Blue and Yellow session

124 Brainstorming green session is

a. Evaluate other's ideas
b. Provides best possible solution
c. Free flow of idea
d. None of these

125 In KASA-------------- ________ last A stands for

a. Attribute
b. Attitude
c. Aspiration
d. Action

126 Important element in evaluation is

a. Collection of information
b. Final solution
c. Criteria for observation
d. All of the above

127 Transactional Analysis was founded by

a. Eric Berne
b. Dr. Wilder Penfield
c. Thomas A. Harris
d. John Dalton

128 Which of the following is related to skill teaching

a. Farm and home visit
b. Radio talk
c. Media forum
d. All of the above

Answer Key

1. a	2. b	3. d	4. d	5. a	6. d	7. a	8. d	9. a	10. c
11. a	12. a	13. a	14. a	15. c	16. a	17. d	18. c	19. a	20. d
21. a	22. d	23. d	24. a	25. a	26. c	27. d	28. c	29. a	30. d
31. d	32. d	33. c	34. b	35. a	36. d	37. d	38. d	39. b	40. d
41. a	42. a	43. c	44. a	45. d	46. c	47. a	48. c	49. a	50. c
51. c	52. d	53. c	54. c	55. c	56. d	57. b	58. b	59. d	60. c
61. d	62. a	63. c	64. b	65. b	66. d	67. a	68. c	69. d	70. a
71. c	72. d	73. c	74. b	75. a	76. d	77. a	78. c	79. c	80. b
81. d	82. d	83. d	84. a	85. d	86. c	87. a	88. d	89. a	90. b
91. a	92. a	93. a	94. d	95. c	96. d	97. a	98. c	99. a	100. a
101. a	102. c	103. d	104. a	105. b	106. c	107. a	108. b	109. a	110. c
111. c	112. c	113. b	114. d	115. c	116. d	117. a	118. a	119. d	120. a
121. b	122. d	123. a	124. c	125. a	126. d	127. a	128. a		

11

Farm Journalism

1 Journalism is basically the communication of news and information to a larger mass at the

a. Same time b. Same day

c. Different Time d. None of these

2 Which of the following are pulled after the matter has been composed?

a. Galley proofs b. Array proofs

c. Systematic proofs d. Synchronized proofs

3 In ABCs of Journalism A stands for Accuracy, B stands for Brevity and C stands for what?

a. Communication b. Charisma

c. Clarity d. Colourful

4 A journal was originally an account of ________ events.

a. Regular b. Daily

c. Periodic d. Weeekly

5 The newsstory is written in ________ person.

a. First b. Second

c. Third d. None of these

6 When assimilation of information comes in technological journalism?

a. First b. Second

c. At the middle phase d. At the last

7 Reading ease is closely connected with which character of reader?

a. Readers' eye sight b. Social belief of the reader

c. Education of the reader d. Ethics of the reader

8 The primary function of the press or print media is to________

a. Publish b. Advertise

c. Maximization of profit d. Inform

9 In Journalism, dissemination of public information should be________

a. Systematic b. Reliable

c. Both a & b d. Peroidic

10 Under which filed of extension science 'Journalism' is considered as one of the tools?

a. Extension programme planning b. Management

c. Research Methodology d. Extension teaching methods

11 A farm journal must be ________ to the eye before reading.

a. Soothing b. Pale

c. Attractive d. None of these

12 NASSDOC stands for

a. National Science Documentation Centre

b. National Social Science Digitisation Centre

c. National Social Science Delivery Centre

d. National Social Science Documentation Centre

13 Which one of the following is a combination of Mass media and interpersonal communication?

a. Campaign b. Radio Rural Forum

c. Exhibition d. Television

14 In which year the Central Information Unit brought under the control of Directorate of Extension?

a. 1985 b. 1992

c. 1995 d. 2001

15 The more readers are affected by the information, its news value will be ________

a. Normal b. Same

c. Greater d. Less

16 The word communication originates from the word 'communis' which means ______

a. Common b. Community

c. Companion d. Shared belief

17 In which city, the second TV station in the country was established?

a. Delhi
b. Mumbai
c. Calcutta
d. Chennai

18 Which of the following characteristic should be possessed by rural newspaper?

a. Participatory
b. People orientation
c. Profit orientation
d. Both a & b

19 A bunch of loose printed papers, properly folded which contains news, views, advertisements etc are-

a. Books
b. Newspaper
c. Folders
d. Leaflets

20 Which one of the following was the first regular magazine on farming in India?

a. Farming Today
b. Kheti Duniya
c. Indian Farming
d. Farming First

21 Journalism is basically communication of information and idea for the benefit of the

a. Farmer
b. Businessman
c. Politicians
d. Society

22 Journalism is considered as-

a. Fourth pillar of democracy
b. Third pillar of democracy
c. Second pillar of democracy
d. First pillar of democracy

23 The term 'Journ' means

a. Week
b. Day
c. Piece of paper
d. Communication

24 Which one of the following was first published periodical on agriculture in India?

a. Agriculture today
b. Farming Today
c. Agriculture farming trends
d. Krishi Sudhar

25 Timeliness is one of the major ingredients which determine the news

a. Truthfulness
b. Function
c. Worthiness
d. Suitability

26 First full fledged printed newspaper in India was brought out by which of the following individual?

a. Job Charnock b. R.N. Tagore

c. Yogesh Dutta d. James Augustus Hicky

27 Television with its unique potential can communicate with which of the following senses?

a. All the senses b. Eyes and Ears

c. Ear d. Eyes

28 The prime purpose of the newsstory is to inform whom?

a. Readers b. Authors

c. Journalist d. Proof readers

29 Dis-embodied communication is considered which form of communication?

a. Spoken b. Body gesture

c. Written d. Posture

30 Journalism is considered as which type of activity?

a. Private b. Social

c. Political d. Educational

31 Which of the following can be considered as ethics of journalism?

a. Wisdom b. Temperance

c. Courage d. All of these

32 Rural literacy in India is showing which type of trend?

a. Decreasing b. Fluctuating

c. Increasing d. Can't say

33 Advocacy journalism was introduced in which of the following country?

a. India b. USA

c. Russia d. Germany

34 Indian Institute of Mass Communication (IIMC) was established in 1965 at New Delhi on the recommendation of ________

a. Asian Development Bank b. UNESCO

c. Ford Foundation d. Both b & c

35 Publishing problems of farm journals in India are mainly because of which of the following reasons?

a. Paucity of advertisement b. Deficiency of readers

c. Both a & b d. None of these

36 Yellow Journalism is also denoted by which of the following?

a. Colored Journalism b. Pale Journalism

c. Sensationalism d. Blind Journalism

37 Feature stories have appeal to the reader's mind in which of the following area?

a. Action b. Imagination

c. Eyes d. None of these

38 Media-embodied communication is associated with which of the following?

a. Friend b. Neighbour

c. Progressive farmers d. Radio

39 In the modern age press is known in which name?

a. First Estate b. Second Estate

c. Third Estate d. Fourth Estate

40 Name the first Hindi farm Journal?

a. Krishi Chayanika b. Krishi Manjari

c. Krishi Safal d. Krishi Sudhar

41 Who has written the book 'Mass media and National Development'?

a. G.L. Ray b. Kelsey and Hearne

c. D.K. Berlo d. Wilbur Schramm

42 News should have which of the following characteristics?

a. Accuracy b. Timeliness

c. Interest d. All the above

43 'Krishi Kathar Asar' is broadcasted by which of the following?

a. Doordarshan b. E TV

c. DD Bharati d. AIR

44 Under which category of media, newspaper can be classified?

a. Electronic media b. Print media

c. Both a & b d. Synchronized media

45 Who among the following have developed readability scale?

a. Louis Fisher
b. Rudolf Flesch
c. Harold Sultz
d. Dimitri Puskinov

46 'Radio Rural Forum' was sponsored jointly by the Ministry of Information and Broadcasting and the UNESCO started in which of the following year?

a. 1950
b. 1955
c. 1960
d. 1956

47 Name the ways Farm Journalism in India is communicated through?

a. Print Media
b. Electronic Media
c. Both a & b
d. TV

48 The first radio programme was broadcasted in the year 1923 by which of the following?

a. Radio club of Calcutta
b. Radio club of Delhi
c. Radio club of Bombay
d. Radio club of Patiala

49 INSDOC stands for

a. Indian National Scientific Documentation Centre
b. Indian Serial Documentation Centre
c. Indian National Scientific Digitalization Centre
d. Indian Scientific Documentation Centre

50 Which of the following Roman emperor started the newspaper?

a. Nero
b. Julius Caesar
c. Julius Augustus
d. Marcus Auralius

51 In the British system of proof reading '**np**' is used for

a. New Paragraph
b. Next Page
c. New Page
d. Next Paragraph

52 The corrections are made by indicating various marks in the proof called

a. Indicating marks
b. Proof marks
c. Standard marks
d. Readers Marks

53 Name one of the oldest newspaper started by Julius Caesar, whose English meaning was 'Daily Events'?

a. Acta Diurna
b. Daily News
c. Dailirium Eventus
d. Eventus Daliycus

54 The person who marks the corrections on the proof is called

a. Marks man b. Proofer

c. Proof reader d. Corrector

55 The rural programme 'Krishidarshan' is broadcasted by which of the following TV channel?

a. Colours b. Doordarshan

c. Zee TV d. E TV

56 In day-to-day conversation all of us use which of the following voice?

a. Active Voice b. Passive voice

c. Inert voice d. Indicative voice

57 Which of the following tells who, what, why, when, where and how and not necessarily all the six, but most of them?

a. Title b. Conclusion

c. Picture d. Lead

58 Truthfulness of the information of the message reported in a journal indicates which of the following aspect?

a. Authenticity b. Fearlessness

c. Acceptability d. None of these

59 The content of farm journal must cover which of the following areas?

a. Documentation b. Communication

c. Coordination d. All of these

60 The extension agency provides advice on request by the farmers by using which approach?

a. Advocacy b. Supremacy

c. Consultancy d. Democratic

61 In which of the following newspaper information on agriculture, family welfare, food and nutrition are covered?

a. Rural newspaper b. Urban newspaper

c. Family newspaper d. None of these

62 Coloured telecast in India started from which date?

a. 2nd October,1980 b. 15th August, 1982

c. 26th January,1985 d. 1st May, 1975

63 Which one of the following is more important with respect to farm journalism?

a. Effective dissemination of agricultural information

b. Development of technical agricultural knowledge

c. Both a & b

d. Varies from situation to situation

64 In which year Indian Farming was first published?

a. 1940 b. 1947

c. 1956 d. 1929

65 In which year the TV station was introduced in Bombay?

a. October1972 b. July 1980

c. August 1982 d. January 1980

66 Directorate of Extension comes under which Ministry?

a. Ministry of Urban Development

b. Ministry of Social Development and Empowerment

c. Ministry of Agriculture and Farmers Welfare

d. Ministry of Information and Broadcasting

67 Which one of the following is considered as the forerunner of PTI?

a. Port Trust of India b. Printing Trust of India

c. Press Trust of India d. Associated Press of India

68 Which personality among the following was associated with first Indian news agency?

a. Balbir Singh b. K.C. Roy

c. Khuswant Singh d. Yegeshwar Dutta

69 Name the largest news agency in India?

a. PTI b. UTI

c. Reuters d. Thompson reuters

70 In which year Associated Press of India was launched?

a. 1947 b. 1955

c. 1910 d. 1935

71 Who is the current chairman of Press Council of India 2019?

a. K. Krishnamuthy b. Chandramauli Kumar Prasad

c. V. Balakrishna d. Ravinder Kichlu

72 In which year Press Trust of India started functioning?

a. 1949 b. 1947

c. 1951 d. 1959

73 In which year PTI was registered?

a. 1949 b. 1947

c. 1952 d. 1957

74 Journal of Rural Development (JRD) is published quarterly by

a. ICAR, New Delhi b. MANAGE, Hyderabad

c. ICRISAT, Hyderabad d. NIRD, Hyderabad

75 National Press Day is celebrated on which date?

a. 16 November b. 1st October

c. 22nd January d. 28th February

76 Which of the following is a monthly farm magazine catering to cash-crop growers in parts of Karnataka and Kerala?

a. Kheti b. Cash crop cultivation

c. Pathrike d. Adike Pathrike

77 'The Agricultural journal of India' was started in which year?

a. 1925 b. 1906

c. 1901 d. 1915

78 Indian Journal of Agricultural Sciences and the Indian Journal of Veterinary Sciences andAnimal Husbandry was started in which year?

a. 1931 b. 1932

c. 1933 d. 1936

79 Agriculture and livestock in India was rechristened as which magazine?

a. Indian Traditional Knowledge b. Kheti

c. Indian Farming d. Phal phul

80 Kheti was started in which year?

a. 1947 b. 1948

c. 1990 d. None of these

81 Which of the following magazine was started in 1973?

a. Krishi Chayanika b. Krishi Katha

c. Kheti d. Kheti duniya

82 Who was the Director General of ICAR when Horticultural quarterly 'Phal Phool' was started?

a. Dr. R.S. Paroda
b. Dr. Mangla Rai
c. Dr. M.S. Swaminathan
d. Dr. Kishan Singh

83 Farm periodicals namely Intensive Farming, Krishi Vistar Samiksha and Unnat Krishi are published by which agency?

a. Directorate of Extension
b. Directorate of Publication
c. Directorate of Printing
d. Ministry of Broadcasting

84 'Shetkari' is published in which language?

a. Bengali
b. Marathi
c. Gujarati
d. Tamil

85 SAARC Agricultural Information Centre is established in 1988 at

a. Dhaka
b. New Delhi
c. Kathmandu
d. Islamabad

86 Name the first American Newspaper?

a. The American times
b. The Chronicles
c. The Chicago Today
d. The Boston News-Letter

87 'Essays of Field Husbandry' the first printed agriculture work in America was written by

a. Jared Eliot
b. Benjamin Franklin
c. Franklin Templeton
d. None of these

88 The first farm magazine in agriculture which was published in Paris in the year 1763, was known as

a. Agri journale
b. Agri De Review
c. Agriculture De Paris
d. Agricultura De Franche

89 At which place, 'Krishi Sudhar' was published?

a. Lucknow
b. Jhansi
c. Agra
d. Allahabad

90 "Basundhara" and "Krishik Jagatt" fam magazines were published in which language?

a. Bengali
b. Marathi
c. Gujarati
d. Oriya

91 Krishimunnade, Sirisambruddhi and Krishimitra farm magazines were published in which language?

a. Kannada b. Malayalam
c. Tamil d. Telugu

92 Which one of the following was the first British daily newspaper?

a. The London daily b. The telegraph
c. The Daily Courant d. The informer

93 The other name of content analysis is

a. Concept analysis b. Module analysis
c. Structural analysis d. Textual analysis

94 Who has formulated the core of content analysis?

a. Issac Newton b. Newcomb
c. Harold Lasswell d. Shannon and Weaver

95 The ease in which text can be read and understood is known as

a. Understandability b. Apprehension
c. Easy d. Readability

96 Which one of the following is a measure of how easily individual letters or characters can be distinguished from each other?

a. Legibility b. Understandability
c. Simplicity d. Readability

97 Who developed the first reading ease formula?

a. Bertha A. Lively b. Sidney L. Pressey
c. Both a & b d. None of these

98 Which one of the following index measures the readability of English writing?

a. GE index b. Gunning fog index
c. Mirage index d. Countability index

99 "The Flesch–Kincaid" formula was first used by whom?

a. US army b. McGraw Hill company
c. British army d. Australian army

100 The readability index of Reader's Digest magazine was about

a. 52 b. 35
c. 65 d. 69

101 A National Knowledge Network project of Government of India has provided link to how many ICAR institutes/SAUs?

a. 9
b. 95
c. 12
d. 49

102 Who is the Project Director of 'Directorate of Knowledge Management in Agriculture'?

a. Dr. Rameshwar Singh
b. Dr. R.C. Tripathi
c. Dr. Tribhubandas Mohanty
d. P.C. Verma

103 Which one of the following was the first printed periodical in the world?

a. The Hindu
b. Bengal gazette
c. Mercurius Gallobelgicus
d. Readers Digest

104 In which year name of the All India Radio has been changed to Akashvani?

a. 1936
b. 1957
c. 1956
d. 1927

105 Agricultural Research Information Centre was established by ICAR in which year?

a. 1967
b. 1975
c. 1977
d. 1957

106 What is the current name of Agricultural Research Information Centre?

a. Directorate of Information Technology Management
b. Directorate of Agriculture Extension
c. Directorate of Knowledge Management in Agriculture
d. Directorate of Information and Publications of Agriculture

107 ARIS was established in the ICAR system in which year?

a. 1985
b. 1995
c. 2003
d. 1998

108 'Indian Forestry' publication by Imperial Forest Research Institute, was started in which year?

a. 1973
b. 1990
c. 1873
d. 1890

109 Indian Farming- is which type of periodical?

a. Monthly
b. Quarterly
c. Annual
d. Half yearly

110 'Krishi Chayanika' is published how many times in a year?

a. 2 b. 12

c. 4 d. 6

111 'Phal Phool' is published how many times in a year?

a. 6 b. 12

c. 4 d. 3

112 Feature stories highlights-

a. Feelings b. Moods

c. Basic facts d. Both a & b

113 In the 'KISS' principle of writing K stands for-

a. Keep b. Know

c. Knowledge d. Kind

114 'Akashvani' has how many stations across the country?

a. 530 b. 409

c. 600 d. 450

115 The Prasar Bharati (Broadcasting Corporation of India) Act, was enacted in which year?

a. 1995 b. 2001

c. 1990 d. 1992

116 Asia-Pacific Institute For Broadcasting Development (AIBD) is headquartered at

a. Kuala Lumpur b. Jakarta

c. Beijing d. Colombo

117 'Yuva Bharati' programme of All India Radio is broadcasted in which day of the month?

a. 1st Monday b. 1st Friday

c. 5th Wednesday d. 2nd Wednesday

118 The Farm & Home programme of All India Radio is broadcasted by the help of which of the following centrally sponsored scheme?

a. Akashvani b. Annadata

c. Kisanbhai d. Kisanvani

119 Kisanvani project was launched in which year?

a. December, 2004 b. February, 2004

c. December, 2005 d. November, 2001

120 All India Radio observes __________ as Radio Kisan Diwas.

a. 15th February b. 23rd December

c. 15th August d. 26th January

121 How many All India Radio transmitters are there?

a. 680 b. 650

c. 580 d. 450

122 ISBN stands for ________

a. Integrated Services Bibliographic Network

b. Indian Standard Book Number

c. International Standard Book Number

d. International Standard for Book and Non- book

123 ISSN stands for ________

a. International Standard Serial Number

b. Indian Standard Serial Number

c. Indian Standard and Safty Number

d. Indian Standard System Number

124 How many digits have in the ISSN?

a. 12 b. 8

c. 10 d. 13

125 How many digits have in the ISBN?

a. 12 b. 8

c. 10 d. 13

126 Modern journalism deals with five departments of mass communication which includes

a. Radio, Newspaper, Internet, Cinema and traditional arts

b. Newspaper & periodicals, Radio, Television, Films and Advertising

c. Music, Film, Internet, Mobile and Photography

d. Photography, Classical dance, Film, Internet and Publicity

127 Principles / canons of journalism are________

a. Sincerity and accuracy b. Impartiality

c. Fair play and decency d. All of the above

128 First newspaper in Roman empire was________

a. Acta Diurd
b. Gazetta in Vernica
c. Acta Dabaca
d. Julius News

129 Which one of the following was second newspaper in Roman empire?

a. Gazetta in Vernica
b. Acta Diurd
c. Cleopatra
d. None of the above

130 China's earliest newspaper in 8th century was________

a. The Ching-pao (news of the palace)
b. The Chinese Expression
c. The Ching-mao
d. The China Herald

131 First printed newspaper in 1457 was________

a. Niurnberg
b. Acta Diurd
c. Gazetta in Vernica
d. The Ching-pao

132 First German Newspaper was ________

a. German Herald
b. Public Relation
c. Avisa Relation
d. German Gazette

133 First American Newspaper in 1690 was ________

a. Public Grievances
b. Public Occurrences
c. Public Opinion
d. Public Outlook

134 Who put the first effort for printing newspaper in 1766 at Calcutta?

a. Raja Ram Mohan Roy
b. James Hickey
c. Ravindra Nath Tagore
d. William Bolts

135 First regular newspaper in India was________

a. Bengal Gazette (or) Calcutta General
b. India Gazette
c. The Hindu
d. Calcutta Advertiser

136 India Gazette (s) Calcutta Advertiser by Peter Reed (1780) was________

a. Second Newspaper of India
b. Third Newspaper of India
c. Fifth Newspaper of India
d. Fourth Newspaper of India

137 Who started first Vernacular periodical – Digdarshan- Bengali in1818?

a. Ravindra Nath Tagore b. S. C. Bose
c. J.C. Marshman d. Raja Ram Mohan Roy

138 Who founded Miratul Akbar-a weekly ?

a. B.C.Roy b. M.K.Gandhi
c. C.V.Raman d. Raja Ram Mohan Roy

139 In which year, first printing press was brought to India

a. 1550 b. 1555
c. 1590 d. 1650

140 Where the first book 'Dourtrina Christa' was printed in 1557

a. Goa b. Calicut
c. Jerusalem d. Rome

141 1st Hindi paper Udunt Martund in Calcutta was printed in which year?

a. 1822 b. 1829
c. 1825 d. 1826

142 Newspaper Act was enacted in

a. 1901 b. 1919
c. 1908 d. 1905

143 Indian Press Act was enacted in which year?

a. 1910 b. 1919
c. 1908 d. 1911

144 Central Bureau of Information (now PIB) was started in________

a. 1921 b. 1920
c. 1919 d. 1925

145 Indian and Eastern Newspaper Society was started in which year?

a. 1939 b. 1944
c. 1943 d. 1947

146 Post graduate diploma course in journalism in Madras University was started in ________

a. 1947 b. 1951
c. 1955 d. 1948

147 Copyright Act was enacted in ________

a. 1960 b. 1947

c. 1957 d. 1967

148 Press Council was set up in________

a. 1965 b. 1956

c. 1976 d. 1966

149 Samachar Bharti – a multilingual news agency was set up in________

a. 1967 b. 1965

c. 1977 d. 1969

150 The Prevention of Publication (Objectionable Matters) Act enacted in________.

a. 1975 b. 1979

c. 1977 d. 1981

151 Employment News (English) and Rojgar Samachar (Hindi) were started in ________

a. 1977 b. 1976

c. 1974 d. 1981

152 Press Council was abolished in 1976 and again revived in______

a. 1978 b. 1977

c. 1981 d. 1980

153 NCERT was started in ________

a. 1961 b. 1951

c. 1955 d. 1957

154 The National Book Development Board was started in ________

a. 1971 b. 1961

c. 1967 d. 1965

155 First World book fair in New Delhi was conducted in ________

a. 1972 b. 1975

c. 1980 d. 1970

156 Audit Bureau of Circulation was started in ________

a. 1948 b. 1947

c. 1955 d. 1951

157 Advertising branch of I & B Ministry (DAVP) was started in ________

a. 1951 b. 1955

c. 1961 d. 1965

158 First Radio News Bulletin in India was in ________

a. 1927 b. 1936

c. 1933 d. 1937

159 Vividh Bharti was started in ________

a. 1957 b. 1966

c. 1955 d. 1959

160 AIR youth service "yuva vani" was started in ________

a. 1965 b. 1959

c. 1969 d. 1966

161 Prasar Bharti Bill was made in ________

a. 1989 b. 1979

c. 1981 d. 1985

162 Calcutta, Madras and Lucknow television stations were started in________

a. 1971 b. 1970

c. 1974 d. 1977

163 Colour TV appeared in India________

a. 1979 b. 1985

c. 1975 d. 1982

164 Pundalik –first Indian Film was made in________

a. 1912 b. 1919

c. 1925 d. 1909

165 The Cinematograph Act was made in________

a. 1918 b. 1919

c. 1915 d. 1921

166 Inverted pyramid story form means ________

a. The climax will be given at first

b. The climax will be given at last

c. The climax will be given at middle

d. None of the above

167 The article will be written by someone else, but published in others name as author- this is known as ________

a. Ghosted writing
b. Guest writing
c. Freelance writing
d. Free writing

168 The structure of the feature article should contain

a. Title
b. Body
c. Lead
d. All of the above

169 If the Human Interest Score is 60-100, its style is described as

a. Dull
b. Dramatic
c. Mildly interesting
d. Highly interesting

170 Sending composed copy to editor for correction, addition and deletion is known as

a. Final proof
b. Edited proof
c. Galley proof
d. Corrected proof

171 Indian Horticulture was started by ICAR in________

a. 1954
b. 1966
c. 1956
d. 1951

172 Indian Journal of Fisheries is published by________

a. Bay of Bengal Programme
b. DADF
c. CIFNET
d. ICAR

173 Agricultural Journal of India (Memoirs of dept. Of Agriculture)- 1906 was published by

a. ICAR
b. Royal Commission on Agriculture
c. Famine Commission
d. Rockefeller Foundation

174 Agriculture Journal of India was renamed in 1931 as________

a. Journal of Agriculture. & Livestock
b. Journal of Indian Agriculture
c. Indian Farming
d. Field Husbandry

175 Circulation of farm magazines in descending order is ________

a. Hindi>English>Bengali>Telugu
b. Hindi> Bengali> English>Telugu
c. Hindi>English>Tamil>Telugu
d. Hindi>Marathi>Bengali>Telugu

176 Agriculture News coverage ranges in India

a. 2-3% b. 7-10 %

c. 15-20% d. 18-25%

177 Karshakan is published in which language?

a. Malayalam b. Marathi

c. Oriya d. Hindi

178 Unnath Krishi, Grahni (House wife), Home Science and Intensive Agriculture are published by whom?

a. Directorate of Extension, GOI b. MANAGE

c. ICAR d. NIRD

179 First farm periodical – Krishi Sudhar was started in which year?

a. 1928 b. 1910

c. 1904 d. 1945

180 Which magazine is being published by Government of Bihar since 1938?

a. Gaon b. Krishak

c. Bihar Kheti d. None of the above

181 In which state, first regional farm journal 'Zamin Ryot' was started in 1928

a. West Bengal b. Karnataka

c. Odisha d. Andhra Pradesh

182 Which magazine was started by Ryot Sewa Sangh of Maharashtra in 1938?

a. Ryot : Kohlapur b. Ryot : Pune

c. Ryot : Nagpur d. Ryot : Nasik

183 Yojana is published by________

a. Ministry of Information and Broadcasting

b. Ministry of Rural Development

c. Ministry of Agriculture

d. Planning Commission

184 Kisan Bharti and Farm Digest are published by________

a. G.B. Pant University of Agriculture and Technology

b. Punjab Agricultural University

c. Odisha University of Agriculture and Technology

d. Allahabad Agricultural Institute

185 Changi Kheti is published by ________

a. HAU b. PAU

c. RAU d. BHU

186 Indian Institute of Mass Communication publishes which of the following?

a. Interaction b. Mass Media

c. Communicator d. Development studies

187 2nd biggest news agency is

a. AP (Associated Press) b. Reuter

c. PANA d. None of the above

188 Which theory says 'Mediamen screen the information before they are processed for print'?

a. Advocate theory b. Media information theory

c. Gate keeper theory d. None of the above

189 Which theory says 'Collecting & publishing the information in the interest of nation (or) oppressed group'?

a. Advocate Theory b. Gate keeper theory

c. Media journalism theory d. Development theory

190 Which theory says 'Mass media has no role to play'?

a. Null theory b. Enthusiastic theory

c. Pragmatic theory d. Caution theory

191 Newspaper stories relies on the elements of ________

a. Novelty b. Pale and variety

c. Directness d. All of the above

192 Basic ingredients the editor of farm magazine should have about make up is

a. Balance b. Contrast

c. Focal point d. All of the above

193 Which one of the following is done to achieve best artistic presentation of a picture and maximum visual impact within the scope of available space?

a. Mapping b. Cropping

c. Masking d. Brightening

194 Who checks and corrects writing for spelling, grammar, punctuation, inconsistencies, inaccuracies and conformity to the requirement of a guide to style?

a. Copy editors b. Clerk

c. Chief editor d. Reporter

195 Which one of the following is correct?

a. Reading proof is more art than science

b. Reading proof is more science than art

c. Reading proof does not require any experience

d. Proof reading concentrates more on style than accuracy

196 What influences the Impact Factor of a scientific journal?

a. Editorial policies of journals

b. Turnover of research in a certain field

c. Influence of article type

d. All of the above

197 The practice of presenting one's own previously published work as though it were new is known as_____

a. Self-plagiarism b. Self propaganda

c. Self satisfaction d. Self centered approach

198 Leaving out authors in an article who should be included is referred as______

a. Jealousy b. Ghost authorship

c. Vengeance d. Revenge

199 Including authors in an article who did not contribute significantly is known as______

a. Gift authorship b. Ghost authorship

c. Loan authorship d. Give and take policy

200 What point should be considered while choosing the right journal for publication?

a. Is the journal peer-reviewed

b. Who is this journal's audience

c. What is the journal's Impact Factor

d. All the above

201 Which one of the following is coming under 4th generation media?

a. Television b. Laptop

c. iPad d. All of these

202 When Doordarshan was started in India?

a. 1st April 1976 b. 1st April 1927

c. 1st April 1977 d. 1st April 1985

203 When Radio broadcasting in India was started?

a. 23rd July 1927 b. 23rd July 1935

c. 23rd July 1931 d. 23rd July 1925

204 The name Akashvani was coined by whom?

a. Valmiki b. Ved Vyas

c. Ravindranath Tagore d. Tulsi Das

205 First Extension Journal in the world was

a. Journal of rural extension service

b. Extension education journal

c. The journal of cooperative extension service

d. Indian Journal of extension education

206 'Mann Ki Baat'-address given by PM of India is expected to be aired________

a. Once a month b. Twice a month

c. Quarterly d. Weekly

207 Which of the following term is used for the space utilized in a newspaper allotted to news and illustrations?

a. News point b. News hole

c. Black hole d. Star point

208 What is the term used for the page opposite to editorial page?

a. Crown page b. Ba-ed-page

c. Op-ed-page d. Page 3

209 The information which is passed to a reporter confidentially is known as

a. Tip b. Top

c. Sincere d. None of these

210 In a newspaper front page of an inside section is known as

a. Narrow page b. Split page

c. Back page d. Cover page

211 Which of the following term is used to denote the first edition of a newspaper?

a. Watchdog b. Spitz

c. Premiere d. Bulldog

212 A very short and amusing story is known as

a. Bright b. Red

c. Light d. Dark

213 Which of the following term is used to denote the area assigned to a reporter for regular coverage?

a. Specialization b. Beat

c. Correspondence d. Area

214 When a short and related story is added to the end of a long story, then it is known as

a. Tail end b. Shirttail

c. Fag end d. Curtail

215 What is the common term used for extended unwanted silence in radio?

a. Dead air b. Sleep time

c. Zero noise d. Silence

216 Which of the following term is used to delete whole or part of news story?

a. Delete b. Cut

c. Kill d. Short

217 'Cloze procedure' which is a newtool for measuring readability has been developed by ?

a. Fredric Wilson b. Wilson Taylor

c. Richard Cloze d William Cloze

Answer Key

1. c	2. a	3. c	4. b	5. c	6. a	7. c	8. d	9. c	10. d
11. c	12. d	13. b	14. a	15. c	16. a	17. b	18. d	19. b	20. c
21. d	22. a	23. b	24. d	25. c	26. d	27. b	28. a	29. c	30. b
31. d	32. c	33. b	34. d	35. c	36. c	37. b	38. d	39. d	40. d
41. d	42. d	43. d	44. b	45. b	46. d	47. c	48. c	49. a	50. b
51. a	52. d	53. a	54. c	55. b	56. a	57. d	58. a	59. d	60. c
61. a	62. b	63. c	64. a	65. a	66. c	67. d	68. b	69. a	70. c
71. b	72. a	73. b	74. d	75. a	76. d	77. b	78. a	79. c	80. b
81. a	82. c	83. a	84. b	85. a	86. d	87. a	88. d	89. c	90. a
91. a	92. c	93. d	94. c	95. d	96. a	97. c	98. b	99. a	100. c
101. a	102. a	103. c	104. b	105. a	106. c	107. b	108. c	109. a	110. c
111. a	112. d	113. a	114. b	115. c	116. a	117. c	118. d	119. b	120. a
121. c	122. c	123. a	124. b	125. d	126. b	127. d	128. a	129. a	130. a
131. a	132. c	133. b	134. d	135. a	136. a	137. c	138. d	139. a	140. a
141. d	142. c	143. a	144. b	145. a	146. a	147. c	148. d	149. a	150. a
151. b	152. a	153. d	154. c	155. a	156. a	157. b	158. b	159. a	160. c
161. a	162. c	163. d	164. a	165. a	166. a	167. a	168. d	169. b	170. c
171. c	172. d	173. a	174. a	175. a	176. b	177. a	178. a	179. c	180. a
181. d	182. a	183. a	184. a	185. b	186. c	187. a	188. c	189. a	190. a
191. d	192. d	193. b	194. a	195. a	196. d	197. a	198. b	199. a	200. d
201. d	202. a	203. a	204. c	205. c	206. a	207. b	208. c	209. a	210. b
211. d	212. a	213. b	214. b	215. a	216. c	217. b			

12

Women Empowerment and Gender Mainstreaming

1 Which day is celebrated as Women in Agriculture Day?

a. 4th December b. 23rd December
c. 8th March d. 8th December

2 Which day is commemorated as International Women's Day?

a. 4th December b. 23rd December
c. 8th March d. 8th December

3 Directorate of Research on Women in Agriculture (currently Central Institute for Women in Agriculture) is established in 1996 at which of the following place?

a. New Delhi b. Pune
c. Madras d. Bhubaneswar

4 Who is the First woman Deputy Director General of ICAR?

a. Dr. B Meenakumari b. Dr. Hema Pandey
c. Ms. Kavita Krishnamoorthy d. Dr. Krishna Srinath

5 First Global Conference on Women in Agriculture (GCWA) was organized in March 2012 at ________

a. New Delhi b. Pune
c. Madras d. Bhubaneswar

6 Who is the First Woman Director of Directorate of Research on Women in Agriculture (DRWA)?

a. Dr. Hema Pandey b. Dr. B Meenakumari
c. Dr. Krishna Srinath d. Dr. Krishna Tirath

7 Who is the first chairperson of Bhartiya Mahila Bank?

a. Ms. Kavita Krishnamoorthy b. Ms. Usha Ananthasubramanian
c. Ms. Usha Thorat d. Ms. Arundhati Bhattacharya

8 Which discipline emphasized the importance of gender in the form of whole family approach?

a. Rural Development b. Agricultural Extension

c. Home science d. Sociology

9 Three-digit emergency women helpline number for all states of the country is

a. 191 b. 181

c. 180 d. 100

10 What is the proportion of assets owned by women in the world?

a. 1/10th b. 1/100th

c. 1/50th d. 1/1000th

11 Who is the chairperson of National Commission on Women (2019)?

a. Mrs. Rekha Sharma b. Mrs. Kiran Bedi

c. Mrs. Sucheta Bhardwaj d. Mrs. Nirula Sindhe

12 Who was the first woman president of India?

a. Mrs. Indira Gandhi b. Mrs. Sonia Gandhi

c. Mrs. Pratibha Patil d. Mrs. Sucheta Kripalani

13 Who was the first woman Chief Minister in India?

a. Ms. Jayalalitha b. Mrs. Mayavati

c. Mrs. Sarojini Naidu d. Mrs. Sucheta Kripalani

14 What percent of the agricultural workforce is contributed by women in the world?

a. 43% b. 53%

c. 49% d. 59%

15 If women have same access as men to land, technology, financial services, education and markets, it would be possible to reduce the number of hungry people in the world by____

a. 10 to 15 million b. 100 to 150 million

c. 500 to 1000 million d. 1 to 2 million

16 Who among the following continues to be comprehensively neglected by extension services despite their focus in agriculture since last 25 years?

a. Women b. Small farmers

c. Marginal farmers d. Large farmers

17 Women are the backbone of workforce in which of the following sector?

a. Industry
b. Service
c. Forestry
d. Agriculture

18 Who among the following often lack capital, information, access to market & technology, knowledge and skill?

a. Women
b. Small farmers
c. Marginal farmers
d. Large farmers

19 From which period attention to women's concerns and priorities in development policy has been evolving?

a. Early 1970s
b. Late 1980s
c. Early 1990s
d. Early 1950s

20 What among the followings hinder the women's productivity and reduce their contribution to the agricultural sector?

a. Gender mainstreaming
b. Gender gap
c. Gender budgeting
d. None of these

21 From which period extension services began paying closer attention to gender issues?

a. Early 1970s
b. Early 1980s
c. Early 1990s
d. Early 1950s

22 During which two decades the role of women was seldom acknowledged or highlighted as being integral to the agricultural landscape?

a. 1960s and 1970s
b. 1980s and 1990s
c. 1970s and 1980s
d. 1990s and 2000

23 Women's needs vary considerably to men's in agriculture due to which of the following?

a. Their differing involvement in agricultural activity
b. Their differing involvement in economic activity
c. Their differing involvement in social activity
d. None of these

24 Many of the agricultural programmes being implemented tend to engage more with which of the following?

a. Male farmers
b. Better off socio economic groups
c. Women farmers
d. Both a & b

25 Who among the following can be expected to provide more and targeted information to women farmers?

a. Male extension officer b. Female extension officer

c. Opinion leader from the village d. None of these

26 Who among the following is most preferred by women farmers?

a. Male extension officer b. Female extension officer

c. Opinion leader from the village d. None of these

27 Women SHGs, are better considered for building ____

a. Social capital b. Monitory benefits

c. Political benefits d. Religious benefits

28 Which among the followings lies in increased number of women opening their bank accounts and better decision making in married households?

a. Increase in women population b. Women empowerment

c. Increase in dowry d. Women urbanization

29 Agricultural projects and programmes are not being formulated with an eye on which of the followings?

a. Diversity of women's group b. Specific interest of women

c. Homogeneity of women's group d. Both a & b

30 ICTs can be used to provide information on which of the followings?

a. Weather

b. Prices

c. Profitable income diversification to women

d. All the above

31 Credit and loan packages should be designed to meet the _______of women throughout their lives.

a. Changing needs b. Aristocracy

c. Negligence d. Dominance

32 Reservation of seats for women in panchayati raj institutions seeks to ensure_________

a. Economic empowerment of women

b. Superiority of women over men

c. Participation of women in public life

d. Strengthening women as an individual

33 Which of the following programs meets the credit needs of poor women?

a. Mahila Samakhya Programme b. Indira Mahila Yojna

c. Rashtriya Mahila Kosh d. Mahila Samriddhi Yojna

34 Which of the following programs aims at the promotion of savings among rural women?

a. Indira Mahila Yojna b. Mahila Samriddhi Yojna

c. Rashtriya Mahila Kosh d. Jawahar Rozgar Yojna

35 As per budget 2013-14, which of the following funds has been set up with Rs. 1,000 crore to empower women and to keep them safe and secure?

a. Mahila Fund b. Malala Fund

c. Nirbhaya Fund d. None of These

36 Reaching the poor women in rural areas require________.

a. Pluralistic extension services b. Single window System

c. Top down approach d. None of these

37 The government has set up a committee of experts to prepare the blueprint of India's firstWomen's bank. The,committee is headed by whom?

a. O P Bhatt b. B A Prabhaka

c. Pratip Chaudhuri d. M B N Rao

38 International Women's Development Agency (IWDA) established in 1985 is situated at which of the following places?

a. Paris b. New York

c. Melbourne d. New Delhi

39 IWDA's work in Asia and the Pacific is mainly focused on which of the following aspects?

a. Gender equality b. Women's rights

c. Gender inequality d. Both a & b

40 When the UN Women was established?

a. July 2012 b. July 2010

c. Jan 2012 d. Jan 2010

41 UN Women is otherwise known as the __________.

a. United Nations Entity for Gender Equality and the Empowerment of Women

b. United Nations Women Organization for Mainstreaming and Empowerment

c. Convention on the Elimination of All Forms of Discrimination against Women

d. International Women's Development Agency

42 What is the full form of CEDAW?

a. Convention on the Elimination of All Forms of Discrimination against Women

b. Conference on the Eradication of All Forms of Discrimination against Women

c. Convention on the Establishment of Dowry Abolishment Act for Women

d. Conference on Enabling Discrimination Abolishment for Women

43 Who among the followings belongs to the UN Women's goodwill ambassadors?

a. Ms. Nicole Kidman, AC Academy Award–winning actress

b. HRH Princess Bajrakitiyabha Mahidol, Thailand

c. Aishwarya Rai: Former miss world

d. Both a & b

44 Which of the following country is the world's female majority parliament with 63.8% parliamentary seats occupied by female?

a. Rwanda b. India

c. Bangladesh d. England

45 Who described the "Woman as the companion of man, gifted with equal mental capacity"?

a. Indira Gandhi b. Indira Nooyi

c. Mahatma Gandhi d. Jawaharlal Nehru

46 Which one of the following can serve as a key pathway and critical source of livelihood to bring women out of poverty?

a. Service sector b. Urbanization

c. Industry d. Agriculture

47 Gender Knowledge Centre is developed by_____

a. CIWA b. UNICEF

c. UN Women d. ICRISAT

48 Who are the principal agents of food security and household welfare?

a. Youth b. Women

c. Both d. None of these

49 Support to Training and Employment Programme for Women (STEP) started in 1986-87, to provide sustainable employment and income generation for which category of women?

a. Marginalized and asset-less poor rural women.

b. Marginalized and asset-less poor urban women.

c. Business entrepreneur women

d. Both a & b

50 Which role of the women remains invisible in the society?

a. As a farmer b. As a mother

c. As a labour d. As a housewife

51 Women are the major producers of food in terms of which of the followings?

a. Value b. Volume

c. Hours worked in agriculture d. All the above

52 The implementation of the Priyadarshini scheme which is a Self Help Group (SHG) based project for holistic empowerment of women and adolescent girls started in ————

a. April, 2001 b. January 2001

c. April, 2011 d. January 2011

53 What is the proportion of women in Indian population?

a. 52% b. 50 %

c. 48% d. 46%

54 Which of the following scheme pertains to Conditional Cash Transfer scheme for pregnant and lactating (P&L) women?

a. Indira Gandhi Matritva Sahyog Yojana (IGMSY)

b. Rashtriya Mahila Kosh (RMK)

c. Sabala Yojana

d. Bhartiya Mahila Bank

55 Which is world Day of the Fight Against Sexual Exploitation?

a. 8th March b. 4th December
c. 4th March d. 8th January

56 Under National Mission for Empowerment of Women (NMEW), the women centre at the village level, the first point of contact for women is known as ________

a. Poorna Shakti Kendra b. Mahila Shakti Kendra
c. Mahila Sahayata Kendra d. Poorna Vikas Kendra

57 What is the motto of Poorna Shakti Kendra (PSK) Under National Mission for Empowerment of Women?

a. Hum Sunenge Naari Ki Baat b. Hum Hai Naari ke Sang
c. Awaaj Uthalo d. Naari ki Pukar

58 When was the Rajiv Gandhi Scheme for Empowerment of Adolescent Girls (RGSEAG) – 'Sabla' started?

a. 2010 b. 2012
c. 2005 d. 2009

59 Which of the following scheme was launched in the year 2001 dedicated to Women's Empowerment in convergence with Self Help Group?

a. Swayamsidha b. Swavalamban
c. Sabla d. None of these

60 Creation of women groups for income-generating activities on a self-sustaining basis is aimed at which one of the following scheme?

a. Self Help Groups
b. Rural Employment Scheme
c. Indira Awas Yojana
d. Development of Women and Children in Rural Areas (DWCRA)

61 Which year declared by the Government of India as the Year of Women's Empowerment?

a. 2010 b. 2001
c. 2011 d. 2000

62 In which year the National Policy for the Empowerment of Women was passed to bring about the advancement, development and empowerment of women?

a. 2013 b. 2009
c. 2001 d. 2010

63 In which year the Government had initiated the formation of Gender Budget Cells within all Central Ministries/ Departments to institutionalize the process of Gender Budgeting?

a. 2005 b. 2000

c. 2010 d. 2004

64 Protection of Women from Domestic Violence Act 2005 came into effect on____

a. 26th October, 2006 b. 26th October, 2005

c. 8th March, 2006 d. 8th March, 2005

65 Which of the following is most accessible financial source to rural women?

a. Macro-finance b. Micro-finance

c. Mortgage d. All the above

66 Protection of Women against Sexual Harassment at Workplace Bill approved in which year?

a. 2011 b. 2012

c. 2009 d. 2010

67 Which of the following is the characteristic of the sex under normal circumstances?

a. Universal b. Biological

c. Permanent d. All the above

68 The difference in status, power, and prestige of women and men in groups, collectives, and societies is referred as____

a. Gender inequality b. Gender equality

c. Feminism d. Patriarchy

69 The process of internalizing the social norms and expectations that correspond to one's sex through social agents such as the family, peers and the media is called____.

a. Feminism b. Gender socialization

c. Gender bias d. Gender gap

70 Which of the following statement is correct?

a. Sex refers to the physical differences in the body, whereas gender concerns the socio-cultural differences between males and females.

b. Sex concerns the psychological, social, and cultural differences between males and females, whereas gender refers to the biological differences in the body.

c. Both a & b

d. None of these

71 The United Nations' gender empowerment measure is ________.

a. Used to identify the enabling factors to achieve some level of economic independence and power for women

b. Used to compare the position of women in different countries based on the percentage of women in parliament, managerial and administrative positions, and the ratio of women's to men's earned income

c. The level of access to women, in different countries, for factors such as education, paid work, and birth control

d. Used to compare different countries' attitudes toward women's role in society

72 Men working in female-dominated professions promoted to top administrative jobs in disproportionately high numbers is referred as________

a. Gender typing b The glass escalator

c. Comparable worth theory d The glass ceiling

73 ________is the difference between male and female earnings.

a. The gender pay gap b The gender gap

c. The gender bias d The gender equality

74 Gender is different________

a. Within the culture b. Between the cultures

c. Both a & b d. None of these

75 Who is the first Indian woman to get Magsaysay award?

a. Kiran Bedi Indira Gandhi

c. Sania Mirza Menaka Gandhi

76 Gender is ________

a. Socially constructed b. Socially learned

c. Socially defined role d. All the above

77 Gender is ________

a. Dynamic b. Change over time

c. Social construct d. All the above

78 Which of the followings is influenced by a wide range of socioeconomic factors?

a. Gender b. Sex

c. Women d. All the above

79 In the common usage gender comes from nature, in academic usage comes from ______

a. Nurture b. Sex

c. Biological world d. None of these

80 ______ are fairly straight forward and formed in the womb at the moment of conception.

a. Gender b. Sex

c. both a & b d. Men

81 Gender deal with both sexes in relation to each other and not ______

a. Only women b. Both men and women

c. Only men d. Either men or women

82 Both men's & women's roles are broadly ______

a. Reproductive role b. Productive role

c. Community role d. All the above

83 Who are the clientele for extension?

a. Only women b. Only men

c. Only youth d. All the above

84 According to World Economic Forum Gender Gap Index report, what is India's rank out of 149 countries (2018)?

a. 108 b. 111

c. 102 d. 91

85 The literacy rate among women and men respectively in India as per Census 2011 ______

a. 65.5% and 82.1% b. 46% and 51%

c. 76% and 85% d. 37% and 54%

86 Institutional barriers preventing women from advancing beyond a certain point in the corporate world, despite their qualifications and successes are referred as ______

a. Gender role b. Feminism

c. Glass ceiling d. The glass escalator

87 The first woman to receive Jnanpith Award________

a. Medha Patkar
b. Taslima Nasreen
c. Ashapurna Devi
d. Margaret Alva

88 The term "gender typing" with regard to work refers to ________.

a. Adopting biased hiring practices for men and women
b. Labeling certain management techniques as "male" or "female"
c. Seeing certain jobs as either masculine or feminine and then become dominated by one gender or the other
d. Discriminating men and women for similar workplace achievements

89 Measuring the relative access to education of males and females is__________.

a. The Gender Parity Index (GPI)
b. The Gender Development Index (GDI)
c. The Gender Education Index (GEI)
d. The Gender Equality Index (GEI)

90 _________implies fairness in the way women and men are treated.

a. Gender equality
b. Gender Parity
c. Gender equity
d. All the above

91 ____________is striving for equal treatment of women and men and for abolishing inequality.

a. Feminism
Gender Studies
c. Rural sociology
Agricultural extension

92 Men and women have different _______

a. Needs
b. Constraints
c. Roles
d. All the above

93 Which of the followings is the correct sentence?

a. Women play diversified roles as compared to the men in the society
b. Men play diversified roles as compared to the women in the society
c. Women and men play equal roles in the society
d. None of these

94 The process of assessing the implications for women and men of any planned action, in all areas and at all levels is known as________

a. Gender mainstreaming
b. Women Mainstreaming
c. Social engineering
d. All the above

95 What is women's average labour contribution in farming?

a. 55-60% b. 45-50%

c. 65-70% d. 70- 75%

96 Research on women in India during 1960's was contributed mostly by_____

a. Home scientists b. Extension scientists

c. Agricultural Scientists d. Women Scientists

97 During 1961 to 1987, which institutes focused mainly on women's research?

a. Farm universities b. Economics institutes

c. Political universities d. All the above

98 Which of the following denotes the equal valuing by society of both women and men?

a. Gender equality b. Gender parity

c. Gender disparity d. None of these

99 Which of the followings is the correct sentence?

a. Women are superior than men by birth

b. Men are superior than women by birth

c. Men and women are born equal in society

d. None of these

100 First Indian woman to win the Booker Prize

a. Arundhati Roy b. Nirja Mishra

c. Vandana Shiva d. None of the above

101 ________is a comprehensive scheme for prevention of trafficking and rescue, rehabilitation and reintegration of victims of trafficking for commercial sexual exploitation.

a. Ujjawala b. Swadhar

c. Nirbhaya d. Sabla

102 Which agencies are responsible for creating gender difference in society?

a. Family b. Social system

c. Religion d. All the above

103 Who among the followings introduced the terminological distinction between biological sex and gender as a role in 1955?

a. Alex MacFarlane b. Swanson

c. John Money d. Judith Butler

104 ________refers to power relations between men and women due to which women occupy a secondary status in society.

a. Gender relation b. Gender promotion

c. Gender demotion d. Gender parity

105 Gender relations have direct bearing on which of the following aspects?

a. Women's mobility

b. Women's decision making capacity

c. Women's right to choice

d. All the above

106 ________refers to the study of the different roles of women and men to understand their activities, resources needs and priorities.

a. Gender analysis b. Gender mainstreaming

c. Gender empowerment d. All the above

107 __________is a strategy for incorporating women's as well as men's concerns and experiences in policies and programmes at all levels so that it will benefit both of them equally and prevent further inequality.

a. Gender mainstreaming b. Gender Parity

c. Gender prosperity d. All the above

108 Practical Gender Needs (PGN) are ________

a. Short term b. Immediate

c. Long term d. Both a & b

109 Strategic Gender Needs (SGN) are________

a. Short term b. Immediate

c. Long term d. Both a & b

110 __________is a person who does not recognize that gender is an essential determinant of life choices available to people in society.

a. Gender bias b. Gender angry

c. Gender blind d. Anti gender

111 _____refers to perception that both sex are not equal and do not have similar rights to resources.

a. Gender bias
b. Gender Role
c. Gender parity
d. Sexualism

112 Which is the ultimate goal of gender mainstreaming?

a. To achieve gender equality
b. To achieve women dominancy
c. To achieve gender inequality
d. To achieve gender parity

113 Practical Gender Needs (PGN) pertains to ________

a. Day to day living conditions of women
b. The position of women vis-à-vis men
c. Both a & b
d. None of these

114 Strategic Gender Needs (SGN) pertains to ________

a. Day to day living conditions of women
b. The position of women vis-à-vis men
c. Both a & b
d. None of these

115 Practical Gender Needs (PGN) includes________

a. Domestic income earning activities
b. Housing and basic services
c. Traditional employment opportunities
d. All the above

116 Strategic Gender Needs (SGN) changes in________

a. The gender division of labour
b. Shared domestic labour and child care
c. Elimination of institutionalized forms of discrimination
d. All the above

117 _____are women-headed households in which the male partner is 'temporarily' absent mostly due to male labour out migration and the women are not the legal household head.

a. De Facto Women-Headed Households
b. De Jure Female-Headed Households
c. Defaulted Women-Headed Households
d. None of these

118 _______ are women-headed household in which the male partner is 'permanently' absent due to separation or death, and the woman is legally single, divorced or widowed.

a. De Facto Women-Headed Households

b. De Jure Female-Headed Households

c. Defaulted Women-Headed Households

d. None of these

119 _______ refers to un-favourable treatment of individuals on the basis of their gender.

a. Gender discrimination b. Gender mobility

c. Gender insecurity d. Gender sensitization

120 _______ refers to right and opportunity of men and women to use the resources as per one's need to carryout his/her activities.

a. Access to productive resources

b. Access to un-productive resources

c. Access to reproductive resources

d. None of these

121 _______ refers to the rights and power of men and women to decide on the use and destination of the resources

a. Control over productive resources

b. Control over un-productive resources

c. Control over reproductive resources

d. None of these

122 _______ focuses on gender with an objective to achieve gender equity, equality and empowerment through practical and strategic gender needs.

a. Gender planning b. Gender sensitization

c. Gender parity d. All the above

123 Millennium Development Goal-1 (MDG -1) is related to_______

a. Eradicate extreme poverty and hunger

b. Achieve universal primary education

c. Reduce child mortality

d. Improve maternal health

124 Millennium Development Goal-2 (MDG -2) is related to________

a. Eradicate extreme poverty and hunger

b. Achieve universal primary education

c. Reduce child mortality

d. Improve maternal health

125 Which of the Millennium Development Goals is related to promote gender equality and women empowerment ?

a. MDG 1 b. MDG 8

c. MDG 3 d. MDG 6

126 Millennium Development Goal-4 (MDG -4) is related to________

a. Eradicate extreme poverty and hunger

b. Achieve universal primary education

c. Reduce child mortality

d. Improve maternal health

127 Millennium Development Goal-5 (MDG -5) is related to________

a. Eradicate extreme poverty and hunger

b. Achieve universal primary education

c. Reduce child mortality

d. Improve maternal health

128 Which of the Millennium Development Goals is related to combat HIV/ AIDS, malaria and other diseases?

a. MDG 1 b. MDG 8

c. MDG 3 d. MDG 6

129 Which of the Millennium Development Goals is related to ensure environmental sustainability?

a. MDG 1 b. MDG 8

c. MDG 3 d. MDG 7

130 Which of the Millennium Development Goals is related to develop a global partnership for development ?

a. MDG 1 b. MDG 9

c. MDG 3 d. MDG 8

131 MDGs Goal 1 indicate that: India must reduce the proportion of people below poverty line from nearly 37.5% (in 1990) to _______about by 2015.

a. 18.75% b. 20.75%

c. 30.50% d. 15.75%

132 Goal 2: India should increase the primary school enrollment rate to by _______2015 against 41.96% in 1991-92.

a. 75% b. 100 %

c. 70% d. 90%

133 According to Millennium Development Goal 3, India will have to promote female participation at all levels to reach a female male proportion of equal level by_______

a. 2015 b. 2020

c. 2030 d. 2050

134 MDG- 4 aims at reducing 'under five mortality rate (U5MR)' from 125 deaths per thousand live births in 1988-92 to___________in 2015.

a. 42 b. 00

c. 50 d. 25

135 According to MDG- 5 India should reduce maternal mortality (MMR) from 437 deaths per 100,000 live births in 1991 to ________ by 2015.

a. 100 b. 109

c. 43 d. 150

136 How many domains have been defined in Women's Empowerment in Agriculture Index (WEAI) to measure the women empowerment in agriculture?

a. 4 b. 5

c. 10 d. 8

137 Which of the following domains have defined in Women's Fmpowerment in Agriculture Index (WEAI) to measure the women empowerment in agriculture?

a. Production, Resources, Income, Leadership, Time

b. Production, Resources, Education, Leadership, Time

c. Production, Resources, Education, Health, Time

d. Production, Resources, Income, Leadership, Education

138 _________ is a new survey-based index designed to measure the empowerment, agency, and inclusion of women in the agricultural sector.

a. The Women in Agriculture Index (WAI)

b. The Women's Equality in Agriculture Index (WEAI)

c. The Women's Empowerment in Agriculture Index (WEAI)

d. The Women's Equity in Agriculture Index (WEAI)

139 Which of the followings concept was first proposed at the 1985 Third World Conference on Women in Nairobi, Kenya?

a. Gender mainstreaming b. Gender equality

c. Gender disparity d. Gender role

140 _______ refers to the modification of behaviour by raising awareness of gender equality concerns.

a. Gender sensitization b. Gender mainstreaming

c. Gender role d. Gender parity

141 "Stree Shakti Puraskar" awards are named after which of the following eminent women ?

a. Rani Laxmi Bai & Mata Jijabai

b. Rani Rudramma Devi & Kannagi

c. Rani Gaidinliu Zeliang & Ahilya Bai Holkar

d. All the above

142 Match the following:

(a) Gujarat	(i) Working Women's Forum
(b) Maharashtra	(ii) Kudumba Sri
(c) Tamil Nadu	(iii) Annapurna Mahila Mandal
(d) Kerala	(iv) Self-Employed Women's Association

a. (ii) (i) (iii) (iv) b. (iv) (ii) (iii) (i)

c. (iv) (iii) (i) (ii) d. (i) (iii) (ii) (iv)

143 Write the sequence of the following programmes for women development. 1. Indira Gandhi Matritva Sahayog Yojana2. Gender Budgeting 3. Swadhar 4. UJJAWALA Scheme

a. 3, 2, 4, 1 b. 1, 2, 3, 4

c. 4, 2, 3, 1 d. 2, 3, 4, 1

144 Which of the following bills provide measures to punish anyone who teases or molests women in public places ?

a. Women and Girl Child Bill 2012

b. Women and Girl Child Protection Bill 2012

c. Women and Girl Child Atrocities Bill 2012

d. Women and Girl Child (Prevention of Atrocities) Bill 2012

145 What do you mean by 'Comparable worth' discrimination ?

a. Pay for farm work

b. Sex segregation in jobs

c. More pay for women's work

d. Sex segregation in jobs and different pay scales for "female" and "male" jobs

146 Which country declares Official National Holiday on 'Women's Day'?

a. Russia b. India

c. Canada d. Australia

147 The First Chairperson of the National Commission for Women was____

a. Jayanti Patnaik b. Krishna Tirath

c. Girija Vyas d. Amrita Patel

148 First Indian Woman President of the Indian National Congress :

a. Sarojini Naidu b. Annie Besant

c. Rajkumari Amrit Kaur d. Sucheta Kriplani

149 What is the correct expansion of ICRW ?

a. International Committee on Review of Women

b. International Centre for the Research on Women

c. International Conference on Research of Women

d. International Council for Research on Women

150 Match the followings :

(a) Rajiv Gandhi Scheme for Empowerment of Adolescent Girls:	i. Ujjawala
(b) Scheme for Women in Difficult Circumstances	ii. SABLA
(c) Scheme for Prevention of Trafficking	iii. Swayamsiddha
(d) Holistic Empowerment of Women in a sustainable manner	iv. Swadhar

a. iii iv i ii b. i ii iv iii c. ii iv i iii d. iv ii i iii

151 Which of the following sentence is correct?

a. Gender Auditing is part of the Gender Budgeting process

b. Gender Budgeting is part of the Gender Auditing process

c. Gender Auditing and Gender Budgeting both are same

d. All the above

152 Gender auditing is the process that is conducted________

a. After the budget has been adopted and implemented

b. Before the budget has been adopted and implemented

c. At the time of budget adoption

d. All the above

153 Women's Empowerment in Agriculture Index (WEAI) is launched in 2012 by _______

a. The International Food Policy Research Institute (IFPRI)

b. The Oxford Poverty and Human Development Initiative (OPHI)

c. The Feed the Future Initiative and the U.S. Agency for International Development (USAID)

d. All the above

154 Who among the followings conduct skill oriented training programmes for farm women?

a. KVKs b. RRBs

c. SHGs d. MNREGA

155 How many women Subject Matter Specialists are provided in each KVK?

a. One b. Two

c. Six d. Three

156 What are the mandates of Directorate of Research on Women in Agriculture (DRWA)?

a. Conducting basic and strategic research on women issues in agriculture

b. Conducting applied research on women issues in agriculture

c. Undertaking technological refinement catering to the needs of farm women with respect to agriculture.

d. All the above

157 When was the NRCWA upgraded to the level of Directorate of Research on Women in Agriculture and later as Central Institute for Women in Agriculture respectively?

a. 2008 & 2014 b. 2011 & 2014

c. 2009 & 2013 d. 2010 & 2015

158 What is correct acronym of 'DAWN' ?

a. Development Association with Women for a New Era.

b. Department of Attention for Women in a New Era

c. Development Alternatives with Women for a New Era

d. Development Association with Women for a New Employment

159 Women Youth Training Extension Project (WYTEP) was implemented in which of the following state?

a. Maharashtra b. Tamil Nadu

c. Karnataka d. Rajasthan

160 When was the Women Youth Training Extension Project (WYTEP) implemented in Karnataka?

a. 1982 b. 1992

c. 2002 d. 2012

161 Training & Extension for Women in Agriculture (TEWA) was implemented in which of the following state?

a. Tamil Nadu b. Odisha

c. Rajasthan d. Maharashtra

162 The recently introduced bill in the Lok Sabha which intends to provide for the gender specific needs of women farmers is known as________

a. Women Farmers Bill 2012

b. Women Entitlement Bill 2012

c. Women Farmers Entitlement Bill 2012

d. Women Farm laborers Bill 2011

163 When was the Tamil Nadu Women in Agriculture (TANWA) initiated?

a. 1982 b. 1986

c. 1996 d. 2002

164 A large number of female extension officers were recruited and trained for the first time as Assistant Agricultural Officers-Farm Women (AAO-FW) under ____________

a. Women Youth Training Extension Project (WYTEP)
b. Training & Extension for Women in Agriculture (TEWA)
c. Madhya Pradesh Women in Agriculture (MAPWA)
d. Tamil Nadu Women in Agriculture (TANWA)

165 Match the Five Year Plan wise Issues for Women as given below :

(a) The Eighth Plan	(i) Women's Component Plan
(b) The Ninth Plan	(ii) Shift from "development" to "Empowerment"
(c) The Tenth Plan	(iii) Gender equality and gender justice goals
(d) The Eleventh Plan	(iv) Gender budget and gender mainstreaming

a. (ii) (i) (iii) (iv) b. (iv) (ii) (iii) (i)
c. (iii) (i) (ii) (iv) d. (iv) (iii) (ii) (i)

166 Multiplier training by the trained farm women and organising women into groups were the special component of _________

a. TANWA programme. b. WYTEP programme
c. TEWA programme d. MAPWA programme

167 Farm Women Groups (FWGs), which were started with about1500 groups, gradually evolved into Self-Help Groups (SHGs) and later, some groups transformed in to "micro entrepreneurs' under which of the following programme?

a. TANWA programme. b. WYTEP programme
c. TEWA programme d. MAPWA programme

168 Training & Extension for Women in Agriculture (TEWA) project of Odisha was started in which of the following years?

a. 1999 b. 2000
c. 1987 d. 1985

169 In which of the following programme, Lady Village Extension Workers (LVEW) under their circle imparted training in 43 skills of agriculture and allied fields?

a. TANWA programme b. WYTEP programme
c. TEWA programme d. MAPWA programme

170 Madhya Pradesh Women in Agriculture (MAPWA) project was started in 8 districts of Madhya Pradesh in which of the following years?

a. 1993 b. 1989

c. 1999 d. 1995

171 Female science graduates were recruited and given a one-year diploma training in agriculture at Jabalpur Agricultural University under which of the following programme?

a. TANWA programme b. WYTEP programme

c. TEWA programme d. MAPWA programme

172 First woman to become Deputy Chairperson of Rajya Sabha was ________

a. Violet Alva b. Meera Nayar

c. Najma Heptullah d. Margaret Alva

173 Training of Farm Women in Agriculture (TWA) project was funded by Government of Netherlands was launched in 6 districts of Gujarat in which of the following years?

a. 1993 b. 1989

c. 1999 d. 1995

174 Training of Farm Women in Agriculture (TWA) project was executed by which of the followings?

a. Farmers Training Centres (FTCs)

b. Krishi Vigyan Kendra's

c. Krishi Gyan Kendra's

d. SHGs

175 Andhra Pradesh Training of Women in Agriculture (ANTWA) project was started in which of the following years?

a. 1994 b. 1989

c. 1998 d. 1990

176 Which one of the following is working for the empowerment of women at global level?

a. UNIFEM b. DAW

c. UNICEF d. UN Women

177 Under which plan, Ministry of Agriculture launched Farmers Training and Education Programme (FTEP) to address specific needs of women farmers?

a. 7th Five Year Plan b. 9th Five Year Plan

c. 4th Five Year Plan d. 10th Five Year Plan

178 How many Farmers Training Centres (FTCs) were established in India under FTEP to bridge the visible gap among farm women's knowledge and skills?

a. 250 b. 150

c. 350 d. 50

179 According to Global Gender Gap Index 2013- what is India's status out of 136 countries?

a. 101 b. 105

c. 110 d. 99

180 When Support to Training and Employment Programme for Women (STEP) programme was launched in 19 states to provide skills and new knowledge to poor and asset-less women working in the traditional sectors?

a. 1987 b. 1989

c. 1983 d. 1982

181 The share of funds under ATMA scheme to be utilized to benefit the women farmers______

a. 30% b. 35%

c. 50% d. 10%

182 ________is the nodal agency for convergence and coordination of gender related issues within Department of Agriculture & Cooperation (DAC).

a. National Gender Resource Centre in Agriculture (NGRCA)

b. Central Instititute for Women in Agriculture (CIWA)

c. SEWA

d. All the above

183 Which agency is responsible for monitoring and assessing the gender contents and impact of various on-going programmes of DAC and suggesting improvements in their strategy and design_______

a. National Gender Resource Centre in Agriculture (NGRCA)

b. Central Instititute for Women in Agriculture (CIWA)

c. SEWA

d. All the above

184 NGRCA developed Gender Sensitisation Modules (GSM) for programme implementers in collaboration with _________

a. MANAGE

b. Central Instititute for Women in Agriculture (CIWA)

c. SEWA

d. NAARM

185 Who is the first woman to receive Bharat Ratna Award ?

a. Lata Mangeshkar　　b. Sarojini Naidu

c. Indira Gandhi　　d. Mother Teresa

186 What per cent of capital linked back ended credit subsidy is provided to women in Agri-Clinics and Agri-Business Centres (AC & ABC)?

a. 33.33%　　b. 50%

c. 75%　　d. 25%

187 Which scheme was launched by the Government of India to empower the women farmers as a sub component of the National Rural Livelihood Mission (NRLM) in 2010-11?

a. Mahila Kisan Sashaktikaran Pariyojana (MKSP)

b. Rural Women Livelihood Mission (RWLM)

c. Mahila Kisan Shiksha Programme (MKSP)

d. Rural Women Literacy Mission (RWLM)

188 ________is aimed to empower women farmers to gain more control over the production resources and manage the support systems in agriculture.

a. Mahila Kisan Sashaktikaran Pariyojana (MKSP)

b. Rural Women Livelihood Mission (RWLM)

c. Mahila Kisan Shiksha Programme (MKSP)

d. Rural Women Literacy Mission (RWLM)

189 ______ scheme is envisaged to enable women farmers gain/ access to the inputs and services and ensuring food security for their families and communities.

a. Mahila Kisan Sashaktikaran Pariyojana (MKSP)

b. Rural Women Livelihood Mission (RWLM)

c. Mahila Kisan Shiksha Programme (MKSP)

d. Rural Women Literacy Mission (RWLM)

190 MKSP project is implemented through Rural Development Departments of the concerned states with help of______

a. Government organizations

b. NGOs

c. Community Based Organizations

d. All the above

191 What per cent of subsidy is provided for women entrepreneurs in Gramin Bhandaran Yojana?

a. 33.33% b. 50%

c. 75% d. 25%

192 How much funds earmarked for small, marginal and women farmers through Macro Management of Agriculture?

a. 33% b. 50%

c. 75% d. 25%

193 Under Programme for Development of Oil palm assistance for drip irrigation component, how much subsidy is given to women farmers?

a. 70% b. 20%

c. 30% d. 50%

194 Which approach has been found effective to address gender issues in extending extension efforts to women farmers?

a. Group approach b. Individual contact approach

c. Both a & b d. None of these

195 Which plan of Union Government gave due importance of a formal cognizance of women's participation in agriculture for the first time?

a. IV Five Year Plan b. V Five Year Plan

c. VI Five Year Plan d. VIII Five Year Plan

196 "Engendering of the Development Process" in agricultural research and extension programmes was stressed for empowerment of women during ________

a. X Plan
b. XI Plan
c. IX Plan
d. XII Plan

197 Women farmer's concerns gain more concern with the start of extension reforms for mainstreaming women in agriculture during ________

a. XI Plan
b. X Plan
c. IX Plan
d. XII Plan

198 ________ helps to institutionalize gender in policy making.

a. Gender budgeting
b. Gender inequality
c. Gender socialization
d. None of these

199 Special Sub-Programme on the "Empowerment of Women Farmers" was launched with UNDP Assistance under UNDP Food Security Programme during 9th Five Year Plan (1997–2002) in which of the following state?

a. Odisha
b. Andhra Pradesh
c. Uttar Pradesh
d. All the above

200 ______ involves dissection of the government budget to establish its gender differential impacts and to translate gender commitments into budgetary commitments?

a. Gender budgeting
b. Gender planning
c. Gender typing
d. Gender prospect

201 The major aims of gender budgeting include ________

a. Seek to create a separate budget for women
b. Provide affirmative action to address specific needs of women
c. Both a & b
d. None of the above

202 Gender budgeting is ________

a. beyond allocation of resources for women
b. limited only to allocation of resources for women
c. refusing allocation of resources for women
d. for reduction of allocation of resources for men

203 ____cover tracking the utilization of allocated resources, impact analysis and beneficiary incidence analysis of public expenditure and policy from gender perspective.

a. Gender budgeting b. Gender typing

c. Women empowerment d. All the above

204 When gender budgeting process was initiated by the Ministry of Finance to tackle gender imbalances and promote gender equality?

a. 2004-05 b. 2010-11

c. 2001-02 d. 2005-06

205 ____is aiming to serve as focal points for coordinating gender budgeting initiatives, both intra and inter-ministerial.

a. Gender Budgeting Cell (GBC) b. Gender Resource Centre

c. Gender Knowledge Centre d. DRWA

206 When was the Gender Budgeting Statement started in Union budget to reflect quantum of budgetary allocation for programmes/schemes that substantially benefit women?

a. 2004-05 b. 2010-11

c. 2001-02 d. 2005-06

207 In two way classification in Gender Budgeting Statement, Part A includes

a. Schemes with 100% allocation for women

b. Schemes with 30 to 99% allocation for women

c. Schemes with <30% allocation for women

d. All the above

208 In two way classification in Gender Budgeting Statement, Part B includes

a. Schemes with 100% allocation for women

b. Schemes with 30 to 99% allocation for women

c. Schemes with <30% allocation for women

d. All the above

209 The gender inequality more deep rooted in society because of ____________

a. Traditional norms

b. Religious beliefs

c. Dominance men folks of the society

d. All the above

210 __________ is a process through which an individual acquiring a gender responsive behavior patterns through exposure to socio-psychological and educational programmes.

a. Gender sensitization
b. Gender role
c. Gender Socialization
d. Gender need

211 Who coined the term 'Gender role'?

a. Ann Oakley
b. Kate Millet
c. Simone de Beauvoir
d. John Money

212 _____ is the process of changing the stereotype mindset of men and women – a mindset that strongly believes that men and women are 'unequal entities'.

a. Gender sensitization
b. Gender typing
c. Gender Socialization
d. Gender bias

213 What is the incidence rate of male pseudohermaphroditism in India?

a. 1 in 20 live births
b. 1 in 200 live births
c. 1 in 20000 live births
d. 1 in 2000 live births

214 What is the incidence rate of female pseudohermaphroditism in India?

a. 1 in 12 live births
b. 1 in 125 live births
c. 1 in 1250 live births
d. 1 in 12500 live births

215 What is the incidence rate of Trisomy X (47, XXX) in India?

a. 1 in 1000 female live births
b. 1 in 100 female live births
c. 1 in 10 female live births
d. 1 in 10000 female live births

216 What is the incidence rate of sex chromosome abnormalities (Most common genetic disorder) in India?

a. 1 in 40-50 live births
b. 1 in 4000-5000 live births
c. 1 in 400-500 live births
d. 1 in 200-300 live births

217 Human biology allows for forms of intermediate levels between the conventional categories of male and female, sometimes referred to as__________

a. Intrasex
b. Pseudosex
c. Intersex
d. All of these

218 Who first domesticated crop plants and thereby initiated the art and science of farming?

a. Men
b. Women
c. Both a & b
d. Intersex

219 ______is a tool to better understand the realities of women and men whose likes are affected by development activities.

a. Gender analysis b. Gender parity
c. Gender inequality d. Gender bias

220 _________ aim to discover dynamics of gender differences across a variety of issues

a. Gender analysis b. Gender parity
c. Gender inequality d. Gender bias

221 _______is generally conceived as physical and mental strain, agony, fatigue, monotony and hardship experienced by human being.

a. Drudgery b. Leisure
c. Madness d. All the above

222 Self Employed Women's Association (SEWA) was formed in 1972 for organisation of poor, self-employed women workers is headquartered at ___________

a. Ahmadabad b. Anand
c. Delhi d. Mumbai

223 In 1977, SEWA's General Secretary, Ela Bhatt, was awarded a prestigious award and this brought international recognition to SEWA. Which was that award?

a. Ramon Magsaysay Award b. Pulitzer Award
c. Nobel Award d. Global Peace Award

224 SEWA Bank was registered as a co-operative bank under the dual control of Reserve Bank of India and State Government and has become a viable financial venture in__

a. 1974 b. 1994
c. 1972 d. 1977

225 Harvard Analytic Framework developed by Harvard Institute of Development is also known as _______

a. Gender Roles Framework b. Gender Planning Framework
c. Gender Analysis Matrix d. Social Relations Framework

226 Caroline Moser Framework developed by Caroline Moser is also referred as ______

a. Gender Roles Framework b. Gender Planning Framework
c. Gender Analysis Matrix. d. Social Relations Framework.

227 Rani Parker Framework developed by Rani Parker is also called as __________

a. Gender Roles Framework b. Gender Planning Framework

c. Gender Analysis Matrix. d. Social Relations Framework.

228 Naila Kabeer Framework is also called as __________

a. Gender Roles Framework b. Gender Planning Framework

c. Gender Analysis Matrix. d. Social Relations Framework.

229 Sara H. Longwe Framework invented by Sara Hlupekile Longwe. It is also called as

a. Gender Roles Framework

b. Women Empowerment Framework.

c. Gender Analysis Matrix.

d. Social Relations Framework.

230 Who was the first woman President of the United Nations General Assembly?

a. Sirimavo *Bandaranayaka* b. Smt Indira Gandhi

c. Mrs. Vijaya Laxmi Pandit d. None of these

231 Women's Empowerment Framework can be used for_________

a. Women participation in decision – making

b. Empowerment of women in isolation

c. Political empowerment of women

d. Economic empowerment of women

232 Socio-Economic And Gender Analysis (SEAGA) is an approach elaborated by ___

a. FAO b. UN women

c. UNDP d. UNICEF

233 Women treated better and enjoyed more rights in which of the following period?

a. Vedic period b. Post Vedic period

c. Both a & b d. None of these

234 Extraordinarily talented women like Aditi, Lopamudra, Gargi, Maitreyi Ghosha and Apaala contributed to which of the following period?

a. Rigveda b. Samveda

c. Ayurveda d. Yajurveda

235 ___________allowed women to choose life partners.

a. Sage Yagnyavalkya b. Valimiki

c. Barahamihira d. Aryabhatta

236 Who choose a husband on her own conditions in Vedic period?

a. Rishika Gargi b. Aditi

c. Maitreyi d. Lopamudra

237 Women in which period made inferior to men?

a. Vedic Period b. Post Vedic Period

c. Pre Vedic Period d. All of these

238 Which goddess are worshipped for scholarship and wealth in Hindu religion?

a. Saraswati & Lakshmi b. Durga & Laxmi

c. Saraswati & Vaishno d. Saraswati & Durga

239 Great ____________________ placed motherhood on a high pedestal.

a. Epics b. Saga

c. Stories d. Novels

240 Sankaracharya says if no shakti, then no _____

a. Shivam b. Bhakti

c. Laxmi d. Mukti

241 Who opined, Gods reside where women are respected?

a. Manu b. Sankaracharya

c. Shukracharya d. All the above

242 Female students were hardly found in Gurukulas during____________.

a. Post Vedic period b. Vedic period

c. Pre Vedic period d. All of these

243 Women were not allowed to learn vedas & chant mantras in________.

a. Post Vedic period b. Vedic period

c. Pre Vedic period d. All of these

244 Women serve husband to attain salvation in _________

a. Post Vedic period b. Vedic period

c. Pre Vedic period d. All of these

245 Society viewed women as a weak (Abala) in _________.

a. Post Vedic period b. Vedic period

c. Pre Vedic period d. All of these

246 Girl child neglect, child marriage, sati, denial of education, barring remarriage, dowry, pattern change in food, dress, appearance & social conduct were found since ________

a. Post Vedic period
b. Vedic period
c. Pre Vedic period
d. All of these

247 Freedom struggle in India was refreshingly__________.

a. Gender neutral
b. Gender biased
c. Gender responsive
d. Gender reformative

248 Which of the following is responsible for higher awareness among Indian women?

a. Western education
b. Liberal Ideas
c. International Attention
d. All of these

249 ________accelerated the process to eliminate skewed perception of the society about women.

a. Freedom movement
b. Agrarian movement
c. Industrial movement
d. All the above

250 What are the recent forms of problems for women at work?

a. Eve-teasing
b. Sexual harassment at work
c. Occupational Discrimination
d. All the above

251 Which of the following is responsible for improving the status of Indian women?

a. Constitutional rights
b. Legislatives action
c. Gender focus in development activities
d. All the above

252 Which article of fundamental rights in Indian constitution ensures equality before law & equal protection by the law?

a. Article 14
b. Article 32
c. Article 41
d. Article 35

253 Which article of fundamental rights in Indian constitution ensures prohibition of discrimination on the grounds of religion, race, sex or place of birth?

a. Article 15(c)
b. Article 14(c)
c. Article 16(c)
d. Article 19(c).

254 Which article of fundamental rights in Indian constitution ensures equality of opportunity in matter of public employment?

a. Article 16 b. Article 19

c. Article 15 d. Article 25

255 Which article of fundamental rights in Indian constitution ensures positive discrimination to make special provisions for women?

a. Article 15(2) b. Article 15(4)

c. Article 16(2) d. Article 17(2)

256 Which article of fundamental rights in Indian constitution ensures protection of life and personal liberty?

a. Article 21 b. Article 19

c. Article 15 d. Article 25

257 Which principles in Indian constitution ensure that citizens not forced to unsuited work due to economic necessity?

a. Directive b. Guiding

c. Binding d. Fundamental

258 Directive Principles in Indian constitution renounce practices that are derogatory to the dignity of which of the following?

a. Men b. Women

c. Hermaphrodite d. Transgender

259 Which of the Directive principles in Indian constitution became law?

a. The Maternity Benefits Act b. Local body reservation

c. RTE d. All of these

260 Which article of Indian constitution guarantees political equality to women?

a. Article 326 b. Article 321

c. Article 344 d. Article 366

261 Which article of Indian constitution prohibits exclusion from electoral rolls on the basis of sex?

a. Article 325 b. Article 321

c. Article 344 d. Article 366

262 Reasons for limited outreach of state legislations to help needy women are due to______

a. Entrenched cultural practices b. Lack of legal awareness

c. Limited access to courts d. All of these

263 Women's rights to land and other natural resources are covered under which of the following laws?

a. General civil law
b. Property, Family and Succession Law
c. Agrarian and natural resource law
d. All of these

264 Statutory law in India mainly reflects which of the following norms?

a. Religious | b. Political
c. Educational | d. Economic

265 The Hindu Succession Act was enacted in which of the following year?

a. 1955 | b. 1967
c. 1956 | d. 1937

266 Muslim Women's (Protection of Rights on Divorce) Act came in to existence in which year?

a. 1985 | b. 1984
c. 1986 | d. 1987

267 Christian Marriage Act, the Parsi Marriage & Divorce Act and the Indian Succession Act of 1925 were amended in which year?

a. 1991 | b. 1992
c. 1993 | d. 1990

268 Legal doctrines in traditional Hindu law namely, Dayabhaga is applied in which state?

a. Bengal | b. Assam
c. Gujarat | d. Both a & b

269 The Dayabhaga system did not envisage________

a. Joint family property | b. Individual family property
c. both a & b | d. None of these

270 Under which system, property was divided in two categories: joint family ("coparcenary") property, belonging to the extended family and separate property?

a. Mitakshara | b. Dayabhaga
c. Both a & b | d. Swabalamba

271 Women had ________ control powers under Dayabhaga than under Mitakshara

a. Wider
b. Lesser
c. Similar
d. None of these

272 The Hindu Succession Act of 1956 applies to Hindus, Sikhs, Jains and Buddhists of all Indian states except for which of the Indian state?

a. J & K
b. Assam
c. Mizoram
d. Goa

273 The Hindu Succession Act of 1956 grants ________

a. Unequal inheritance rights to men and women
b. Equal inheritance rights to men and women
c. Inheritance rights to only women
d. Inheritance rights to only men

274 Legislation usually fixes a land ceiling for each________

a. Household
b. Village
c. Society
d. Subdivisin

275 Special protection during pregnancy and paid maternity leave, and the right not to be dismissed on grounds of pregnancy or maternity leave comes under ________

a. CEDAW, art. 11(2)
b. PEDAW, art. 11(2)
c. CEDAW, art. 19(2)
d. PEDAW, art. 19(2)

276 Equal Remuneration Act of 1976 prohibited________

a. Sex discrimination
b. Age discrimination
c. Skill based discrimination
d. Colour based discrimination

277 Plantations Labour Act of 1951 prohibits the employment of women between 19 hours and 6 hours except for ________

a. Midwives
b. Nurses
c. Permitted by the state government
d. All the above

278 MGNREGA ensures________

a. High wages for male
b. High wages for female
c. Equal wages for both men and women
d. A lot of leisure during work

279 Employers with more than 50 women workers must provide crèche facilities under_____

a. Plantations Labour Act of 1951

b. Indian Contract Act of 1872

c. Equal Remuneration Act of 1976

d. None of these

280 Which act ensures full contractual capacity for both men & women at the age of majority?

a. Plantations Labour Act of 1951

b. Indian Contract Act of 1872

c. Equal Remuneration Act of 1976

d. None of these

281 According to the Banking Regulation Act of 1949 Legislation concerning credit is_____

a. Gender neutral b. Gender biased

c. Women focused d. Men focused

282 The Self-Employed Women's Association (SEWA) Co-operative Bank, established by SEWA in 1974, provides deposit and credit facilities for especially self employed_______

a. Men b. Women

c. Both a & b d. Youth

283 When the Child Marriage Restraint Act, was came into force?

a. 1921 b. 1935

c. 1929 d. 1934

284 When Hindu Marriage Act was come in force?

a. 1956 b. 1955

c. 1966 d. 1969

285 When Special Marriage Act was came into force?

a. 1956 b. 1955

c. 1966 d. 1969

286 When The Indian Christian Marriage Act was came into force?

a. 1872 b. 1972

c. 1893 d. 1927

287 When Indian Divorce Act, 1969 came into force?

a. 1956 b. 1955

c. 1966 d. 1969

288 When Converts Marriage Dissolution Act, came into force?

a. 1986 b. 1886

c. 1994 d. 1987

289 When the Dowry Prohibition Act was came into force?

a. 1961 b. 1956

c. 1955 d. 1966

290 When was the Family Court established?

a. 1984 b. 1999

c. 2001 d. 1994

291 When the Married Women's Property Act came into force?

a. 1874 b. 1887

c. 1888 d. 1885

292 Government passed the Prenatal Diagnostic Techniques (Regulation and Prevention of Misuse) Act to prevent female foeticide in_____

a. 1994 b. 1996

c. 2001 d. 2005

293 Which Act says- "A person must be paid at least that amount of wages as fixed by the government"?

a. The Equal Remuneration Act, 1976
b. The Minimum Wages Act, 1948
c. The Maternity Benefit Act, 1961
d. The Married Women's Property Act, 1874

294 ________ensures payment of equal wages for equal work or similar nature of work for women and men.

a. The Equal Remuneration Act, 1976
b. The Minimum Wages Act, 1948
c. The Maternity Benefit Act, 1961
d. Married Women's Property Act, 1874

295 The Maternity Benefit Act, 1961 provides__ for maternity leave with pay.

a. 25 weeks b. 20 weeks

c. 30 weeks d. 15 weeks

296 In which Five Year Plan a specific chapter was devoted to women and development

a. Fifth Five Year Plan b. Sixth Five Year Plan

c. Seventh Five Year Plan d. Fourth Five Year Plan

297 What per cent of beneficiaries and credit made available is reserved for self employed women In IRDP?

a. 40 % b. 33.33 %

c. 25 % d. 50%

298 DWCRA targeted women belonging to families ________

a. Below the poverty line b. Above the poverty line

c. From slum area d. Urban middle class

299 What per cent of reservation for women was provided in TRYSEM?

a. 40 % b. 33.33 %

c. 25 % d. 50%

300 In which year Women's Development Corporations were established at state level to provide women entrepreneurs with technical assistance and training, improved access to credit, support for marketing and for women cooperatives?

a. 1987 b. 1999

c. 1985 d. 1990

301 National Commission for Women (established under the National Commission for Women Act of 1990) can investigate violations________

a. *Motu proprio* b. Upon Complaint

c. Both a & b d. None of these

302 In India, the 73rd and 74th Constitutional Amendment Acts of 1993 reserved how many seats to women in local government institutions?

a. One-third b. Two-third

c. Half d. One fourth

303 Legal services authorities act of 1987, which explicitly lists women among possible legal aid beneficiaries (sect. 12(c)) was amended in which of the followings years?

a. 1994 b. 2000

c. 1995 d. 1990

304 What is the gender related Index that have been developed and used by United Nations in 2010?

a. Gender Related Developed Index (GDI)

b. Gender Inequality Index (GII)

c. Gender Empowerment Measure (GEM)

d. Human Gender Index (HGI)

305 What do you mean by gender-neutral technology?

a. The technology is not influenced by gender of both the user and developer

b. Technology providing priority to women

c. Technology, providing priority to men

d. Technology providing priority to technical people

306 Gender roles are ________

a. Result of differences in biological aptitude

b. Roles ascribed by men and women in society

c. Roles assigned by the society to women

d. Roles assigned by the society to men

307 Which is the correct expansion of UNIFEM ?

a. United Nations Development Fund for Education of Women

b. United Nations International Fund for Education of Women

c. United Nations International Female Evaluation and Monitoring

d. United Nations Development Fund for Women

308 Among the following pair which is not correctly matched?

a. Sonia Gandhi – Political leader

b. Medha Patkar – Eco-Feminist

c. Jayanti Patnaik – Chairperson, NCW

d. Vandana Shiva – Booker Prize Winner

309 What is the expansion for IWRAW ?

a. Indian Women's Association for Women's Rights.

b. International Women's Rights Action Watch.

c. International Women's Rights and Welfare Association.

d. Indian Women's Rights Action Watch.

310 'Women's Component Plan' was adopted in which five year plan ?

a. 9th five year plan
b. 5th five year plan
c. 7th five year plan
d. 6th five year plan

311 Among the following which is not an objective of Rashtriya Mahila Kosh ?

a. To advise the government on all policy matters affecting women.
b. To promote the provision of micro credit to poor women.
c. To promote the organisation of women's groups.
d. To link with thrift and savings with credit.

312 According to the National Rural Employment Gaurantee Act, the percentage of women beneficiaries shall be ________

a. 50 %
b. 75 %
c. 33 %
d. 100 %

313 Which article of the Constitution of India provides 'The State to make any special provision in favour of women and children'?

a. Article 39
b. Article 14
c. Article 19
d. Article 15 (3)

314 Which is the Creche Scheme introduced by the Ministry of Women and Child Development for the children of working mothers in 2006?

a. Indira Gandhi National Creche Scheme
b: Rajiv Gandhi National Creche Scheme
c. Sishu Vikas Creche Scheme
d. Jawahar National Creche Scheme

315 Sex is a/an ________ because a person is born with it ; Gender is a/an ________ because it has to be learned.

a. achieved ; ascribed
b. attained ; achieved
c. ascribed ; achieved
d. achieved ; adopted

316 Which dimensions are considered to calculate the Gender Inequality Index (GII) ?

a. Gross national income, education and health
b. Long and healthy life, knowledge and a decent standard of living
c. Health, education and standard of living
d. Health, empowerment and labour market

317 Which of the following pair is not correctly matched ?

a. Indira Gandhi - First Woman received the Ramon Magsaysay Award

b. Fathima Beevi - First Woman Judge in the Supreme Court

c. Kalpana Chawla - First Indian Woman went into the space

d. Punita Arora - First Indian Woman done the highest rank of Lt. General

318 Match the following :

List – I	List – II
(a) National Policy on Empowerment of Women	(i) 1992
(b) National Mission on Empowerment of Women	(ii) 2001
(c) High Level Committee on the Status of Women	(iii) 2010
(d) National Commission for Women	(iv) 2012

a. (iii) (ii) (iv) (i) b. (i) (iv) (iii) (ii)

c. (iv) (ii) (iii) (i) d. (ii) (iii) (iv) (i)

319 Which Constitution (Amendment) Bill was passed by Rajya Sabha in 2008 that provides reservation for women in Parliament and State Assemblies?

a. 102nd Amendment Bill b. 108th Amendment Bill

c. 81st Amendment Bill d. 110th Amendment Bill

320 Beti Bachao Beti Padhao Yojana was launched on January 22, 2015 from____

a. Panipat, Haryana b. Howrah, West Bengal

c. Nasik, Maharashtra d. Guntur, Andhra Pradesh

321 In India seats are reserved for women in

a. Village Panchayats b. District Panchayats

c. Nagar Panchayats d. All the above

322 Assertion (A) :Not sex but gender has been defined as a form of social stratificationReason (R) :Biologically females are not similar to males

Codes :

a. (A) and (R) both are correct and (R) is the correct explanation of (A)

b. (A) and (R) both are correct but (R) is not the correct explanation of (A)

c. A) is correct but (R) is wrong.

d. (R) is correct but (A) is wrong.

323 Assertion (A): Skill training and development programme are being given priority for women by the Government.

Reason (R): A considerable skill gap is noticed among farm women

Codes :

a. (A) is correct and (R) is wrong.

b. (A) is incorrect and (R) is correct

c. Both (A) and (R) are correct and (R)is a correct explanation of (A)

d. Both (A) and (R) are correct but (R) is not a correct explanation of (A)

324 Assertion (A): Infant mortality rate has correlation with population growth rate.

Reason (R): Decrease in infant mortality rate does not help in decreasing birth rate

Codes :

a. (A) and (R) both are correct

b. (A) and (R) both are wrong.

c. (A) is correct but (R) is wrong

d. (R) is correct but (A) is wrong.

325. Assertion (A): Extension is a continuous educational process for farm women in which both farm women and extension agents contribute and receive

Reason (R): The purpose of extension education is to change the attitude and practices of the farm women.

Codes :

a. (A) is true but (R) is false

b. (A) and (R) both are true but (R) is not the correct explanation of (A)

c. Both are false

d. (A) and (R) both are correct and (R) is correct explanation of (A)

326 Assertion (A) :Motivation is not an integral part of learning for farm women

Reason (R) :Motivation improves the pace of adult learning especially for women

Codes :

a. (A) is correct but (R) is wrong

b. (R) is correct but (A) is wrong.

c. (A) and (R) both are correct.

d. (A) and (R) both are wrong.

327. Assertion (A) : Farm Women are matured and rigid to learn

Reason (R): Learning is a slow process and requires continuous feedback and motivation for matured farm women

Codes :

a. (A) is correct but (R) is wrong.

b. (R) is correct but (A) is wrong.

c. (A) and (R) both are correct but (R) is not correct explanation of (A)

d. (A) and (R) both are correct but (R) is the correct explanation of (A)

328 Arrange the following important days in the order in which it celebrated from January to December :

I. International Women's Day

II. World Habitat Day

III. National Youth Day

IV. World Environment Day

Codes :

a. I, II, III, IV b. II, I, IV, III

c. III, I, IV, II d. I, II, IV, III

329 Assertion (A): Prevailing socio-cultural barriers prevented the women empowerment in India

Reason (R) : Idealism, Rationalism and Pragmatism failed to influence the mindset of males even after several years of independence.

Codes:

a. Both (A) and (R) are correct, but (R) is a correct explanation of (A)

b. (A) is correct and (R) is wrong

c. (A) is wrong and (R) is correct.

d. Both (A) and (R) are wrong

330 Assertion (A): Capacity building of farm women can serve as an instrument of positive social change

Reason (A): Social change is not a slow process.

Codes :

a. (A) and (R) both are correct

b. (A) and (R) both are wrong

c. (A) is correct, but (R) is wrong

d. (R) is correct, but (A) is wrong

331 Who was the first male appointee to the National Commission for Women (NCW) in India?

a. Alok Nath b. Alok Kumar

c. Alok Rawat d. Alok Chatterjee

332 Which of the following is true about 'Gender Audit'?

a. Social Audit b. Quality Audit

c. Tool and a process d. All of these

333 Which of the following term is used to denote disparity between women and men's condition and position in society?

a. Gender inequality b. Gender gap

c. Gender parity d. None of these

334 Set of implicit and explicit rules which governs gender relations are known as

a. Gender norms b. Gender contract

c. Gender folkways d. Gender fluidity

335 Which is the most commonly accessed resource by women in rural India?

a. Land b. Cattle

c. Machinery d. Capital/ Money

336 The situation where and individual fails to recognise roles of women and men are known as

a. Gender insensitive b. Gender blindness

c. Gender volatility d. Gender non recognition

337 In which year Swayamsiddha scheme was introduced by replacing the erstwhile Indira Mahila Yojana?

a. 2001-02 b. 2004-05

c. 2010-11 d. 1998-99

338 Swa-Shakti was funded by

a. World bank and IFAD
b. Central bank
c. NABARD
d. RBI

339 Assertion (A): The percentage growth of education among girls and women has contributed to their empowerment.

Reason (R): The increase in education of girls does not contribute to postponement of the age of marriage and to a reduction in the size of families.Codes:

a. Both (A) and (R) are correct.
b. Both (A) and (R) are wrong.
c. (A) is correct and (R) is wrong
d. (R) is correct and (A) is wrong.

340 An initiative for Rural empowerment in a local language is ____

a. India Development Gateway
b. Millennium Development Goal
c. SarvSaksharata Mission
d. None of these

341 Ultimate aim of gender mainstreaming is ____________

a. Gender equality
b. Gender Bias
c. Women empowerment
d. None of these

342 Expand WEAI

a. Women Empowerment in Agriculture Index
b. Western Economic Association International
c. Weatherhead East Asian Institute
d. None of these

343 In India Women Entrepreneurs' percentage is

a. 20%
b. 14%
c. 34%
d. 50%

344 Women is an incarnation of "shakti" – goddess of power. If she is bestowed with education, India strength will double, this sentence said by

a. Pratibha Patil
b. Indira Gandhi
c. Narendra Modi
d. Sharad Pawar

345 ___has given training to women's association and working member club.

a. James Stuard
b. Young *Women's* Christian *Association*
c. American *Association* of University *Women*
d. Dr. MusimbiKanyoro

346 Making awareness about Gender is called

a. Gender Sensitization
b. Gender empowerment
c. Gender identity
d. All of these

347 In which of the 'World Conference on Women' the landmark document 'Beijing Platform for Action' came out?

a. 1st
b. 2nd
c. 4th
d. 5th

348 Physical / Biological role is occurs in

a. Sex
b. Gender
c. Gender binary
d. All of above

349 On the basis of nature and normal, put the role of gender in media (book) is

a. Gender Sensitization
b. Gender stereotype
c. Gender reveal
d. None of these

350 Hinder factors of women empowerment is known as

a. Shyness
b. Expression
c. Discrimination
d. All of the above

351 Which SDG is related to gender equality?

a. SDG 5
b. SDG 7
c. SDG 8
d. SDG 10

352 Under one stop centre- scheme women can complain after .... days

a. 7 days
b. 3 weeks
c. 5 days
d. 10 weeks

353 Women component plan was the concern in which plan?

a. 8th five year plan
b. 5th five year plan
c. 9th five year plan
d. 3rd five year plan

Answer Key

1.	a	2.	c	3.	d	4.	a	5.	a	6.	a	7.	b	8.	b	9.	b	10.	b
11.	a	12.	c	13.	d	14.	a	15.	b	16.	a	17.	d	18.	a	19.	a	20.	b
21.	b	22.	a	23.	a	24.	d	25.	b	26.	b	27.	a	28.	b	29.	d	30.	d
31.	a	32.	c	33.	c	34.	b	35.	c	36.	a	37.	d	38.	c	39.	d	40.	b

41. a	42. a	43. d	44. a	45. c	46. d	47. a	48. b	49. d	50. a
51. d	52. c	53. c	54. a	55. c	56. a	57. a	58. a	59. a	60. d
61. b	62. c	63. a	64. a	65. b	66. d	67. d	68. a	69. b	70. a
71. b	72. b	73. a	74. c	75. a	76. d	77. d	78. a	79. a	80. b
81. b	82. d	83. d	84. a	85. a	86. c	87. c	88. c	89. a	90. c
91. a	92. d	93. a	94. a	95. a	96. a	97. a	98. a	99. c	100. a
101. a	102. d	103. c	104. a	105. d	106. a	107. a	108. d	109. c	110. c
111. a	112. a	113. a	114. b	115. d	116. d	117. a	118. b	119. a	120. a
121. a	122. a	123. a	124. b	125. c	126. c	127. d	128. d	129. d	130. d
131. a	132. b	133. a	134. a	135. b	136. b	137. a	138. c	139. a	140. a
141. d	142. c	143. a	144. d	145. d	146. a	147. a	148. b	149. b	150. c
151. a	152. a	153. d	154. a	155. a	156. d	157. a	158. c	159. c	160. a
161. b	162. c	163. b	164. a	165. a	166. a	167. a	168. c	169. c	170. a
171. d	172. a	173. b	174. a	175. a	176. d	177. c	178. b	179. a	180. a
181. a	182. a	183. a	184. a	185. c	186. a	187. a	188. a	189. a	190. d
191. a	192. a	193. d	194. a	195. a	196. c	197. b	198. a	199. d	200. a
201. b	202. a	203. a	204. a	205. a	206. d	207. a	208. b	209. d	210. a
211. d	212. a	213. c	214. d	215. a	216. c	217. c	218. b	219. a	220. a
221. a	222. a	223. a	224. a	225. a	226. b	227. c	228. d	229. b	230. c
231. a	232. a	233. a	234. a	235. a	236. a	237. b	238. a	239. a	240. a
241. a	242. a	243. a	244. a	245. a	246. a	247. a	248. d	249. a	250. d
251. d	252. a	253. a	254. a	255. a	256. a	257. a	258. b	259. d	260. a
261. a	262. d	263. d	264. a	265. c	266. c	267. a	268. d	269. a	270. a
271. a	272. a	273. b	274. a	275. a	276. a	277. d	278. c	279. a	280. a
281. a	282. b	283. a	284. b	285. b	286. a	287. d	288. a	289. a	290. a
291. a	292. a	293. b	294. a	295. a	296. b	297. a	298. a	299. a	300. a
301. c	302. a	303. a	304. b	305. a	306. b	307. d	308. d	309. b	310. a
311. a	312. c	313. d	314. b	315. c	316. d	317. a	318. d	319. b	320. a
321. d	322. b	323. c	324. a	325. d	326. b	327. b	328. c	329. a	330. c
331. c	332. d	333. b	334. b	335. b	336. b	337. a	338. a	339. c	340. a
341. a	342. a	343. b	344. c	345. a	346. a	347. c	348. a	349. b	350. d
351. a	352. c	353. c							

Model Paper for ARS Agricultural Extension

Total marks: 240 Time: 3 Hours

i. All questions are compulsory

ii. There are three parts in the question papers i.e. A, B, and C. Part A contains 40 questions @ 2 marks/question, Part B contains 20 questions @ 5 marks/question and Part C contains 6 questions @ 10 marks/question

PART – A

20 questions x 2 marks = 40 marks

(Please write your answer in given space)

1. Farmers first was first proposed by-

   a. Niels Rolling b. Robert Chambers

   c. M. S. Swaminathan d. Paul Leagans

2. Extension approach is ________

   a. Individual is the end

   b. Individual is a means to an end

   c. Rural development

   d. transfer of technology

3. Match the following

i. Journal of Rural development	( )	a)	NIRD
ii. Yojana	( )	b)	Ministry of information and Broadcasting
iii. Kurukshetra	( )	c)	Ministry of Rural Development
iv. Krishi Chayanika	( )	d)	ICAR

4. Formal cultural structure devised to meet basic social needs is called as ________.

5. Communication IQ test was proposed by Bhanja. **True/False**

6. What should be the motto of rural development:
   (a) Economic development
   (b) Growth with equity
   (c) Development of elite class
   (d) Development with growth
7. Mach the followings

i. Nominal	( )	a)	Average milk yield
ii. Ordinal	( )	b)	Arbitrary zero
iii. Interval	( )	c)	Likert scale
iv. Ratio	( )	d)	Member of football team

8. When a new crop variety advocated to farmers suits the agro-climatic condition then it indicates cultural compatibility. **True/False**
9. _______________ helps us to better plan an exact extension programme.
   (a) Evaluation (b) Determination
   (c) Observation (d) None of the above
10. Match the followings:

i. AICTA	( )	a)	Boss & Das Gupta
ii. NAIDTEA	( )	b)	Wilkening
iii. AIETA	( )	c)	Wilson and Gallup
iv. AIDCAS	( )	d)	Singh & Pareek

11. The number of subordinates a superior can effectively manage is
    (a) Principle of span of management
    (b) Principle of local control
    (c) Principle of delegation
    (d) None
12. Planning and organizing are called as Siamese twins of management. **True/False**
13. The gap between what is and what what ought to be known as ___________.
14. Match the followings:

i. Gender disaggregated calender	( )	a)	Cause effect relationship
ii. Venn Diagram	( )	b)	Socio physical situation
iii. Transact Walk	( )	c)	Role relationship
iv. Flow diagram	( )	d)	Workload assessment

15. Starting point of programme building process is ______________.

16. Use of lurid features and sensational news lacking credibility for increased circulation is referred as yellow journalism. **True/False**.

17. Decision to cease the use of an idea in order to adopt a better idea which supersedes it is called as____________________..

18. An innovation with low relative advantage may have

i. Slow rate of adoption

ii. High rate of adoption

iii. Low rate of discontinuance

iv. High rate of discontinuance

Select the correct answer using the below mentioned codes

(a) 1 & 2 (b) 1 & 4

(c) 2 & 3 (d) 2 & 4

19. Judgment before due examination and consideration of fact and based on certain assumption is called as stereotype **True/False**

20. A marginal farmer is one who owns ____________________ land

21. Match the followings:

i. Validity	( )	a)	Freedom from individual bias
ii. Reliability	( )	b)	Consistency of results
iii. Objectivity	( )	c)	Correctness or accuracy
iv. Subjectivity	( )	d)	Chances of bias

22. An abstract formed from generalization from particular is called ______________.

23. For motion picture, sitting arrangement is fixed by 4X6 formula. **True/False**

24. Match the followings:

i. ERG Theory	( )	a)	V H Vroom
ii. Valance theory	( )	b)	Clayton Alderfer
iii. Two factor theory	( )	c)	F. Herzberg
iv. Reinforcement theory	( )	d)	B F Skinner

25. Ordinal alpha is used for

(a) Reliability testing (b) Validity testing

(c) Predictability testing (d) Conformity testing

26. In the concept of FARMERS FIRST full form of FIRST is 'Farm, Innovation, Recourses, Science and Technology' **True/False**

27. Which of the following is not a measure of central tendency

    (a) Mean (b) Mode

    (c) Median (d) Variance

28. Rejecting null hypothesis when it is true is known as __________.

29. 108th Amendment Bill passed in the Loksabha intends to provide for the gender specific needs of women farmers. **True/False**

30. ______________variable is the presumed cause of the ______________ variable, the presumed effect

31. Match the followings:

    i. National Policy on Empowerment of Women ( ) a) 1992

    ii. National Mission on Empowerment of Women ( ) b) 2001

    iii. High Level Committee on the Status of Women ( ) c) 2010

    iv. National Commission for Women ( ) d) 2012

32. Trustworthiness and competency are the elements of

    (a) Credibility (b) Fidelity

    (c) Empathy (d) sympathy

33. In exploratory field studies hypothesis are formulated to predict empirical inquiry. **True/False**

34. A farmer brings infected cauliflower to the extension scientist for solution of the diseases. Here, the infected cauliflower is an example of:

    (a) Chart (b) Model

    (c) Specimen (d) Mock-up

35. Match the followings:

    i. Operant Conditioning ( ) a) Aristotle

    ii. Trial and Error the ( ) b) Pavlov

    iii. Classical Conditioning ( ) c) E.L Thorndike

    iv. Theory of Mental Faculties ( ) d) B.F Skinner

36. While writing for farmers, sentences generally considered ideal are those which have:

    (a) Less than 8 words (b) Less than 18 words

    (c) Less than 30 words (d) Less than 50 word

37. To test the superiority or inferiority of two groups by indicating a direction of difference, One tail t-test can be used. **True/False**

38. Match the followings:

i. Kinesics	( )	a) Assigning of meanings to voices
ii. Proximics	( )	b) Say more in less words
iii. Conciseness	( )	c) Space around the speaker
iv. Deciphering	( )	d) Study of body language

39. Brainstorming session has two stages and these are ________________ and ________________.

40. Match the followings:

i. Minikit demonstrations	( )	a) Observability
ii. Result demonstration	( )	b) Trialability
iii. Crop insurance	( )	c) Relative advantage
iv. Multiple use machinery	( )	d) Preventive innovation

PART – B

20 questions x 5 marks = 100 marks

(Please write your answer in blank A4 page)

1. What is chasm model of adoption?
2. Can we change the level of measurement of variable? If yes, the, explain with a suitable example.
3. Write down the constitutive and operational definition of the followings:

   (a) Knowledge (b) Attitude

   (c) Education (d) Adoption
4. What are the differences between experimental research and non-experimental research?
5. Write a short note on 'Grapevine communication'
6. Briefly explain "Stratified random sampling method"
7. What are the differences between PERT and CPM?
8. What is full form of TRIPs and write down its different parts?
9. Write a short note on ATMA-KVK convergence

10. What are the key points that will be kept in mind during planning /formulation of farmers' training programme

11. How you will improve/build capacity of dairy farmers?

12. What are the important characteristics of agripreneurs? Explain different types of agripreneurs?

13. Write a brief note on "Farmers'-Producers' Company"

14. What are the basic characteristics of ITKs and name one technique to validate ITK through farmers' participatory approach.

15. What are the different dimensions of women empowerment?

16. Explain different models of contract farming with suitable example

17. Briefly describe the basic structure of logical framework analysis (LFA)

18. What is media mix and briefly explain its importance in extension service?

19. What is "Hub and Spoke Model"?

20. Write down the different tools of Participatory Rural Appraisal.

PART – C

6 questions x 10 marks = 60 marks
(Please write your answer in blank A4 page)

1. Describe in short, the genesis and growth of extension education in India since independence and what in your opinion, its future vis-à-vis agricultural and rural development of our country in the decades ahead.

2. Write an essay on "Application of social media in information dissemination".

3. Briefly explain different adoption behaviors.

4. Explain importance of research design in extension research. Briefly outline different research designs applicable in extension research with suitable example.

5. How you will identify the training needs of progressive dairy farmers and how you will meet these identified needs?

6. Name the ICAR programmes launched by Prime Minister on 25th July 2015. Write short paragraph on each of these programmes.